HOSPITALITY DIGITAL MARKETING ESSENTIALS:
A Field Guide for Navigating Today's Digital Landscape

The study guide for the Certified Hospitality Digital Marketer (CHDM)
certification, 5th Edition | www.hsmai.org/chdm

Published May 2019 By:

HOSPITALITY DIGITAL MARKETING ESSENTIALS:

A Field Guide for Navigating Today's Digital Landscape

Dear Colleagues,

This book is the study guide for the Certified Hospitality Digital Marketer (CHDM) certification (www.hsmai.org/chdm).

If you've gotten this far, you're interested in refining your skills and becoming a certified digital steward – congrats! Whether you have been in your role for years, are just entering the exciting space of hospitality marketing, or are considering expanding your sales and/or revenue management background into digital, the investment to become CHDM certified will pay off.

In our work to provide hospitality professionals with information on the most pertinent, relevant and in-demand topics, we are proud to deliver an updated 2019 edition which includes expanded material throughout Part 4 (Paid Media) and the addition of a comprehensive Glossary.

As part of its mission, HSMAI's Marketing Advisory Board seeks to inspire success for HSMAI members and those they serve through the creation, curation, and promotion of relevant knowledge in the digital marketing space. We hope you agree that this book is a strong step toward that goal.

See the Acknowledgements for a full accounting of the individuals who contributed countless hours to make this edition possible, and please refer to the next page for a roster of all advisory board members as of the printing of this edition.

WHY BECOME CHDM CERTIFIED?

- This globally-recognized digital marketing certification administered by HSMAI will set you apart as having legit digital literacy + skills.
- It's one of the few digital marketing certifications specializing in hospitality.
- Leaders with CHDM Certification have increased confidence. Being certified means that you know what you're talking about – inspiring more trust in you and your recommendations.
- The curriculum was carefully built by fellow hospitality marketing experts who know the space, the pitfalls, and all the in-demand digital marketing skills. Who could be better to help guide you through everything from the basics to the most advanced practices and skills?
- Invest in yourself and your career. You won't regret learning more about how digital has and will continue to impact the hotel industry.

REASONS YOUR ORGANIZATION SHOULD INVEST IN YOUR CHDM CERTIFICATION

- The curriculum provides an increased comprehension in the digital space which can lead to improved performance and overall revenue for your organization.
- The CHDM can be used as a continuing education piece proving that your organization is invested in your professional growth. Because the certification requires resubmission every two years, it's a given that you'll always be up to date on the latest trends and news. Every CHDM whose certification is current receives a copy of the new edition of the study guide whenever it is updated.
- You'll be a part of a community of over 7,000 HSMAI members worldwide which leads to peer interaction, advanced networking, and a larger company footprint within an esteemed cadre of professionals.

HSMAI AMERICAS MARKETING ADVISORY BOARD

- Chair: Dan Wacksman, CHDM, Principal, Sassato
- Anil Aggarwal, CEO, Milestone, Inc.
- Dustin Bomar, Head of Industry, Travel, Google
- Tiffany Braun, CHSP, Chief Strategy Officer, Kinship
- Katie Briscoe, President, MMGY Global
- Aimee Cheek, CHDM, Director of eCommerce, OTO Development
- Robert Cole, Founder-CEO, RockCheetah
- Jessica Davidson, CHDM, SVP, Digital, Wyndham Hotels & Resorts
- James Hansen, CHA, CHDM, Director, Marketing, Best Western Hotels & Resorts
- Benjamin Hoeb, CHDM, Corporate eCommerce Manager, PCH Hotels & Resorts
- Theodore Holloway, CHDM, Director of eCommerce, Remington Hotels
- Carolyn Hosna, CHDM, Vice President, Marketing, White Lodging,
- Ryan Hudgins, Director, Performance Marketing, IHG
- Michael Innocentin, Vice President, E-Commerce & Digital, North & Central America, Accor
- John Jimenez, CHSP, VP of E-commerce, Noble Investment Group
- Meghan Keough, CRME, CHDM, Senior Director, Hotel Strategic Accounts, Expedia Group Media Solutions
- Sarita Mallinger, Regional Director, Digital Marketing, Kimpton Hotels & Restaurants
- Delana Meyer, CHDM, , DRM Consulting, LLC
- Amy Mierzwinski, CHDM, Director, Horwath HTL
- Natalie Osborn, Director, Marketing, SAS Institute, Inc.
- Olga Peddie, SVP, Client Strategy & Success, Cendyn
- Mandy Penn, VP, Marketing, Universal Orlando Resort
- Lisa Ross, President, rbb Communications
- Mariana Safer, CHDM, SVP, Client Success, HEBS Digital
- Jeff Spaccio, VP, Sales and Strategic Partnerships, Tambourine
- Paolo Torchio, CHDM, VP Digital Operations, Two Roads/Hyatt
- Misty Wise, CRME, CHDM, Corporate Director, eCommerce Strategies, Atrium Hospitality
- Michael Wylie, SVP, Head of eCommerce, Interstate Hotels & Resorts
- James Zito, Chief Commercial & Revenue Officer, Club Quarters Hotels
- Holly Zoba, CHDM, VP, Technology Resources, Hospitality Digital Marketing

HSMAI EUROPE DIGITAL MARKETING ADVISORY BOARD

- Chair: Paul Mulcahy, SVP Commercial, Member of Mövenpick Hotels and Resorts Executive Committee, Mövenpick Hotels & Resorts
- Niklas Schlappkohl, Global Senior Director, Digital Travel Solutions
- RJ Friedlander, Founder And CEO, ReviewPro
- Riko Van Santen, Vice President Digital Strategy, Loyalty & Distribution, Kempinski Hotels
- Frank Reeves, CEO and Co-Founder, Avvio
- Torsten Sabel, COO, Customer Alliance
- Suzie Thompson, Vice President Marketing, Distribution & Revenue Management, Red Carnation Hotels
- Adrian Hands, Senior Director Key Accounts EMEA, TripAdvisor
- Roman Sucharzewski, Director Hotel Distribution & Marketing – Europe, Diamond Resorts International
- Edward Lines, Industry Manager, Google

TABLE OF CONTENTS

PART 1: INTRODUCTION

CHAPTER 1
Hospitality Digital Marketing Essentials: A Field Guide for Navigating Today's Digital Landscape...the CHDM Study Guide

From print to radio to TV, the mediums and methods of marketing have changed dramatically over the years, but no medium has had such a huge impact so quickly as the internet and the emerging field of digital marketing.

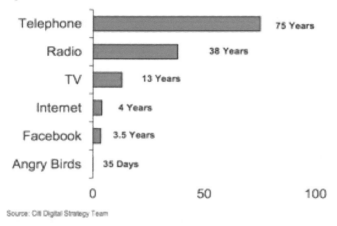

Figure 5. Time to reach 50 million users

Telephone — 75 Years
Radio — 38 Years
TV — 13 Years
Internet — 4 Years
Facebook — 3.5 Years
Angry Birds — 35 Days

Source: Citi Digital Strategy Team

The year 1995 is often pointed to as the start of the "internet revolution." It was in this year that the Netscape internet browser went public, Amazon.com began selling books, and a company, then known as Backrub (later to be called Google) was founded.

Fueling this growth was the constant increase in bandwidth and the introduction of more powerful and sexier devices, like the iPhone which was introduced in 2007 followed by android phones in 2008.

As indicated by Jackob Nielson and his "Nielsen's law of internet bandwidth," users' bandwidth has grown by 50% per year from 1983 to 2016.[2]

The following screen shot illustrates this "law" and will continue to evolve annually at https://www.nngroup.com/articles/law-of-bandwidth/.

The dots in the diagram show the various speeds with which I have connected to the net, from an early acoustic 300 bps modem in 1984 to an ISDN line when I first wrote this article (and updated to show the 300 Mbps upgrade I got in 2018. It is amazing how closely the empirical data fits the exponential growth curve for the 50% annualized growth stated by Nielsen's law. (The y-axis has a logarithmic scale: thus, a straight line in the diagram represents exponential growth by a constant percentage every year).

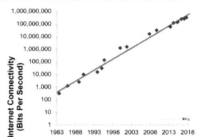

Nielsen's law is similar to the more established Moore's law. Unfortunately, comparing the two laws shows that bandwidth grows slower than computer power. Moore's law says that computers double in capabilities every 18 months, which corresponds to about 60% annual growth. As shown in the table, bandwidth will remain the gating factor in the experienced quality of using the internet medium.

		Annualized Growth Rate	Compound Growth Over 10 Years
Nielsen's law	Internet bandwidth	50%	57x
Moore's law	Computer power	60%	100x

After the initial years of "irrational exuberance" and the popping of "the internet bubble" it became very clear that the internet was a new and powerful marketing tool, that was (and is) constantly changing; from email marketing to banner ads; to search engine marketing to social media marketing; and from simplistic ROI calculations to algorithmic attribution models. In 2016 it was estimated by eMarketer[3] that 37% of total media spend in the U.S. that year was being spent on digital marketing. While specific numbers are not available for hotels, we believe that this number is even greater for that vertical.

Important Milestones in Hospitality Marketing & Technologies

1995
- Netscape Goes Public
- Microsoft Internet Explorer 1.0 Launched
- Backrub (later to be called Google) Formed
- Amazon.com begins selling books online

The Rest Is History...
- Expedia launched (1996)
- CTRIP launched (1999)
- TripAdvisor launched (2000)

- Email for Blackberry launched (2001)
- WordPress released (2003)
- LinkedIn launched (2003)
- Myspace founded (2003)
- First commercial mobile SMS (2003)
- Facebook launched (2004)
- YouTube founded (2005)
- Twitter launched (2006)
- iPhone introduced (2007)
- Android smartphone launched (2008)
- Airbnb started (2008)
- UBER founded (2009)
- Instagram launched (2010)
- Facebook Chat launched (2011)
- Google+ launched (2011)
- iPad introduced (2011)
- Device responsive website design became the new website standard (2012)
- Expedia purchased Travelocity and Orbitz (2015)
- Snapchat went public (2017)

As we updated this 5th edition of the CHDM Study Guide, we came to the realization that formatting it in a linear approach does not provide the most efficient resource for the student. Since the field is constantly changing with new technology and entrants, we must create a "field guide" that is easily updatable. There is also so much overlap between different areas of digital marketing that dividing topics into understandable chunks can often become overwhelming. One example of this would be social media. When discussing social media, we need to discuss paid media, review sites, engagement, influencer's, website integration, on-property activation, and so on. Based on this we have decided to break down the course work in a different way. This guide will focus the reader on where the specific tactic or strategy fits within these three buckets:

1. **Paid Media:** This includes any media that requires that you pay the "publisher" for that media unit. This includes paid search, display advertising, social media advertising (including "boosting posts"), subscription services (e.g., Trip Advisor Business Listing), and the myriad of other paid advertising vehicles.

2. **Earned Media:** It is called "earned" media because it often requires effort and know-how to get it; you can't buy it — you must earn it. In a traditional sense it might be PR or word of mouth advertising but in the digital world this becomes mentions in blogs, posts, websites, review sites, and so on. While it takes effort (and sometimes cost) to garner earned media, it is often among the most powerful because it is deemed by consumers as "unbiased" information.

3. **Owned Media:** This is any media that is directly controlled by you. The most obvious is your website but can also include social sites, database/email marketing, blogs, and so on.

We believe by dividing into these areas the content becomes more understandable and hopefully a little less overwhelming.

The following diagram illustrates how different marketing vehicles fit into this structure.

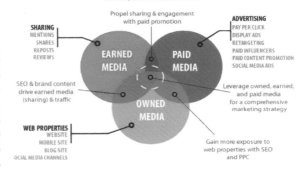

Source: https://www.titan-seo.com/newsarticles/trifecta.html

Why are these labels important? Marketing lingo comes in and out of fashion and some might even question the use of these terms, but this is an easily understandable way to help divide the course, and we also believe it is useful for digital marketers to be thinking in these terms (or terms similar to this). Everything the digital market does should be for a reason; once this goal is determined then these terms give you a good way to consider your options and determine how you will get your message out. For example:

Hotel A has a soft period in the next month and needs to do its best to fill those rooms. The GM comes to the digital marketing team with a budget (or not) and asks, what can we do? The digital marketer then should ask him/herself these questions:

- What should we do in paid media?
- What should we do in earned media?
- What should we do in owned media?

After going through this exercise, the digital marketer may choose tactics in all three or perhaps just one of these areas.

The guide that ensues is meant to touch on the most important elements of digital marketing for hoteliers and represents the base of knowledge required to be considered a Certified Hospitality Digital Marketer (CHDM).

We hope you enjoy the study guide and good luck with the certification process!

Important Note: This guide was published in May 2019 and will be updated again within 2 years. At the time of publishing all the information was accurate, but it is important, as a digital marketer, that we all keep up to date on the changes in the discipline.

Chapter 1 Endnotes

[1] Kamath, Maya. "To reach 50 million users Telephone took 75 years, Internet took 4 years however Angry Birds took only 35 days!!" TechWorm. March 13, 2015. www.techworm.net/2015/03/to-reach-50-million-users-telephone-took-75-years-internet-took-4-years-angry-birds-took-only-35-days.html. January 5, 2018.

[2] Nielsen, Jakob. "Nielsen's Law of Internet Bandwidth." Nielsen Norman Group. 2018. https://www.nngroup.com/articles/law-of-bandwidth/. January 8, 2018.

[3] US Digital Ad Spending to Surpass TV this Year. eMarketer. September 13, 2016. www.emarketer.com/Article/US-Digital-Ad-Spending-Surpass-TV-this-Year/1014469. January 5, 2018.

Today's technologically advanced travel marketplace sees travelers interacting with multiple digital devices, while expecting those encounters to address their personal needs and interests. This behavior is understandable, given the rise of always available mobile apps and voice-based personal assistants. As a result, hoteliers are finding that engaging travelers and satisfying their expectations is an increasingly complex endeavor.

Some context is required to fully appreciate the challenges facing today's hospitality marketer. See "Important Milestones in Hospitality Marketing & Technologies" in Chapter 1 for a listing of significant hospitality industry advancements juxtaposed with important general technology advancements.

A Historical Perspective

A century ago, Ellsworth Statler, the father of the modern hotel industry, proclaimed the keys to success using three maxims that remain relevant today:

- "Location, Location, Location" — still the first rule of hotel Real Estate Investment Trusts (REITs)
- "Life is Service" — a mantra of every successful luxury hotel operator
- "The Guest is Always Right" — one that continues to be problematic for digital marketers

If a hotel offered a good product, in a good location, and treated guests well, word-of-mouth referrals could sustain adequate traveler demand.

Fifty years ago, as travelers became more mobile via increased automobile and commercial air travel, hotel brands emerged, creating expectations of consistency across a breadth of destinations. These brands incorporated new technologies including computerization and central call centers to simplify and add consistency to the booking process across growing property portfolios.

Brand messaging was tightly controlled by the hoteliers through advertising and public relations. It largely highlighted product features, and was broadcast to consumers largely based on the demographics of a particular distribution channel.

Two decades ago, hotel distribution continued to be largely focused on traditional consumer media, travel agency, corporate travel management company, and group meeting planner channels. But the internet changed everything. At first, Travelocity, the first Online Travel Agency (OTA) touted a "Shop, Check, Book" process for consumer self-booking that mirrored methods employed by travel agents.

Six major step-changes have required hoteliers to adapt since the birth of the Internet:

1. World Wide Web
2. Interface Standards
3. Social Networking
4. Free Web Analytics
5. Smartphones
6. Machine Learning/Big Data/Voice Interfaces

The first phase of the internet's impact on the hotel industry was the World Wide Web. Early hotel websites began to propagate, presenting rates and inventory availability, along with basic descriptive information and photos shared over the internet. As familiarity with the technology advanced, hoteliers gained powerful new tools.

Email campaigns powered by Customer Relationship Management (CRM) tools offered more customized communications based on enhanced guest profile information. Search engine marketing enabled messaging tailored to the topics being searched. Rich media and video eventually provided more immersive and compelling story telling by hoteliers.

A second, and much more subtle, impact was put into motion in the early 2000's — resulting from travel industry interface standards. Pioneered by the OpenTravel Alliance, XML-based messaging specifications facilitated the ability of organizations to more easily exchange travel-related data.

These standards soon ushered the ability for technology vendors and digital agencies to more easily marry Internet Booking Engines (IBE) with the Content Management Systems (CMS) powering websites. Channel Management Systems (ChMS) were then created to more efficiently manage the growing number of systems capable of booking a hotel.

This new level of automation allowed the flexibility of either pushing the information from the hotels to the OTA, or the OTA pulling the data from the hotels, replacing reliance on cumbersome manual update processes via extranet. Websites became efficient at booking hotels, offering a greater variety of rates, with more accurate pricing and availability, resulting in more customer adoption and improved booking conversion rates.

A third phase of impact, between 2004 and 2006, saw the widespread adoption of social networks, featuring user-generated content sharing. Changes were led by TripAdvisor's pivot to consumer review forums, the launch of YouTube, and Facebook opening its network beyond students. The internet radically democratized the aggregation, communication, and consumption of information. For hoteliers, this was an unnerving development. Customer conversations might not involve management of the hotel, even though the property was a primary subject of discussion.

Brand positioning transitioned from the controlled messaging that a hotel published to what consumers believed, based on descriptions, photos, and videos shared by fellow travelers. This significant loss of control was countered with new reputation management tools that helped to proactively manage conversations, address customer service issues, and improve guest satisfaction.

The fourth phase of technological advancement arose around the same time frame with the launch of Google Analytics, which allowed webmasters to better understand the sources and behaviors of site visitors. Basic analytics metrics that were once only available to large organizations able to fund support for Omniture SiteCatalyst (now part of Adobe's Marketing Cloud) were available to any website for free.

The ability to leverage tracking pixels and browser cookies to monitor and track user actions provided online advertising with an advantage over traditional offline broadcast media by offering clearer evidence of Return on Investment (ROI). One challenge that arose however was determining the attribution of booking intent from tracking data that extended across plural touchpoints, across multiple websites and sessions.

Determining cause and effect remains a considerable task, even for those sporting the most comprehensive tracking technologies. In many cases, travel apps and websites use extensive A/B or multi-variate testing to compare results of experiments designed to improve usability, engagement, and conversion opportunities.

The introduction of the smartphone, most notably the launch of the Apple iPhone in 2007, produced a fifth phase of internet-induced change for hotels. Beautiful websites designed for a guest's desktop computer did not translate well to the cramped real estate and less reliable bandwidth of a handheld mobile device. Notoriously impatient mobile users required a better user experience tailored to fingers and taps as opposed to the point and click of a mouse.

Native applications (Apps) designed specifically for mobile devices evolved to take advantage of new mobile technologies including Global Positioning Systems (GPS), wireless networking (WiFi/Bluetooth), messaging (SMS), cameras, fingerprint readers, and contactless payments (NFC), in addition to voice telephony. Mobile-web friendly websites now offer many capabilities that were once exclusively the domain of native apps.

Even a decade later, hotels, OTAs, and Metasearch websites continue to struggle with optimizing booking conversion on mobile devices, despite the fact that mobile website traffic in many cases now exceeds desktop traffic.

Today, leading brand and property websites take advantage of all past advancements offered by internet-based technologies. Tracking user behaviors, they learned to present personalized content and alter website experiences based on customer profiles, navigation, and purchase behavior to appeal to specific traveler personas for a particular property, destination, or customer segment. Behavioral retargeting presents context-relevant advertising across advertising exchanges for users who have previously visited a hotel website.

Major travel websites, whose business models are powered by data-driven strategies, adapt digital experiences based on a combination of historic and exhibited behaviors, even before they may recognize the complex underlying motivations driving those user decisions. They employ a Test-and-Learn philosophy that knows no fixed objective — they seek continual improvement through a cycle of more data yielding better understanding to produce improved results.

Sophisticated digital marketers can dynamically create specialized promotional offers and alter Cost-per-Click (CPC) bidding strategies depending on the expected booking value, probability of conversion, and ultimately customer lifetime value of a traveler.

However, in 2017 the hotel industry entered a sixth phase of internet technology impact, with the emergence of Machine Learning, Big Data, and Voice Interfaces.

Using big data technologies to capture massive quantities of information from a broad range of sources, machine learning algorithms identify patterns and signals to improve user experiences and optimize conversion rates using predictive models that would be too labor intensive and take too long for humans to calculate. This capability now informs everything from pricing and product sort orders to tactical promotions based on weather patterns or news events.

Advanced deep learning technologies, now utilizing neural networks, are being applied to the challenge of voice (natural language processing) and image (computer vision) recognition, tackling not only identification of content, but context. Artificial Intelligence (AI) is the natural extension of machine learning, the point where systems are trained to make decisions and ultimately enhance their own applications without human assistance.

Where web searches originally produced a list of links deemed best suited to offer relevant information, voice interfaces for mobile devices and home smart speakers are designed to leverage big data and artificial intelligence to offer what the user ultimately seeks — the BEST answer to their query. Hotel marketers will need to again adapt to a dramatic change in societal behavior and expectations prior to, during, and following a guest's stay.

Digital Marketing = Business Model + Strategy + Measurement

A hotel must consider appropriate marketing strategies based on market conditions, competitive positioning, and product differentiation. However, the resources available to fund strategic initiatives depend on the business drivers of the enterprise.

Hotels are not built to earn revenue; the ultimate objective is to produce a profitable return on investment. Hospitality digital marketing executives must understand the underlying business model of the hotel or brand to create value by attracting and sustaining profitable business.

As with all businesses, organizational strategy has three foundational pillars — Business Model, Performance Measurement, and Risk Tolerance. From a pragmatic perspective, strategies supporting well-defined, measurable goals more readily earn funding approval by helping decision makers understand risks.

Business models represent how a corporate strategy creates value. One of the major trends in the hotel industry has been the shift from capital intensive to service-based business models. Major hotel groups that once owned and managed large property portfolios have gone "asset light," divesting the real estate assets on their balance sheets in favor of fee-based revenue streams.

The fragmentation of the hotel industry into hotel owners, third-party management companies, and hotel brands has created multiple parties that may have differing revenue streams, cost structures, and risk exposure emanating from a single property. It is critical for hotel marketers to understand how business strategies impact the profitability of these various constituencies.

The increased share of branded properties results from the same trend toward a services orientation. While an independent hotel may be able to establish awareness within a particular area or market segment, its core demand may not be sufficient to drive adequate profitability. Hotel brands can extend a hotel's marketing reach substantially across a broader geographic region or additional market sectors, especially when able to successfully cross-sell to frequent guests of sister properties.

Property-level marketing and branding expenditures can represent risky propositions for hotel owners, particularly during times of economic uncertainty. Paying a franchise and/ or marketing fee can reduce the financial exposure and cash flow impact of developing and executing marketing programs by basing expenditures on achieved sales and shifting some responsibility for driving revenue to a partner hotel group. This is why many hotel financing term sheets often require some form of brand relationship.

The growing market share of OTAs results from similar structural factors. OTAs expend billions of dollars to global marketing initiatives and technology platforms designed to convert travel demand into any hotel sale, not specifically for a particular brand or property. As hotel brands extend the marketing reach of a property, an OTA can extend the distribution of both a property and brand — again, with limited risk exposure. Compensated only on arrived business, OTAs have successfully developed a business model that is best described as "Guests as a Service." While some hoteliers may complain about OTA fee levels (or brand fee levels, for that matter), in many cases, those complaints discount the pricing premium typically associated with any business model that creates value by eliminating risk.

All intermediary compensation levels are dictated by market conditions — if insufficient value is created, there is downward pressure on fee levels. Following nine years of economic recovery after the global financial crisis, the hotel industry is generally performing very well. That strength is reportedly translating into pressure on OTA margins.

However, during economic downturns when hoteliers become highly motivated to seek incremental market share as core demand sources wane, intermediaries gain an opportunity to grow margins as risks increase for hotel owners, especially if limited alternatives exist.

Pulling It All Together

Hospitality marketing has evolved into a discipline that encompasses every facet of the lodging business ranging from product design, service delivery standards, and competitive positioning, to more traditional marketing disciplines of pricing, promotion, and distribution. In order to efficiently execute successful marketing campaigns, hospitality marketers now need to get a lot of things right. For example:

- Offering the Right PRODUCT (beachfront hotel)
- In the Right PLACE (Jamaica)
- Including the Right EXPERIENCE (all-inclusive package)
- To the Right GUEST (family with young children)
- Providing the Right VALUE (ocean view upgrade)
- Via the Right MEDIA (retargeting ad)
- On the Right PLATFORM (mobile)
- Using the Right CONTENT (family beach GIF)
- For the Right PRICE ($299 per night)
- Rewarding the Right BEHAVIOR (clicking on an offer)
- At the Right TIME (weekend evening)
- Through the Right CHANNEL (direct to hotel website)

Every strategy should be mapped to a desired outcome, which may range from a principal business objective to a specific tactical result. Regardless of magnitude, goals must be measurable. When success can be measured, success can be rewarded. Even if a strategy is not successful, measurable results offer an opportunity for future refinement and improvement. It should also be noted that if success can't be measured, it becomes simpler for critics to describe it as failure.

The following chart presents examples of common metrics used to measure the success of several business objectives that are matched with a phase of the traveler lifecycle.

Examples of Goals and Metrics by Traveler Lifecycle Phase

Phase	Objective	Example Metric
Dreaming	Acquisition	Click-Through & Bounce Rate
Planning	Engagement	Week 1 Retention Rate
Booking	Conversion	Arrived Conversion Rate
Experience	Satisfaction	Net Promoter Score
Sharing	Evangelism	Shares, Amplification & Applause Rate

Technology is a Tool to Support Strategy

In a digital world, success requires the appropriate alignment of strategy and technology. This does not mandate that a hotel have access to the latest and greatest tools (although that helps). Technology is merely a tool to fulfill the strategy — businesses with good technology rarely survive bad strategies.

Effective digital marketing strategies must consider the hotel's technological capabilities to efficiently target the desired customer, deliver appropriate messaging, and measure performance with sufficient detail to allow the marketer to learn and refine future efforts. If technology gaps exist, unnecessary complexity should be avoided. Good strategies supported by good technology create opportunities.

Over the years, the internet has enabled the tech industry to embrace highly scalable Software as a Service (SaaS) business models that reduce capital expenditures and risk profiles associated with technology investments. Cloud computing — using internet-based services to replace local servers (including the hardware and labor required to maintain it) — serves as the foundation for SaaS platforms.

The primary technological challenge facing hoteliers is keeping up with the accelerating pace of technology innovation in a complex industry with a highly fragmented control structure and geographically dispersed product portfolio. Core hotel operational technologies such as Property Management System (PMS), Point of Sale (POS), Private Branch Exchange (PBX), Heating, Ventilation & Air Conditioning (HVAC) control systems were traditionally proprietary, requiring expensive custom interfacing to communicate.

Scrubbing fully depreciated technology assets off balance sheets when transitioning from legacy systems to modern Cloud/SaaS platforms is conceptually compelling, especially when avoiding large upfront capital expenditures in the process.

However, the reality of replacing the full operational tech stack within 24/7 hotel operations can be a daunting task. Replacing one system can create a functional gap with another interfaced "mission critical" legacy system. Writing a temporary "throwaway" interface between the new platform and the old system that may also soon be replaced is rarely cost effective.

Superlative coordination is required across brands, owners, and management (who may control various systems), especially when decisions are made regarding who expends the funds, as compared with who reaps the benefits. The complexity of multiple partners, possessing different business models with diverse revenue streams, expense exposure, and risk tolerance can complicate technology decisions.

Similar dynamics impact the hotel marketing technology stack. Many marketing and operational systems must be integrated to provide a cohesive guest experience. Complicating matters further, hoteliers want to avoid costs related to retraining staff and establishing new processes to replicate tasks that are already reliably executed.

The following table offers a summary of the major components of the growing hospitality marketing technology stack (excluding operational systems like PMS, POS, etc.).

Marketing Tech Stack

Business Intelligence
Campaign/Website/Sales Analytics | Frequency Program
Guest Profile Management | Management Dashboards
Rate Shopping | Surveys and Guest Reviews
Yield & Revenue Management

Digital
Booking Engine | Content Management System
Customer Relationship Management | Database Marketing
Digital Marketing Platform | Search Marketing |
Social Media Marketing Website Development/Management

Distribution
Call Center Services | Central Reservation System
Channel Management | Global Distribution Systems
Internet Booking Engine | Internet Distribution System

Sales Office
Meeting and Event Planning | Catering and Event Management
Sales/Catering/Event Management | Casino Player Tracking

Source: Channel Optimization in Hospitality, Secrets of Data-Driven Hoteliers — Phocuswright, 2017

Every marketing strategy now has a digital dimension. Digital permeates every aspect of guest engagement, from pre-arrival shopping online to the in-real-life on-property experience, and the sharing of those experiences with others. A critical consideration is how well its marketing technology stack can effectively manage initiatives advancing the hotel's business strategy.

The successful digital marketer must consider not only the direct marketing results, but how they translate into enterprise profitability through the most efficient deployment of available technology.

Historically, a marketing funnel looked like this:

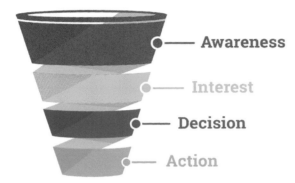

Typically, awareness was created by placing print ads or running direct mail campaigns. Once some interest was established, the ball was placed in the hands of salespeople or operations. Marketing's role was really just to lead the prospects to the point of contacting the individual hotel or brand.

In today's digital world, the funnel has changed significantly. Today, digital marketing likely has a role in every single step of this funnel.

What is "digital marketing" or "eCommerce?" What do you think of when you hear those terms? Many of you will think first of your hotel or brand website. Others will consider online travel agencies such as Expedia or Booking.com, and metasearch sites such as Kayak or Trivago. Or is it customer review sites such as TripAdvisor and Yelp? Social media? Facebook? Or is it search engine optimization, online marketing, paid media channels? Perhaps email marketing? What about mobile apps and digital guest services?

The truth is, "digital" encompasses all of these areas — and much more — and is the fastest evolving and ever-changing area of the hotel business. Digital now covers all phases of the customer "journey" in regard to booking a hotel (as well as staying at a hotel), and for many brands and hotels, it is quickly becoming the largest single source of customer traffic and bookings.

Let's quickly cover the 4 main "phases" of the digital customer journey:

The Acquisitions Phase

How do we "acquire" customers on our end digital channel — our hotel website? How do potential customers find us and where do we need to engage those customers to capture their attention and bring them to our sites? Examples of these areas that will be discussed in this program include natural (or organic search), paid search, local search, third-party sites such as TripAdvisor and metasearch engines, social media, and many others.

The Conversion Phase

Once we capture those customers and bring them to our hotel website, we still need to "convince" them to book with us and "Convert" them into "bookers." While, as digital marketers, we may not be able to control all guest considerations such as price and location of the hotel, we have direct control over the display of content on our website that would convince a potential guest that our hotel is, in fact, the correct choice for them. Content may include textual information about the hotel, surrounding area, maps and directions, and airport and transportation information to name a few, as well as professional imagery that relays visual information about the hotel, it's facilities, rooms, area attractions, and more.

Other content areas may include customer reviews, social media links, benefits of booking on your channel, and more. In the end, your hotel website should serve as your "virtual lobby." More travelers will see your website than will ever walk through your physical doors. Also keep in mind that many customers who choose to book your hotel on other channels will visit your hotel website to view much of the above information, either before or after their booking.

The "Stay" Phase

This is the "newest" area of digital business... how can we leverage "digital" post-booking? We have seen initial efforts into this space through engagements such as confirmation and pre-arrival emails and ancillary sales efforts. However, there are many more ways we can engage with and service our on-property guests once they arrive at our hotels. More recent and future engagement areas in this phase include mobile check-in and check-out, keyless room entry, guest service requests and chat through our apps, in-room entertainment options, guest messaging, and more. This is an exciting area for hoteliers as we better leverage digital and mobile technology to provide more enhanced customer service to our guests and provide them with the more streamlined digital options that they have been asking for from all of us.

The Post-Stay Phase

This is the period where you attempt to build a long-term relationship with the guest. Even if they booked through a third party, if you are able to get the guests email address you can directly talk to them and engage them, and the next time they look to book, they will likely book direct. While we cannot get every guest to book direct, the holy grail is being able to ensure that the second time they book, they book direct.

This customer journey is also referred to as the purchase funnel, and while different people and organizations have different takes on it, at the end of the day it is all very similar with the ultimate goal of driving conversion.

The Customer Journey and Funnel

The average consumer visits 12 to 36 websites before booking a hotel. So, where are they going...and, more importantly, what is impacting their end decision? Let's walk through a simple example a customer journey — taking a family of two adults and two kids looking for somewhere to go for their summer vacation:[1]

Let's return to the first part of the customer journey — the Acquisitions Phase — to illustrate the many influencers to which today's digital customers are exposed. Where are our guests going and what are they seeing as they navigate the digital landscape during their search? Why is this important?

This family has decided they need a much need vacation. At this point, they have no idea where to go and begin their research on line.

Their first "Google" search may be for something very generic as they first need to decide on where they are traveling...say "Family Vacations" or "Best places to travel with kids." The results may be a host of articles, travel blogs, top 10 lists, informational sites, as well as travel sites such as Expedia, TripAdvisor, and brand sites, among others. In this discovery phase alone, they may well visit dozens of websites.

Once they decide on a location...for this example, let's pretend Orlando as it's time to get those kids to Disney and Universal... the next step may be to research airfare (is this trip affordable?). They may find themselves visiting multiple airline sites as well as Online Travel Agencies such as Expedia and Booking.com to check airline prices and flight schedules. From these sites, they may also start looking at hotels or be exposed to offers, deals, and other marketing from relevant travel companies.

Once the decision is made that this is indeed a great trip destination, they may return to Google with a slightly more detailed search — "hotels in Orlando." They begin to check hotels in the market, prices, locations, imagery, and review scores. They may again visit the Octa's, but also brand.com sites such as Marriott, Hilton, IHG, and independents. They may visit metasearch sites such as Kayak and Trivago to better compare prices and availability.

Through all of this, many customers will now also engage social media. From simply asking friends for travel information and advice, social media has now become a larger influencer on the decision-making process. So, our family goes to Facebook to ask for recommendations on where to stay, what to do, etc. (possibly being exposed to retargeting and travel ads in the meantime).

Keep in mind that this family may visit many of these sites multiple times, and during their journey, will also be exposed to marketing and advertising, offers, rate displays, targeted and retargeted ads, and other influencers.

Their final visit, if not one of the above sites to make their booking, may be to return to Google and search on the exact hotel name, again with results from many of these sites for booking options. What they see first on Google will highly depend on paid advertising (SEM or paid search), or organic rankings in search results, highly depended on SEO activities.

For the moment, let's assume the family made this final search on Google for the hotel they decided on…and then clicked on the link to the hotel's own website. From a reporting perspective, this would be tracked as a branded search from Google and attributed to that in reports. However, the truth is that the customer visited dozens of sites and was exposed to a large number of influencers along the way.

As you move into the following sections of the CHDM study guide, ask yourself "where in the journey/funnel is the customer?" This may help you understand how best to market to this customer. Remember, while it is easy to think of the funnel as linear, it is not — people can bounce around. Consider the customer who has booked your hotel and continues to search to confirm their decision and check pricing. This customer went from booking back to inspiration and research, and this has to be taken into consideration.

The following represent different ways to think about and visualize the customer journey and the funnel.

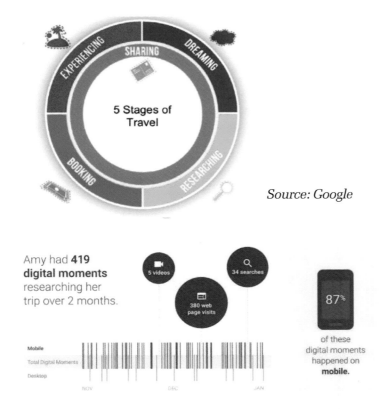

Source: Google

Source: Think with Google[2]

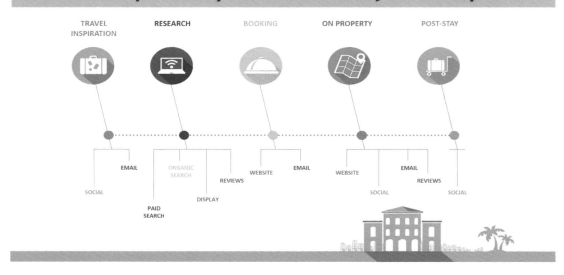

Hospitality Customer Journey

| TRAVEL INSPIRATION | RESEARCH | BOOKING | ON PROPERTY | POST-STAY |

Source: Milestone Internet Marketing

Customer Journey Evolution

Old Model

Awareness

Trust

Engagement

Bookings / Conversion

New Model

Source: Milestone Internet Marketing

In truth the process is not linear — especially today when people, even after booking, continue to search, explore, talk about, and potentially even change their decision.

Chapter 3 Endnotes

[1] Used by permission of Shawn Paley. https://spark.adobe.com/page/Qw6IcN8kdKolA/

[2] Travel Trends: 4 Mobile Moments Changing the Consumer Journey. Think with Google. November 2015. www.thinkwithgoogle. com/consumer-insights/travel-trends-4-mobile-moments-changing-consumer-journey/. January 5, 2018.

CHAPTER 4
The Hotel Website

KEY POINTS

- Regularly updated content and professional imagery are important for a successful, revenue generating website.

- Best practices for optimum revenue-generating websites include travel booker friendliness, user friendliness, search engine friendliness, mobile optimization, and social interactivity.

- Understand additional features available and functionality required for an effective site.

SUMMARY

"When I started in the hotel business 52 years ago, the first impression customers had of our hotels was the lobby when they walked through the front doors. But in this digital age, often the first impression comes when they visit Marriott.com. It's our digital front door." - Bill Marriott

Currently, the hotel website represents the best opportunity for high-volume, low-cost bookings. It is your most valuable owned asset in the digital landscape. Properties must ensure that their hotel websites are optimized for search engines, best represent their selling points, and are geared to an online customer.

There are essentially three types of websites:

- **Brand.com** – If your property is part of a brand, in all likelihood, your property will be included in the brand website and booking engine; the property will have some level of control over content and rates but for the most part control is with the brand.

- **IndependentHotel.com** – Hotels that are not part of a brand, in all likelihood, will build an independent website and utilize a third party or homegrown booking engine for their property.

- **VanitySite.com** – Sometimes also called microsites, these sites are sometimes created by properties that already have presence on a brand site but for some reason have decided that having an additional property specific site is needed. Reasons include uniqueness of property that cannot be represented on brand.com, language needs that may not be represented on brand.com, search engine strategy, etc. While vanity sites may be a good option, they should be carefully considered as there are also drawbacks to having these sites. Please note that different brands have different guidelines as they relate to vanity sites; some may allow them while others strictly forbid them.

Once the investment decision is made to build (or re-build) a website, there is a finite list of must-haves to ensure your website is user friendly, search engine friendly, and booker-friendly.

What began in the early '90s as simply a digital brochure has evolved into a complex collection of marketing content, keywords, meta tags, visual images, widgets, and booking engines. Within this platform, you are not only telling your story to your potential guests through visuals and text, there is a lot more going on. Your website – and social presence – should communicate a specific vision that speaks to search engines, Google, Siri, your customer's and their friends and family, other influencers, and of course, your owners. And these elements exist for two reasons – to acquire and convert more customers.

The first step in any hotel digital marketing strategy should be a review of (or creation of, in the case of a new hotel) the hotel website. Today's hotel website carries the burden and responsibility of generating or initiating the bulk of online bookings for the property. The property website has become the backbone of the hotel marketing mix and is the primary digital asset of any hotel. In this age of multi-channel marketing, any type of hotel marketing initiative (from search engine marketing and banner advertising to email and social marketing) ultimately drives travel consumers to the hotel website. In short, the best ROI can currently be found by creating or maintaining a well-optimized, user-friendly, mobile optimized, booking-friendly, property-specific website.

Independent vs. Franchise/Branded Properties

Each brand or franchise has a website typically referred to as its brand.com site. For example, when you franchise a Holiday Inn, your property has an individual presence on the IHG.com branded site. For these branded hotels, maintaining an up-to-date branded site should be the primary focus and centerpiece of your online presence. In some cases, a stand-alone site, often referred to as a "vanity site," may be a necessary supplement. In the case of independent, non-branded properties, a stand-alone site is a necessity.

This chapter first addresses branded hotels with a presence on the brand.com website, then independent hotels and resorts responsible for their own website creation. While in some cases, branded hotels will also create and maintain a stand-alone ("vanity") website, hotels should always discuss this with their brand to be sure they understand the brand's position on vanity websites, as well as possible issues this may cause versus the potential benefits.

Brand.com

Typically, hotels that are part of a large brand (such as Marriott, Hilton, Starwood, etc.) are automatically provided a website on the brand.com site. These sites follow the brand templates (design, color schemes, and navigation), and have many of the important features already built in, including booking widgets and other appropriate technology, textual content, and imagery placements as well as additional marketing components.

While the brand provides the framework, it is the responsibility of the property to ensure the website is well maintained from a content perspective, including:

- Well-written and effective textual content from both a marketing and SEO standpoint
- Up-to-date, professional hotel and room imagery
- Use of other ancillary components offered by the brand for promotions & deals, additional hotel information, "product" highlights, and other "news and updates" for the hotel

IndependentHotel.com (also for branded properties with stand-alone websites)

The decision is simple for an independent hotel or resort – a website is an absolute necessity. The primary strategic decision in this case is the level of investment appropriate for the vanity site based on projected returns. In order to determine the level of investment you should make, consider the following factors:

- Does your website have the most accurate descriptions of your hotel product and services from both a textual content and imagery perspective?
- Are your year-over-year (YOY) website booking contributions growing, level, or slipping? How does that compare to industry benchmarks and within your market?
- Are your website traffic and search rankings deteriorating? When was your website last re-optimized for SEO?
- Is your website integrated with the property's social media profiles?
- Does your website include a blog (and are you posting to that blog)?
- Does your website support open graph tags (snippets of code that cause your selected picture and marketing text to appear when users share content from your site on Facebook, tweet links to your content, or post to Instagram)?
- Does your website have a robust Content Management System (CMS) to allow you to manage visual and textual content, set up new specials and packages, post events and happenings, create new landing pages, and push fresh content to your social media and mobile site? Does your CMS support social media integration, such as updating Facebook from within the CMS?
- Is your website responsive? In other words, is the site built in a way that automatically adapts to the various devices and screen sizes used by today's consumers? Most search engines, such as Google, are now favoring responsive sites in their ranking algorithms. In fact, Google penalizes websites that are not mobile friendly.
- Do you find that you and your staff like the websites of your competitors better than your own?

- Do you have any staff capacity and capability to manage the site in-house, or will you need to outsource the site management?
- If your hotel website was last redesigned more than two years ago, remember that the rate of change in the industry is high. In the last few years we saw the deployment and adoption of schemas, open graph tags, new algorithm updates including penalties for non-mobile friendly sites. Change is continuous and rapid. Hoteliers no longer have a choice of whether to redesign their website. A website redesign is a must and should be considered in the upcoming budgeting season if not budgeted for the current year.

VanitySite.com

For branded properties, a number of factors must be considered prior to electing to allocate resources for a vanity site.

First, it pays to understand the chain/brand policies regarding property vanity websites. Several brands discourage their franchisees from creating stand-alone sites, preferring the resources be channeled through a central brand site or other online marketing activities. This enables product consistency, and in some cases is the wisest decision for a property. In either case, the best practice is to review your chain/brand's policies and recommendations regarding vanity websites before investing time and resources. Maintaining current information on a branded site is time consuming, and regardless of whether a stand-alone site is needed, this should be a priority for any digital marketing strategy. Keeping photos, information, keywords, and market niches up to date is primarily the responsibility of the property.

Does the chain/brand provide adequate marketing exposure and promotional support for all of your key customer segments? Typically, branded hotels have similarities. Residence Inn is known for extended stays. Hyatt is known for meeting and catering space. If your hotel matches your brand's typical profile, it is likely their branded site will provide you the support you need. However, if you are a hotel with an unusual ratio of meeting space, have unusual or different facilities outside the brand norm, or a location near a strong demand generator, the branded site may or may not support your needs.

Does your hotel offer packages and special offers that can't easily be accommodated on the brand site? If so, a vanity site can help in featuring and selling these packages and special offers better than the brand site.

After analyzing property location and composition of visitors (e.g., leisure, business, group, etc.) to your destination, is every significant visitor segment sufficiently addressed by the chain/brand site? Sometimes resorts and full service properties in primary markets may not be adequately supported by a brand site. There are resort brands that support their properties perfectly, but a resort property is often unique in that it targets a very specific mix of customers due to its location and activities. This may necessitate a more specific targeted approach to the website than the brand can provide.

Does the chain/brand provide adequate marketing exposure for your property in your main feeder markets? More specifically, do you know where they are marketing your hotel? Most brands run extensive search marketing campaigns, but it is the responsibility of the property to communicate your targeted feeder cities to the brand.

How competitive is your location on the chain/brand website? If you are in a primary or even secondary market with a strong brand presence — meaning multiple properties flying the same flag – a vanity site may be necessary to stand apart. Also, as noted previously, if your property has a non-standard brand component, a vanity site may be necessary to target your right customer mix.

Are your booking contributions via the web competitive — are you receiving your fair share of online bookings? Bottom line, if you are receiving more than your fair share on your branded site, is a vanity site necessary? If, on the other hand, you see that your share is lagging, a great boost would likely be a new or upgraded vanity site.

How easy is it for a customer to find your specific hotel on the brand site? In some cases, there are franchise naming issues – Hotel X airport south, airport southeast, etc., that may be confusing to consumers, and a vanity site may more clearly differentiate your property.

What is the referral process of your brand site? If your hotel is sold out, what properties will be recommended? When will you be recommended?

What investment does the brand require of you to support the website and what investment does the brand make in local search efforts? The percent of spend on organic versus paid search should be relatively easy for a property to discover. Again, look at your return – are you getting a reasonable ROI?

Best Practices: Textual Content

Content should be written, first and foremost, with the customer in mind. The hotel should be positioned appropriately with the top selling features and informative descriptions of the hotel and its services. What you write matters as much as any keywords you use.

You and your brand may have invested a lot of time, effort, and budget into driving traffic to your website…now that you have a possible customer on your website, it's time to effectively market to and convince them that your hotel is the best choice for their trip. Search engine optimization (SEO) is also extremely important for your hotel website and definitely will have an impact on your textual content and metadata; thus striking a strong balance between the use of content for marketing and SEO is very important. SEO will be covered in more detail in Chapter 7.

It is also important to understand when creating content WHY the customer is considering your hotel and, thus, how you should market to them. There are obviously large differences, for example, between a city center hotel, an airport hotel, and a resort hotel. Each has a different audience, a different reason for "being" (trip purpose), and various amenities and services. Your content should best relate to those differences and speak in the appropriate "voice"… allowing visitors to quickly understand who and what you are…and what impression you wish to give of your hotel. One way to approach this is to think of your website in terms of how a Director of Sales (DOS) markets the hotel. Does your website reflect the demand generators that bring customers to your area? Are you appropriately featuring proximity to local attractions, amusement parks, stadiums, etc.? Are you a venue for weddings, family re-

unions, etc.? Make sure your website reflects the reasons why consumers travel to you or your area.

Keep It Brief

As you write your copy, keep in mind that web copy is a very different animal than print copy. Web copy is "scanned" or glanced through… not "read" in the traditional sense. This is even more true on mobile platforms, which will soon be the primary source of your online traffic and where visitors have much shorter attention spans. Most consumers will not read your website content word for word but look for appropriate "keywords" or phrases.

You should ensure that all text relates important features and selling points quickly and upfront and avoids long lists and heavy-handed, overly-promotional content that visitors won't read. Content should be easily scannable and paragraphs and sentences kept short and concise so visitors can find what they're looking for quickly. Your most important points should always come first, whether written in paragraph format or bulleted lists (for branded hotels, the formatting is typically pre-determined at the brand level template).

In addition, it is best to avoid needless repetition, jargon, and unnecessary words in your copy…keep it as simple as possible. As effective online copywriting can be seen as an "art," some properties will choose to hire professional copywriters or vendors to handle this area for them. Check first with your brand to see if they have any internal services or vendor recommendations.

Keep It Fresh

The "freshness" of your content is also extremely important, both from a marketing and an SEO perspective. All content areas should be up-to-date and include the latest information on the hotel itself, new services and amenities, and the most recent local area content. Not only is this important from a consumer perspective, but it is also extremely important from an SEO perspective as Google and other search engines weigh the "freshness" of content in their ranking algorithms.

Also, all promotional or event dates should be constantly updated (e.g., is your website still promoting a New Year's Eve event in February?). While content should always be reviewed and refreshed on a regular basis from a marketing and business perspective, especially when your property's facilities and amenities are changed or updated, the question is tougher when it comes to SEO. For SEO, it can be important to keep the addition of new content at a steady pace, keeping your page dynamic and continuously offering fresh content when and where possible. You should consider updating at least once to twice a year on key pages (those pages with the highest visitor view rates). For branded sites that include customer reviews, the constant addition of customer reviews also helps in this area as it is technically new content (as are responses by the hotel to those reviews).

It is important to have proper room descriptions as these will help drive conversion and upsell the customer into paying for a premium room.

In summary, is your website offering what your potential customers are looking for, is it current, and can they find it quickly (at a glance)?

Best Practices: Imagery

Imagery sells…and can make all the difference. Strong photography may be one of the most important aspects of your digital presence and your hotel website. Numerous studies show that photography is one of the primary influencers of bookings on a hotel website and, aside from price and location, ranks with reviews as one of the most important aspects in the customer decision-making process. Imagery should be professionally shot, using a photographer experienced in architectural photography. Neither handing a General Manager a high-end digital camera nor using a wedding photographer is an example of "professional" hotel photography.

Your hotel website photo gallery and header images should contain images representing all architectural features of the hotel, including the exterior, meeting space, lobby, fitness centers, pools, recreational areas, business centers, etc., and should provide the website visitor with enough visual knowledge to understand the offerings and services provided by the hotel. Pictures can tell a story, and a single image, if shot correctly, can convey information faster and more effectively than a paragraph of text.

Room photography is especially important. At the end of the day, the room is what the customer is "purchasing." It is important for them to understand the features of the room, the size of the room, and the differences between various room types. If you are selling a suite, focus on the size and layout of the room. If you are selling a "view" room, show the view. Too often, hotels simply repeat the same images (typically a bed shot) across various room types, in essence telling the customer that regardless of description and price, the rooms are all the same. We know that this is not the case and should show the rooms accordingly. This will assist in both conversion as well as upsell opportunities. If you can show a visitor how much bigger the "Junior Suite" is than a "Standard" room, or what that "City/Ocean View" looks like versus the "Standard" room through imagery, a customer will be much more likely to respond to upselling opportunities.

Effectively impact revenue generation through imagery.

- Tell the whole story with professional architectural photos. Be careful of over-staging, unnatural lighting, or props.

- Display a minimum of 2-3 images for each room type. The more high-quality images of the rooms and the hotel, the better; and trends have shown the number of images has an impact on customer engagement and bookings.

- Document the space with the best angles to give guests the visual information they look for when booking a room…show context.

- Capture the "benefits" of the room to show layout, features, and amenities…and, yes, bathroom shots are important as well.

- Document what is unique about a room type and visually represent the differences.

- Ensure that new photo shoots are scheduled as soon as possible during the opening process or after major renovations and enhancements.

- Avoid any stock hotel imagery. If customers realize you are showing them stock images and not actual images of the hotel, they will lose trust.

- If the website has the capability to show videos, 360's, and more immersive type imagery the property should take full advantage of this, as video (in particular) has been shown to have a big impact in the guest's purchase decision.

Be honest…do not "trick" customers through the use of photo cropping or Photoshop type enhancements, etc. Color correction, cropping for size, etc., is one thing…but providing false impressions of facilities to guests will result in lost trust or, worse yet, very unhappy customers at a hotel.

One area of hotel photography often debated is the use of models in your imagery. While models can often convey the hotel "experience," there are downsides as well. Models are expensive, can "date" your photos fairly quickly (clothing, hairstyles, etc.), and release rights are needed and must be kept up to date. Perhaps more importantly, models can provide unexpected perceptions of your hotel to possible guests. Think of that image of the family with small children enjoying the pool. To some, that might mean loud and splashing children running amok, and not a great hotel for a quiet retreat or work trip. Or, think about the image of the young couple at the bar. To some, that might mean it's not a great hotel for families with kids. While possible perceptions may not always align with the intent (or how we may view the same images), they must be considered.

To look at hotel photography a different way, compare hotel shopping to how we act when shopping for other retail products online. If you searched on Amazon.com for a product – let's say an Espresso machine – would you consider purchasing any of your resulting choices if they had no images attached? Do you learn more about the product with highly professional and multiple images (the machine's size, materials, color, and build) or those with only a single image? Are there specific features you're looking for – perhaps stainless steel – that are conveyed through the imagery more effectively than in the text description?

In summary, imagery may be the single most effective tactic you have on your hotel website to increase conversion. Today's consumers are more visual than ever and will gain most of the knowledge they need to know in their decision-making process from the website imagery. Your imagery serves as your "virtual" lobby (and will be viewed by far more people than

will ever walk through your physical lobby) and should present the very best of the hotel in the most professional way possible. If not done professionally and appropriately, and if once on your website the customer is provided a lack of, or poor, imagery, all those traffic generating efforts from SEO to PPC to display advertising may be for naught.

Best Practices: Ancillary Content

In addition to textual content and imagery, many brand.com sites offer additional opportunities for adding ancillary content on your hotel website. These may include the ability to add "product" pages to the website (think spa, golf, restaurants, meetings, historic, etc.), additional promotional pages or elements beyond the typical "deals" listings, various timed marketing messages, renovation and new hotel alerts, and posting of PDF/informational items (menus, A/V service listings, directions, etc.). Be sure to check with your brand to ensure you are aware and knowledgeable on all available enhanced products for your website.

Best Practices: User-Friendliness

Website user-friendliness refers to the quality of the user experience on the website (i.e., the website usability). In human-computer interaction, usability usually refers to the elegance and clarity with which the interaction with a computer program or a website is designed.

Website user-friendliness encompasses several key components that are crucial to the user experience, including:

- site architecture and page layout for both desktop and mobile usage
- tiered navigation structure (e.g., top/main navigation, subnavigation, actionable navigation, footer navigation, etc.)
- logical flow of information
- content addressing all of your key customer segments
- rich media, videos, and quality imagery
- page download speeds
- design aesthetics
- on-page/internal links
- call to action
- quick links

WELCOME TO HOLIDAY INN CHICAGO MART PLAZA RIVER NORTH

Make sure your pages load quickly – if it's too slow, your visitor will move on. This typically means you have to carefully determine the number of images per page. And for every image, determine if it is inviting, and is it worth the load time? And remember, mounting evidence suggests that mobile users are even more impatient than desktop customers. With mobile, page load time is just as, if not more, important than the image.

Text is important for search optimization factors, but text should always be relevant for your visitor. On your location page, are you telling your visitor what they need to know about your location? If you are an airport property, how clear is your proximity to the airport?

Every page should have a clear and easy way for visitors to make a reservation. Some sort of "Book now" or "Click here to make reservations" should have a prominent position on every single page. It may seem redundant but the primary function of your hotel website is to generate bookings, and you want to make it easy for the visitor to make the reservation whenever they feel they have enough information. It may be once they visit your home page, or once they see the restaurants you offer onsite, or directions from the airport – make it easy to book.

Another opportunity doesn't have as obvious an ROI, but it has a potential cost of noncompliance. Making your website accessible to users with disabilities is critical. Threats of lawsuits for noncompliance aside, some marketers feel that Google is rewarding sites who are trying to focus on universal accessibility factors. To learn more, search for the topic at www.hsmai.org or visit the Web Accessibility Initiative website at https://www.w3.org/WAI/. There are some simple best practices to implement immediately.

The same principle can be applied for those hotels that focus on group business. Prominently include clear navigation to information about event space and sales contacts so that meeting and event planners can find the information they need no matter how they have come into your site.

Redundant navigation is important. Show the main content areas across the top and duplicate them in text on the bottom of each page. Don't make the visitor scroll too far to find what they are looking for. The most relevant information should be top left, then top right. If you have a call to action (other than to make a reservation) give it a clear spot near the top. Don't bury it in the content.

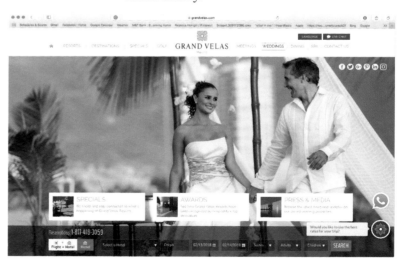

- Provide sufficient contrast between foreground and background.
- Don't use color alone to convey information.
- Ensure that interactive elements are easy to identify.

- Provide clear and consistent navigation options.
- Include image and media alternatives in your design – create visible links to transcripts of any audio you have, visible links to audio described versions of videos.
- Text along with icons and graphical buttons.
- Caption and description for tables or images.

Best Practices: Travel Booker Friendliness

The booker-friendliness of a hotel website is a direct result of how well the hotel website handles a whole range of complex issues that can influence the purchasing behavior of the website users.

Build trust and credibility. Visitors are savvy; they will search between 17 - 22 sites during the booking process. How is your rate integrity? If you offer any sort of lowest rate guarantee, place this in a prominent position on your website, repeatedly. A Best Price guarantee is all you may need to say to build some trust.

Focus on the ease-of-use of your booking engine and the smoothness of the booking process. How hard do you make it for someone to book your property? Is checking availability tedious? If it is, they will move on and book elsewhere.

Put a reservation widget on your home page and include it as part of the global navigation of the site. Use a customized look-and-feel design that "mimics" the website design. When a customer clicks to book your property, are they worried they have gone to another site because the look and feel is different? That doesn't help with trust and credibility. Most usability studies and industry best practices suggest that the booking widget should be placed at the top left of the page. This is where you will find most widgets on brand websites for example. If your reservation widget is located on the right hand side of the page, lower down on the screen, or in a difficult to find place, you will pay a penalty in revenue and conversions.

Highlight the availability of bookable unique special offers, packages, and promotions with excellent perceived value propositions. You know your guests and your property better than anyone. Do your packages reflect what is unique about you, or are they what you can find anywhere? Keep your specials up to date. If they are expired, remove them. Otherwise, again, your credibility is in question.

Ensure good security and privacy policies, posting your privacy policy for visitors to see.

If one of your conversion goals is to receive RFPs from your site, make sure it is easy to submit them on your site. Conduct an annual update of customer segmentation optimization to fully address all key customer segments, from meeting and group planners, to corporate and leisure travelers, social event planners and family travel planners.

Shopping Cart Abandonment

Taking a cue from retail, hotels have become more sophisticated about tracking and engaging with lookers who don't make it all the way through the booking process.

First, you should track what percent of your visitors go to your booking engine, and then what percent of those visitors actually make a reservation (or request an RFP if that is a goal). If you have a high abandonment rate, you should research to find out why. Is it a technical issue, or a rate parity issue?

There will always be a percentage of prospects who will go to your booking engine and then change their mind. One tactic is a trigger screen that will appear as they try to close out your website. A popup can appear that offers a further special, or invites the visitor to sign up for a newsletter.

A second common practice is sending a follow-up email later the same day or the next, again with a special incentive to return to complete the booking.

Finally, retargeting is an option – an ad for your hotel will again appear when the visitor is on another site.

All three methods can increase your ultimate conversion rate, but the key is to understand why your visitors are leaving in the first place. If it is cumbersome to book online, they may pick up the phone to call or simply go to a competitor's site. If your rate is not in line with what they have seen on the OTA sites, they will likely leave to find the better deal. In both of those cases, the traditional shopping cart abandonment practices will not be effective.

In order to test your site's booking friendliness, there is a service at usertesting.com that will allow you to test your site with visitors matching your customer demographics.

Best Practices: Search Engine Friendliness

The search engine-friendliness of the hotel website is as important as user friendliness and travel booker friendliness. You may have a very user-friendly site that makes booking easy as pie, but if you never show up in search engine results for the right keywords, no one will find you.

See the Chapter 7 for a more in depth discussion of on search engine optimization (SEO). Also, consider the following best practices to ensure your website is search friendly.

- Make your hotel name, address, and phone number consistent on the site, and across all the places, websites, directories, and locations that feature your hotel across the web. This becomes relevant for local results. There are tools that will help you do this like YEXT.
- Ensure your navigation is clear and logical. Use an html sitemap to outline all searchable pages on your site.
- Use meta tags that are your most relevant keywords, and have them vary based on the page being displayed.
- Be sure your content is relevant. If you are found, visitors who can't find what they want will bounce away quickly, harming you in the long run. Make sure your content changes are up to date and relevant to your unique selling points.
- Have strong links to your site. If you are located next to a university, does that university link back to you? How about local corporate headquarters? Conduct search engine optimization (SEO) updates regularly (every twelve months is recommended) in order to take full advantage of the evolving search dynamics.

Site load time is important to consumers, and so it is important to Google and their search results. Several years ago, Amazon released a study that showed that every one-second delay in their site load time negatively impacts that product's revenues by 10%. Current research suggests that 50% of users expect a website to load within 2 seconds, and at 3 seconds you will start to see users abandoning your site. To check the download speed of your website, try this free tool — https://www.uptrends.com/tools/website-speed-test

Speed is even more important on mobile and Google is showing some preferential treatment to mobile sites who have taken advantage of AMP – Accelerated Mobile Pages. AMP is a project that was backed by Google and was designed as an open standards project for any developer to access that will help your mobile pages load faster. In February of 2016, Google officially began integrating AMP listings into its mobile search results. This is a marketing investment with a strong ROI if you believe ranking high on Google is worthwhile. Written in what is referred to HTML lite, the entire concept is to encourage companies to deliver the product that consumers want – fast loading mobile sites.

Sites are written in compliance with AMP, and hosted by Google – which also adds an element of speed. They don't need to go and fetch it from you but instead, just present it.

Voice search is a growing opportunity. Today, mobile searches account for about 50% of all searches but starting in 2018, 50% or more of mobile searches are expected to be via voice – like Siri or Alexa. The opportunity is, for now, that these search results are all organic, not yet paid, so you have the chance to optimize your website to appeal to this growing segment. Don't be confused, voice search is the same as a text search, the real difference is in the way we speak vs. how we write. You might type "hotels near downtown Charleston" but you might say, "Siri, find me a hotel that's in downtown Charleston and that has Jacuzzi's in the rooms." As you know, Siri (or Alexa) is going to tell you about one, and then the next. So how can you be first? (See Chapter 9 for more information on voice search.)

There are two ways. First, you should involve your web development team because they need to ensure a lot of schema categories are built into your website. Voice search is looking for specific categories, and if your website has this built into it in the right manner, it will help. Second, a FAQ is a user-friendly way to be found. For example, the Hotel Nikko San Francisco (http://www.hotelnikkosf.com/faq.aspx) offers a FAQ in five categories:

Doing a voice search of "find a hotel near Union Square" provides the Hotel Nikko a better chance of being displayed because the website has built the answer in the FAQs section. You want to try to provide content on your site that addresses the potential voice searches your target audience may use. And this will be a lot easier if you know what and why your current guests are staying with you.

Best Practices: Social Interactiveness[1]
Hoteliers must align the interactivity of the hotel website with the hyper-interactive behavior of today's travel consumer both on the hotel website and on the social web. The social

interactivity of the hotel website is dependent on how well the website can intrigue users and enable them to provide comments, share content, and interact with various features and functionality. For a hotel to have a strong brand voice on the web, the relationship with customers must be a two-way street.

- Social interactivity features should be regularly implemented/updated to improve customer engagement on the site. For brand.com websites, much of this may have already been implemented by the brand, including Facebook sharing functions, links to social sites, etc.

- Include a blog on your website (it's one of the best ways to incorporate social interactivity). Content can (and should) be changed frequently, it encourages comments, and it is also helpful for search optimization.

- Consider posting real reviews on your website. This is risky; if there is a negative review posted it will be front and center on your site, but from a credibility standpoint, mostly positive reviews on your website go a long way to inspire confidence. Most major brands have already implemented reviews on their hotel websites. The property responsibility in this case will lie in the need for the hotels to be sure they're responding to those reviews through the brand's approved process or platforms.

- Have links to your social sites (YouTube, Twitter, Facebook, LinkedIn, etc.) if you have them. Link easily and often back and forth between these channels and your website.

- Make it easy for your visitors to "share" information, to like it, and to post it to their Facebook pages, etc.

- Use open graph tags so that a photo and marketing text you determine is displayed when users post your content to their Facebook page, re-tweet links to your website, and post your content on Instagram. For more information on how to create open graph tags see https://blog.kissmetrics.com/open-graph-meta-tags/. While the use of open graph tags doesn't directly impact your website SEO, it had a dramatic impact on how shareable your social content will be, which should ultimately lead to an increase in website traffic.

Best Practices: Selecting a Website Design/Development Vendor

Remember that your hotel website's primary objective is to generate as many direct bookings and group leads as possible. This objective requires not only building a website according to the industry's best practices, but also marketing this website according to the industry's best practices. Some prefer to work with a full-service website design and internet marketing agency specializing in hospitality that will build and then market your website, while others may look to choose multiple agencies in an attempt to find "best of breed" in each of the disciplines. Either way you go, vendor management is a very important aspect of building and maintaining your website. For further information, see Chapter 30 on Vendor Management.

Start by preparing an RFP outlining your vision of, and expectations for, the new website. Be sure to think about and address the weaknesses of your existing website, as well as any design elements, features, and functionality you like from your comp set's websites.

From the proposals you receive, select the best three and require the vendors to make in-person or web-based presentations.

Best Practices: Features and Functionality

Ensure that your new website is fully responsive across the range of devices and associated browsers your customers will use. Responsive sites automatically resize to fit the device they are displayed on, meaning you don't need to think in terms of a separate mobile site. Some vendors provide the option to display unique content by device type.

A hotel website should have a related content management system (CMS) that allows the property to, at a minimum:

- manage textual and visual content on the desktop site and the mobile site
- create new landing and content pages
- initiate real-time content push to social media
- update an interactive calendar of events
- manage a photo gallery
- feature special promotions

Functionality that should be built into a hotel website includes:

- the ability to accept RFPs
- a reservation widget on the home page (and many other pages as applicable)
- email capture functionality
- videos and rich media
- call-outs to Facebook, Twitter, Google+, and social media feeds to the site
- a blog on the website with "share this site" and RSS functionality
- A/B testing functionality

Best Practices: Tracking Performance with Web Analytics

Digital marketing is all about results. Unlike offline marketing, in the online and mobile space we can track and analyze bookings, room nights, revenue, and ROI results from your website performance and online marketing campaigns quickly and accurately over the internet. Best practices and common business sense require hotel digital marketers to constantly track and analyze website and campaign conversions as well as ROIs, pathing, and behavioral metrics to shift marketing funds from less effective marketing campaigns to campaigns with higher ROIs.

For a brand.com website, the brand will most likely have a suite of reporting tools and reports available to hotels. They may even have reports that can track traffic and web analytics from a stand-alone website to the brand's booking path. For a stand-alone site, choosing the right website analytical tool is an important first step. For franchised/branded hotels, inquire with your brand about web analytics solutions for your vanity website. Many major chains offer that. For independent properties, when budgeting for internet marketing, it is recommended that you include a separate line item for website and marketing analytics. A good place to start is with your online booking engine vendor or website developer. Ask if they support an advanced web analytical tool such as Google Analytics or Adobe Analytics, and have your website developer implement it on your site.

See Chapter 28 for more information on website analytics.

Best Practices: Connect with your global customer through your website.

In the ever-competitive world of travel, website localization is the key to success for a hotel to connect with new consumers, gain market share, and communicate a competitive differentiator. As more companies expand into new markets, competition grows. Hotels that don't localize will be left behind while competitors embrace translation as a means of growth.

In their report, "Can't Read, Won't Buy," the Common Sense Advisory (CSA) notes that 55% of global consumers only make online purchases on websites that offer content in their native language. And these consumers will spend more time browsing on sites in their own language, so a localized website is a must-have for engaging new customers around the world.

With many detailed requirements, website localization can seem like a daunting task. But with careful planning and preparation, you can simplify the process and create a more impactful global website.

When tackling web localization, plan for these key tasks:

- Define your target markets and determine the most relevant languages for consumers in each locale. But be careful not to confuse a country for a locale. A locale refers to a region in which people speak a particular language—and it's not always defined by country borders.
- Evaluate your website technology—particularly your content management system (CMS) and property booking engines—and ensure that it supports multilingual content.
- Check that your web content is written for translation—a method that prevents errors and re-work. This means using clear, short sentences without idioms; they're easier to translate and are better understood by global readers. Be cautious when using humor; it doesn't always translate linguistically or culturally.
- Perform a content audit to determine what web content should be translated—and if any should be locale or region specific. Content that is specific to a locale should be customized to meet local norms, regulations, and reader expectations. For

example, local promotional content, visa requirements, weights, currencies, and payment processing should all be adapted by locale rather than language.

- Define a multilingual URL/domain structure so your site will be well indexed and SEO friendly. You have three options to choose from: a country code Top Level Domain (ccTLD) structure, e.g., travelwebsite.mx; a subdomain structure, e.g., mx.travelwebsite.com; or a folder structure, e.g., travelwesite.com/mx/. Each option has its pros and cons in terms of complexity, cost, and SEO performance.

- Identify your global gateway strategy and decide how translated content will be delivered to the right consumer, in the right language—in each locale. Assume that visitors won't be in their home country, will speak a number of languages, and will use a variety of devices. You'll need a user-friendly solution that guides visitors to locale- and language-specific content — no matter where they are or what language they speak.

- Select your in-region review team and develop a plan for including these team members in the translation process.

- Prepare for international SEO to boost search rankings and ensure that your localized content will be found online.

Chapter 4 Endnotes

[1] This section was adapted with permission from Max Starkov from an original article by Max Starkov and Denis Strekalov titled "Hyper-Interactive Consumers," originally published in HOTELS magazine.

KEY POINTS

- Your content exists to answer guest questions and help them choose your property.
- All modern marketing depends on high-quality content; without content, your customers have nothing to find in search and nothing to share on social.
- Merchandising involves presenting your content — text and visuals — in an appealing and persuasive manner designed to encourage guests to consider and book your destination and property.

SUMMARY

Content matters. It represents one of your hotel's key "salespeople," available to guests whenever and wherever they are along their purchase path. Whether your guests are dreaming, planning, booking, experiencing, or sharing, content performs a vital role in the process. It inspires guests when they're dreaming. It answers questions when they're planning. It provides assurance when they're booking. It offers guidance while they're experiencing your destination. And it inspires, reminds, and delights them and others as well when they're sharing their experience with friends, family, and colleagues.

What is Content?

Content represents a cornerstone destination and hotel marketing tool. Regardless of where your customers choose to book, they will interact with content about your destination and hotel on desktop and mobile, through paid, earned, and owned channels, and at each step of the purchase funnel.

Fundamentally, your guests rely on four broad categories of content to help them decide where to stay.

Destination Content

The first rule of selling travel to consumers remains "sell the destination first." Research from Google shows that travelers tend to start their travel planning by searching destination-related terms[1]. Whether you use blog posts highlighting area attractions, dedicated destination guides offered on your website, email marketing campaigns featuring local hot spots, or themed-content targeting key audiences, guests must first want to travel to your destination; you cannot get guests to consider your hotel if they're planning to travel to another destination altogether.

Property Content

Often referred to as "descriptive" content, or less commonly "static" content, this includes information about your property itself, such as the number and type of guest rooms and meeting rooms, available amenities, its physical location and proximity to attractions, property name, brand affiliation, and other necessary attributes.

Promotional Content

Promotional content includes the many offers, specials, and packages your marketing team designs to attract customers to book, enroll in loyalty programs or email lists, or respond to any other call-to-action you can imagine.

Availability, Rates, and Inventory (ARI)

Finally, availability, rates, and inventory present guests with information about what they'll actually book — descriptions and details of the room types, rate plans, and packages your property offers — as well as the dates when guests can book their stay. While ARI typically refers only to room types and suites, additional amenities, add-ons, and upsell items — including such varied items as bottles of wine, flowers, golf tee times, ski lift tickets, restaurant reservations, and the like — may also represent inventoried items within your property management system, central reservations system, or booking engine.

This chapter will focus primarily on Destination, Property, and Promotional content. For information on ARI, see *Evolving Dynamics: From Revenue Management to Revenue Strategy* published by HSMAI.

Why Does Content Matter?

Knowing what content is, however, is only half the battle. What's more important is how your hotel's content works as an "on-demand salesperson," telling an effective and entertaining story about your destination and property to guests whenever and wherever they may be. Most marketers understand the importance of search and social in selling their property. But without content, your property cannot appear in search. Without content, your guests have nothing to share across their social networks. Even "future" technologies such as chatbots and voice-powered tools like Amazon's Echo depend on quality content to answer guest questions. High-quality content is what makes search and social media work.

As you use content to fuel your property's marketing, it's important to think about how each touchpoint assists guests in their purchase decision. Think about what questions your customers ask — and what answers they're looking to find. Google recently extended their travel marketing framework, adding "micro-moments" that explain what customers want as they move through each stage of the journey[2], and encourages marketers to "be there and be useful," offering answers to the questions your potential guests will ask as they make their decision. Whether using Google's "Dream-Plan-Book-Experience-Share" framework, the "Acquisition-Conversion-Stay" framework, or something else altogether, your content must support guests before, during, and after their stay.

Guest Content Needs Before Reservation and Stay

Early in their shopping process, guests seek inspiration. While leisure travelers may understand that they're ready for a vacation or business travelers may wish to visit customers, these potential guests still have many questions. Research from Google says that "37% of travelers in the U.S. think about vacation planning once a month"[3] and that many have not yet selected their destination. This is your opportunity to capture their attention — and your content plays a crucial role in helping you do just that.

This inspirational content can range from something as simple as a curated itinerary of things to do in your destination as illustrated in Figure 1 to fully staged films like Marriott's popular "Two Bellmen" YouTube series (see Figure 2), the third installment of which has attracted over 9 million views and four thousand likes on YouTube since its launch.

Figure 1: Iron Horse Hotel's (Milwaukee, WI) "Biker Bests" curated itinerary

However, all kinds of content can work to encourage guests to consider key destinations at this stage in their decision-making process and contribute to long-term brand engagement.

Figure 2: Marriott Content Studio's "Two Bellmen" short film https://www.youtube.com/watch?v=ZOgteFrOKt8 *at 2:16*

Most importantly, your "Dream" content must move customers along the funnel and help them move to the next step in their travel decision.

Once guests have narrowed their options, they typically begin putting together the elements of their trip, a process Google refers to as a series of "time-to-make-a-plan" moments. A variety of studies show that guests visit as few as 4.4 websites[4] but may visit travel sites 140 or more times[5] and may have 850 or more "…digital travel touchpoints" in just three months[6] while planning their trip.

Regardless of the actual number of sites and sessions, you have your work cut out for you to connect with guests during each interaction to convince them your property represents the right choice for their stay. Again, following the mantra of "be there" and "be useful," your property content and promotional content must work together to answer the key questions your guests have about the features of your room product and the specific amenities you offer.

Figure 4: 1888 Darling Harbour accompanies its room details with both photos and floor plans.

Figure 3: Highlight key room features to answer guest questions

If your room types are sufficiently diverse and distinct, consider creating separate landing pages on your property's website for individual room types and suites to merchandise the specific benefits your guests will enjoy.

Don't forget to use outstanding images and photos to visually merchandise your product as well. Data from Trivago shows that "...hotel profiles featuring high-quality images receive 63% more clicks than those with low-quality photos" and those hotels with a "high-quality main image" receive the lion's share of all clicks[7]. Or, in simpler terms, "pretty pictures sell hotels."

Best Practices: Content to Support Booking Decisions

It will come as no surprise that the book stage of the guest journey represents a critical moment for your property — and for your content. While the number of visits and searches and sessions guests conduct prior to booking provide you multiple opportunities to catch their attention and interest, any missed chance during the booking process itself may send guests to seek a "better alternative." This is your shot at addressing their concerns and assuring them that your property will make their stay a pleasant one.

As you have likely seen, OTAs have invested heavily in this stage of the customer journey, focusing heavily on merchandising to close the sale.

Figure 5: _Booking.com_ uses social proofs and urgency to merchandise room inventory

Verbiage such as "In high demand — only 1 room left," "Great value today," "Last booked: 5 hours ago," "See our last available rooms," "x people booked this property in the last 48 hours," and other messages, as well as prominent ratings and reviews, signal to guests that they can feel comfortable that they're getting the right room at the right price and the right value for their trip.

Many hotels use tactics such as "Best Rate guarantees" and fenced rates to successfully convert guests. Work with your booking engine provider or brand to test additional message options designed to create desire, urgency, and confidence among guests that booking directly with your property will provide them a satisfactory stay.

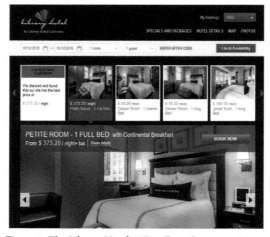

Figure 6: The Library Hotel's "Best Rate Guarantee"

Best Practices: Guest Content Needs During Their Stay

Remarkably, research shows that most leisure travelers wait until after they arrive at their destination before deciding exactly how they'll spend their time while there. And almost 90% "…expect their travel provider to share relevant information while they are on their trip."[8] Once again, this creates a great opportunity for you to provide useful content to guests that will improve both their stay and their view of the value they've received from you during their stay.

By far, the most common form hotel marketers use for providing content to guests on-property are pre-arrival emails, with some hotels also delivering post check-in emails highlighting directions to the hotel, and amenities and special offers in effect during their stay. Increasingly, major chains use their apps to connect with guests on-property to enhance the stay as well.

Figure 7: citizenM provides useful pre-arrival messaging.

Content useful during earlier guest research phases can also help guests to enjoy their stay. Similarly, content from destination partners such as restaurants, museums, concert venues, and tour guides can provide useful and engaging information for guests while at your location. Look to work with those partners to remind guests why they've chosen your destination — and entice them to return in the future.

Best Practices: Content for Sharing and Post-Stay Actions

Finally, you're not the only source of content for potential guests. Thanks to the rapid growth of mobile, your existing guests carry the internet in their pockets, and with it the equivalent of a printing press, professional camera, and HD television studio as well. They're using these tools to create immense amounts of "user-generated content" (or UGC) every day and during every stay. You can persuade guests to share their experiences with their friends, family, and colleagues via social media in the form of photos, videos, ratings, and reviews.

According to social media aggregation firm Stackla, 76% of consumers say "…online reviews from fellow travelers give them inside knowledge" about their destination while 40% of millennials say that they rely solely on user-generated content when making their purchase decision[9]. Additionally, your guests connect with an average of over 150 friends on Facebook[10]. Every one of your guests can promote content about your property and increase the number of potential customers you can reach — but only if you give them something positive to talk about.

By far the most common way to engage guests in the process of telling your property's story is through ratings and reviews on TripAdvisor, OTA's, and Google Local. Most hotel management teams actively ask for reviews from guests throughout their stay, but especially at check-out and in the post-stay email. Make certain your operations team has addressed any issues prior to asking for the review to avoid negative comments on ratings and review sites.

Some properties have expanded beyond traditional ratings and reviews though, and have developed "Instagrammable moments"[11] — cool visuals, distinctive artwork, and unique experiences on-property — designed to encourage guests to snap selfies and share them with their friends across social channels. Seek out opportunities to entice customers with visuals and experiences. Then build on these moments and ask guests to share them with their social networks to help you reach entirely new audiences. And consider whether social media engagement platforms tools such as Flip.to or Sprout Social will work for your property to drive the discussion forward with guests.

How Do You Make Content Work?

Providing great content — useful, informative, and entertaining content — increasingly is "table stakes" for online marketing. But how can you do it well? Do you simply start writing blog posts, taking photos, or shooting video of your property? How do you know what to create and in which formats? And, once you have content, should you place it on your website, send in an email, share on Facebook, or post on Pinterest? The following sections will help guide you through that process.

Content Marketing Process

For starters, content marketing is a process. And it doesn't just involve creating content. Experts recommend that any content marketing process[12] includes four major components:

- planning
- production, management and maintenance
- distribution and merchandising
- measurement and metrics

While the amount of detail needed in each component may vary depending on the size and scale of your organization, you will use these same basic steps whether you work for a 10-room inn, a 750-room resort, or a chain representing tens of thousands of rooms. As such, let's look at each of these steps in detail.

Planning

Research suggests[13] that a failure to develop an effective strategy represents one of the biggest barriers to successful content marketing. Planning helps you put together an effective content marketing strategy, drives each subsequent step in the process, and can easily make or break your overall success.

Consider the following questions when putting together your plan:

- What business objective(s) are you trying to address with your content initiative? This may represent the single most important question in any content marketing plan. Are you looking to drive leisure reservations, increase your wedding or meetings business, grow your loyalty program, or something else altogether? While content can help you do each of these things, it's unlikely that a single piece of content — or even a single campaign — can do all of them. Make sure you know what problem you're trying to solve before you begin.

- Who is the intended audience for your content? Once you know which objectives you're trying to address, think about the customer segment or segments for which your content is intended. Are you looking to reach new or repeat guests; business or leisure travelers; consumers or the travel trade? Each audience will have different questions they need answered and preferred ways of finding answers to those questions. Define your audience up front to guide you to the optimal content, formats, and distribution channels for your content initiative.

- What will you need to produce the content? The answers to this question help drive your project plan. Think about where the content will come from, what resources you'll need, who will do the work, and who owns the result. Many organizations maintain an editorial calendar that outlines the key content they'll develop each season, month, or week, the audiences that content will target, and the roles and resources needed to manage their content initiatives. Think about who and what you'll need before starting to create content to improve efficiency and prevent waste during the process.

- How will you promote the content? A recent Accenture study[14] found that, across industries, "…20% of all content produced is never distributed." In other words, customers never even can interact with content after it's created. Don't let that happen to you. Just because you build it, doesn't mean customers will come. Ensure your plan accounts for distribution and promotion opportunities to ensure your content reaches its maximum potential audience — and delivers on your objectives.

- How will you measure the success of the program? Finally, think about how you'll know your content worked before you begin. As the adage states, "you can't manage what you can't measure." Make sure you've defined what you'll measure and that you have any necessary tracking in place prior to launching your content to avoid the risk that you won't know what worked.

A proper plan can help you overcome one of the significant barriers to content marketing success. It helps you to understand the out-comes you're looking to achieve as well as the necessary path to reach them. As the old saying goes, "by failing to plan, you are planning to fail." Make sure you're planning for success with your content efforts.

Production, Management, and Maintenance

Once you have your plan in place, the next major step is to produce your content. However, "producing" content is not the same as "creating" content. Creating new content from scratch can be expensive and time-consuming. Additionally, your team may lack the skills or time — or both — that is necessary to create great content. Instead, ask yourself, "what is the best way to get the content we need?" The "4C Framework"[15] provides a simple way to think about where your content might come from:

- COLLECT: Reuse and repurpose existing content, such as organizing photos into an interactive video, to lower the cost and time needed to produce content that answers guest questions.

- CURATE: Organize and share destination and property content from partners or local experts. The "curated itineraries" first shown in Figure 1 or tools like Renaissance's Navigator platform represent excellent examples of leveraging others' expertise to produce quality content quickly and inexpensively.

- CROWDSOURCE: Let your guests tell your hotel's story. For example, gather ratings, reviews, feedback from comment cards, or guest photos and videos and share that information with potential audiences on Facebook, Instagram, or Pinterest as in Figure 8. Or record an interview on video with your property's chef, concierge, general manager, or other staff about common questions they receive from guests or their favorite experiences at your destination, then transcribe that interview into a blog post or "curated experience" on your property website. Even better, the video can be reused on YouTube, Facebook, and Instagram to increase your reach and attract interest from new audiences.

- CONTRACT: Clearly, cases will exist where the content you need neither exists nor can it easily be gathered from other sources. In those situations, look to contract with local travel writers, bloggers, PR firms, or agencies for your new content. These resources can often provide a cost-effective means to augment your team on an as-needed basis.

Kings Courtyard Inn
February 10, 2017

We love it when our guests share their Kings Courtyard experiences with us! "This January marked our third trip to Charleston and our third stay at Kings Courtyard Inn. We are repeat visitors to Kings Courtyard Inn because it is so charmingly quaint (dates from 1853) and the location on King Street is perfectly situated near the upscale shops and art galleries. The historic homes in The Battery are just a few short blocks south of the property. They have a very dedicated staff and we see same familiar faces every time we return." TripAdvisor

Figure 8: Kings Courtyard Inn uses guest comments for social promotion.

During your content development process, think about the full content lifecycle as well. While some content pieces can last for years, others age quickly. A guide to beaches and national parks near your property may rarely change, while a list of the "best restaurants in town" might need updating every year. Your website's content management system (CMS) often provides tools to allow you to schedule when pages will be retired from your site. Use website analytics, social media management tools, or your content calendar to periodically revisit older content on your site and social channels for relevance to your customer and alignment with updated business objectives. Once you've reviewed your existing content, update, replace, or retire it as appropriate.

Regardless of the method you use to produce and maintain your content, ensure it remains focused on the audience you defined during the planning stage. Speak to the needs of that audience, using the language they use. Unless you're producing content for the travel trade, avoid jargon and industry terms. And even then, keep it clear and simple so less experienced travel agents and meeting planners can easily understand your message.

Finally, ensure that your content aligns with your brand and quality standards. As a "digital salesperson" for your property, make sure that your content presents an accurate view of the experience guests will have with your brand overall.

Distribution and Merchandising of Your Content

One significant limitation for developing successful hotel and destination content is the sheer volume of it that exists online. Your content may be great, but it can't help your business if no one sees it. Author Mark Schaefer refers to "content shock," stating, "there is just too much content and too precious little time for people to consume it." However, Schaefer argues compellingly[16] that "the real power only comes to those who can create content that connects, engages, and moves through the network through social sharing," search, and other distribution channels.

It's not enough to build it and expect "they will come." Your plan must consider ways to put content in front of your intended audience. This is the core of your content distribution strategy.

While this chapter is in the "Owned Media" section of this book, it is important to note that content distribution can occur across paid and earned media as well. The specific channel you'll use may vary based on your audience and objectives. However, one commonly-used and highly-effective approach follows a "hub and spoke" model that leverages the reach of paid and earned media to drive traffic to your owned website (Figure 9 illustrates what this looks like in practice).

Providing a permanent home for your content on your website increases the value of your site in search engines, demonstrates value to your guests, and establishes you as a trusted information source. At the same time, using "spokes" enables you to get your message in front of the widest possible audience. It also makes it easier for guests to share your content with their friends, family, and colleagues, extending that reach and trust even further.

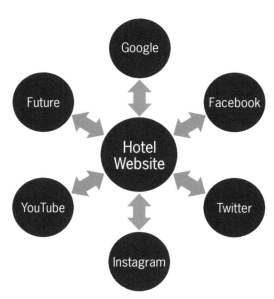

Figure 9: "Hub and Spoke" Content Distribution Model

What Do We Mean by Merchandising?
Merchandising represents the practice of making your content attractive and persuasive to potential customers. While it's debatable whether "the medium is the message," the medium undoubtedly plays a role in what people think about your message. And, no matter which channel you use, your merchandising must support what you want guests to think, feel, and do when seeing your message.

Techniques for improving merchandising continue to evolve with changing customer behaviors, but several key approaches consistently produce results:

- **Define a clear call-to-action.** For any individual piece of content your team produces, make sure you've made it clear what you expect guests to do next. Whether it's "learn more," "enroll," "book now," or something else altogether, help guide your guests to the next step on their journey. Additionally, ensure your call-to-action aligns with where your guests are in that journey. "Book now" may be appropriate in some cases, but not others. Test to see which calls-to-action support guests based on their current step in the buyer's journey.
- **Test urgency.** Which of these calls-to-action do you think generates more bookings: A call-to-action that states, "Only 1 room still available at this rate. Book now to save" or "Plenty of rooms available. Book whenever"? Most people would correctly

guess that the first tends to drive more reservations. Asking guests to act works; asking guests to act now works even better. Urgency drives results. Incorporate a sense of urgency into your content at appropriate points in the guest journey to increase action.
- **Use social proofs.** Human beings are inherently social. We all like to share experiences with our friends and family. At the same time, we want to feel like we belong. This entirely human need to connect often leads us to be influenced by the actions of other people. Social proofs use others' views of our property to influence our potential guests. We've already looked at examples of OTAs showing the number of people who've viewed or booked a given hotel. That's a social proof at work, frequently causing potential guests to say, "If everyone else likes this hotel, it must be a good one." Ratings and reviews work the same way. Look for opportunities to include social proofs in your messages to drive engagement and action.
- **Work towards personalization.** Of course, the best messages speak to each potential guest on an individual basis. Would you rather be addressed by your name or as a generic customer? If you're like most people, a personal touch works more effectively and produces stronger results. Work with your agency and technology vendors to begin the process of personalizing your content at each touchpoint to improve interactions with your guests and grow your bottom line.

Best Practices: Content Formats
Content can take many forms. Hotels have successfully used tactics as diverse as blog posts, infographics, slideshows, destination guides, and interactive tools like trip planners, incorporating text, images, and video to drive engagement, loyalty, and reservations from guests. No single rule exists that says you must use a specific format to achieve your objectives. Marketers have used the same formats to deliver both effective and ineffective content alike. A few basic guidelines exist though to help guide you to the right format for your messaging:

- **Align format with the correct stage in the customer journey.** While no one format consistently works better than others, some tend to support guests based on where they are in their journey. Presenting a detailed list of property amenities in a downloadable document probably won't help guests who've yet to decide whether they'd rather lie on a beach or hit the slopes. By contrast, a harried business executive may not want to sit through a video – no matter how beautifully crafted – just to learn how close your property is to the airport. Think about your guest's questions at each stage and consider the formats that best help them answer their questions.

- **Make each moment earn the next.** A common statement about online content states "shorter is better." While it makes a handy rule of thumb, it's also not entirely true. What is true is that customers don't have lots of time on their hands. Your content must provide support quickly and easily. As seen with Marriott's "Two Bellmen" film series, though, longer-form content can work. What all content must do is continue to provide value at each increment of time or risk losing the guest's attention and interest. When done well, you may find that longer content can prove effective for your guests. Yes, when in doubt, shorter is better. But understand why that's so and challenge yourself to make sure each extra moment you ask your customers to read, watch, or listen to your content is worth their time.

- **Think visually.** As we've already discussed, visuals help sell hotels. Where the channel and message allow, incorporate images or a brief video alongside your other content to let guests experience your property with their own eyes while making their decision.

- **Test and learn.** Finally, test what works with your guests and learn from those tests. Build on your successes to find the content and formats that help answer guests' questions and improve your results. There's no one guaranteed path to success – and the pace of change suggests that even if there were, it would likely evolve in short order. Instead, learn to measure your efforts and apply the lessons learned to continue to grow.

Best Practices: Measurement and Metrics

The process of making content work for your property is relatively straightforward. But to understand what "making content work" means, you must ensure you have the right measurements and metrics in place too. As the Content Marketing Institute points out[17], "Content marketing is often no faster, cheaper, or more effective at moving customers down the funnel than other marketing techniques. However, **its greater power lies in its ability to produce a better customer, a more loyal customer, or a customer more willing to share his or her story with others** – which compounds the value he or she provides to the business."

Similarly, your measures should focus on understanding how content is helping you connect with better, more loyal, and more engaged customers for your property.

To that end, your metrics should seek to answer at least one of these questions:

- **Did your customer see the message or the content in question?** Many marketers speak in terms of "engagement." In other words, did the customer view your content or spend time with it (in the form of time on site or additional pages viewed). While these are useful first steps, try to move your metrics deeper into the funnel to determine whether customers share your content or move towards a conversion. It's not enough to "go viral." Work to understand how visibility leads to business results.

- **Did the customer take action?** Action demonstrates the real value of content marketing success. These actions don't have to be bookings, but might include clicking through to your website; opting-in to your email marketing or loyalty program; sharing your content or property information with friends, family, and work colleagues; downloading meeting room specifications or wedding planning information; or other valuable steps towards doing business with your property. Ensure you've set objectives for action — and that your analytics are in place to measure those actions.

- **Did the customer convert?** Conversions equal the holy grail of any marketing effort for many hotels. These conversions may include bookings or sales leads for weddings and group business. Tracking a customer's entire journey from their first view of your content through to a reservation isn't easy. But it is worthwhile to begin testing which actions — whether shares, downloads, or opt-ins — correlate with increased conversion rate. Follow a "crawl, walk, run" process and continue building on your success to gain a clearer picture of the customer journey.

■ **Is your hotel seeing increased business?** This may take the form of additional reservations, greater repeat business, longer length of stay, increased on-property spend, and so on. As you build out your content marketing initiatives, note whether you're seeing increased business benefit along with your engagement and action metrics. Give your efforts some time to gain traction with customers, then adjust as necessary to drive value for your hotel.

Measuring the success of your content efforts takes time. But you must begin by working backwards from your objectives and putting in place the necessary analytics to assess its value for your hotel. Your content's job is to answer questions for potential guests 24 hours a day, 365 days per year. Ensure you're measuring its effectiveness at helping guests answer their questions to achieve your goals, too.

See Chapter 28 for additional information on measurement and analytics.

Conclusion

Content and merchandising work together. For each piece of content your property creates — whether text, images, or video — consider its intended audience and how that content can help inspire, attract, or convert its viewer into a great customer for your hotel. Evaluate the appropriate next step in the guest journey and ensure you've presented effective calls-to-action to continue the dialogue with your customer and move them from simply dreaming to booking and from experiencing to sharing. Help your guests to make the right choice for their stay and you'll both receive the benefits.

Content represents the cornerstone of all your digital marketing activities. And it's the key to unlocking your hotel's success at every stage of the guest's journey.

Chapter 5 Endnotes

"The 2014 Traveler's Road to Decision." Google. http://storage.googleapis.com/think/docs/2014-travelers-road-to-decision_research_studies.pdf. November 22, 2017. Also, McGuire, Caroline. "Google reveals the top 10 travel searches of 2016 in the US." The Daily Mail. http://www.dailymail.co.uk/travel/travel_news/article-4047968/Was-listening-geography-class-Google-reveals-10-travel-searches-2016-Grand-Canyon-them.html. November 22, 2017.

2 "How Micro-Moments Are Reshaping the Travel Customer Journey." Think with Google. https://www.thinkwithgoogle.com/marketing-resources/micro-moments/micro-moments-travel-customer-journey/. November 19, 2017.

3 Gevelber, Lisa and Oliver Heckmann. "Travel Trends: 4 Mobile Moments Changing the Consumer Journey." Think with Google. November 2015. https://www.thinkwithgoogle.com/consumer-insights/travel-trends-4-mobile-moments-changing-consumer-journey/. January 10, 2018.

4 DiMaio, Pete. "How Hotels Can Adapt To a Dramatic 88% Drop In the Number of Sites a Traveler Visits Before Booking." Fuel Travel Blog. February 21, 2017. http://www.fueltravel.com/blog/hotels-can-adapt-dramatic-88-drop-number-sites-traveler-visits-booking/. January 10, 2018.

5 "Consumption of Digital Travel Content Sees Double-Digit Growth Year-Over-Year." Expedia Media Solutions. https://advertising.expedia.com/about/press-releases/consumption-digital-travel-content-sees-double-digit-growth-year-over-year/. January 10, 2018.

6 "How the Travel Research Process Plays Out in Time-to-Make-a-Plan Moments." Think with Google. July, 2016. https://www.thinkwithgoogle.com/consumer-insights/travel-research-process-make-a-plan-moments/. January 10, 2018.

7 "How Quality Online Content Impacts Your Hotel's Performance: Webinar Highlights." trivago Hotel Manager Blog. April 27, 2017. http://hotelmanager-blog.trivago.com/en-us/trivago-online-content-webinar-recap-2017/. January 10, 2018.

8 "How Mobile Influences Travel Decision Making in Can't-Wait-to-Explore Moments." Think with Google. July 2016. https://www.thinkwithgoogle.com/consumer-insights/mobile-influence-travel-decision-making-explore-moments/. January 10, 2018.

9 Feldkamp, Jeanne. "Travel UGC: A Goldmine Hiding in Plain Sight." Stackla.com. https://stackla.com/blog/travel-ugc-a-goldmine-hiding-in-plain-sight/. January 10, 2018.

10 Knapton, Sarah. "Facebook users have 155 friends - but would trust just four in a crisis." The Telegraph. January 20, 2016. http://www.telegraph.co.uk/news/science/science-news/12108412/Facebook-users-have-155-friends-but-would-trust-just-four-in-a-crisis.html. January 10, 2018.

1 Anderson, Chris. "In the millennial, social-media-centric age, Instagrammable hotels stand out." Hotel Management. September 19, 2017. https://www.hotelmanagement.net/sales-marketing/millennial-age-instagrammable-hotels-stand-out. January 10, 2018.

2 Adapted from "2017 Content Marketing Framework: 5 Building Blocks for Profitable, Scalable Operations." Content Marketing Institute. http://contentmarketinginstitute.com/2016/10/content-marketing-framework-profitable/. November 11, 2017.

13 "How to Overcome Content Marketing Struggles." eMarketer. March 23, 2015. https://www.emarketer.com/Article/How-Overcome-Content-Marketing-Struggles/1012255. January 10, 2018.

14 "You Are Your Content: State of Content 2017." Accenture Interactive. https://www.accenture.com/us-en/_acnmedia/PDF-44/Accenture-You-Are-Your-Content-Survey-Screen.pdf?la=en#zoom=50. January 10, 2018.

15 "The 4C Content Production Framework." Tim Peter & Associates. January 31, 2017.

16 Schaefer, Mark W. The Content Code (Louisville, TN: Mark W. Schaefer, 2015).

17 Rose, Robert Rose. "The 2017 Content Marketing Framework." Content Marketing Institute. October 27, 2016. http://contentmarketinginstitute.com/2016/10/content-marketing-framework-profitable/. January 10, 2018.

CHAPTER 6
Mobile Websites & Marketing

KEY POINTS

- Understand the differences between mobile optimization and compatibility; mobile apps versus mobile websites; and responsive versus device-specific design.

- Understanding when and where mobile devices are used – what drives the decision of the device and the activity, and how it is relevant for hoteliers.

- Seven best practices for mobile optimization.

SUMMARY

In 2015, mobile surpassed PC/desktop users for search according to Google. For our purposes, we can divide mobile into two categories: smartphones and tablets. Consumer behavior varies broadly depending on the mobile platform they use, and to capture a fair share of the mobile market, we must not only understand why and how our customers use their devices, but how we can integrate our own digital assets into their individual buyer journey to create a seamless purchase experience as well as add value to their overall travel experience.

Today's consumers live multi-faceted lives. They wake up in the morning, get coffee, and check their phones for texts and emails. On to work they go, logging onto laptops or desktops, all the while keeping their phones and tablets nearby to take a call or text, or to take notes during their first meeting of the day. They return home at night, relax in front of whatever TV programming grabs their attention, but now they keep a second or even third screen close at hand to tweet about the episode they're watching or to "Google" the company whose commercial just caught their interest.

According to eMarketer, digital travel sales will reach $189.62 billion in 2017, and 40% will come from mobile devices, with approximately 81% of all mobile travel bookers using a smartphone to book a trip.[1]

Transactional growth in mobile is only part of the shift in the travel marketplace. Increasingly, consumers see their mobile devices as an extension of their overall travel experience, whether it's preparing for their trip and creating activity agendas, looking around on-site for activities or restaurants in the area, or finding ways to include their social network in everything they're doing while they're on their trip. According to Google SmartThink Insights, 40% of unique page visits to U.S. travel sites and 60% of destination information searches now come from mobile devices.[2] And while the buyer journey continues to see a shift toward a seamless transition between desktop and mobile, more and more of the perceived value in digital assets is found in smartphone technology. See chart below.

As a result, hotel marketers shouldn't view mobile and desktop in silos, but rather as a consistent consumer experience across channels from the dreaming stage of travel planning all the way through post-purchase activity. By considering how users use mobile technology at each stage of the process, hoteliers can integrate their content seamlessly into the guest's experience, rather than forcing the guest to con-

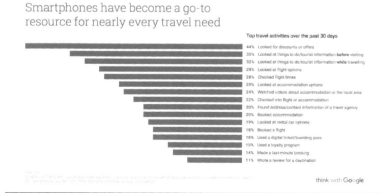

Smartphones have become a go-to resource for nearly every travel need

Top travel activities over the past 30 days

%	Activity
44%	Looked for discounts or offers
35%	Looked at things to do/tourist information before visiting
32%	Looked at things to do/tourist information while travelling
29%	Looked at flight options
28%	Checked flight times
25%	Looked at accommodation options
24%	Watched videos about accommodation or the local area
22%	Checked into flight or accommodation
20%	Found address/contact information of a travel agency
20%	Booked accommodation
19%	Looked at rental car options
18%	Booked a flight
18%	Used a digital ticket/boarding pass
15%	Used a loyalty program
14%	Made a last-minute booking
11%	Wrote a review for a destination

think with Google

Source: Think With Google

form to the hotel's experience, delivering amazing personalized guest experiences that can lead to better vacations, increased brand loyalty, and more bookings over the customer's lifetime.

This section will provide insights into current mobile behavior, helping hoteliers understand the mobile platform and, most importantly, how it can be leveraged to their properties' advantage. Additionally, it will offer further rationale for making mobile a key component in marketing planning, along with a sense of urgency to act now.

Mobile Defined

Mobile consists primarily of two main platforms: smartphones and tablets. It's important to recognize that people use smartphones differently than they use tablets due in large part to screen size, device size, and context.

Those factors will dictate how users interact with each device, and integrate all of their devices, depending on the context. For example, today's consumer might watch TV while at the same time accessing mobile web on her tablet to look up additional information, play games, or check email. At the same time, she might be texting on her smartphone. All devices involved might play a part in a buying decision, which could begin with any of them.

Smartphones tend to become much more of the "all-in-one" device once users start to move around. While tablets offer much more mobility than desktops, they still may be limited by access to wireless, and they can still be cumbersome to carry around without a pack. So a vacationer on tour is more likely to want to take photos, create blog posts, make reservations, view images and video, and look for area information all on their smartphone.

Tablets come into play much more once the user is indoors, usually with easy access to their room. They might carry a tablet with them to the property restaurant or lounge – someplace where they are likely to be stationary and in range of the property's wireless internet.

How Consumers Use Mobile Devices… and Why It Matters to You

Increasingly, potential guests are visiting and transacting on hotel websites through mobile channels, not just on desktops. Consider the findings in Google's report: "The New Multiscreen World: Understanding Cross-platform Consumer Behavior." Interestingly, 47% of people start their travel planning from their smartphone.

This shift creates many challenges, which we will discuss in this chapter, but it also opens new opportunities for business growth.

For example, mobile has become particularly strong for last-minute hotel bookings. Hotel Tonight leverages the last-minute and spontaneous nature of many mobile-mediated travel bookings. Orbitz noted that "over 70% of reservations coming through smartphones are being done within a day of check-in." Expedia reported that 68% of its mobile hotel reservations are done within 24 hours of the planned stay. Hotel operators now have a powerful tool to help move inventory that once might have been considered "dead."

It is no longer a question of whether you will have a mobile strategy. Consumers already have one, and that means they set the parameters on how, when, and with what they will engage your brand and attempt to use your services. In a marketplace where brand loyalty is decreasing in favor of experience quality, any hotelier who has fallen behind in terms of creating a quality front-to-back mobile experience risks being passed over.

According to Google research, bad mobile websites are the No. 1 deterrent to making online bookings.[3] The next big issue is unplayable content. For example, a video file embedded using Flash will not render on an iPhone or Android 4.01, or newer device, making the video unplayable on many mobile devices.

- 50% of people admit they use websites less if the site is not mobile friendly.
- 61% of users are likely to leave quickly if your site is not optimized well for mobile devices.
- 67% of users are more likely to buy from mobile-friendly sites. [4]
- 92% of mobile users share videos with others. [5]
- Mobile and tablet shoppers are three times more likely to view a video than laptop or desktop users. [6]

Creating the Optimal Mobile Experience

Because low mobile quality is becoming a barrier to entry in the travel industry, hotel operators must understand how their customers want to use their devices to interact with their brand – whether that is searching price and amenities, searching available dates, booking, and receiving confirmation info, preparing for their trip, or getting the most out of their vacation experience.

Website design requirements vary dramatically between desktop and mobile, for multiple reasons. Desktop navigation is typically geared toward point-and-click functionality, while mobile requires touchscreen capability. A device-responsive approach (also known as Device Agnostic, Responsive Design, or Liquid Design) involves the development of the primary hotel website in such a way that the navigation and layout morph based on the screen resolution of the device being used to view it. A point-and-click navigational schema intended for a consumer on a desktop would convert to a touchscreen interface for a consumer on the same website using a tablet.

All the major hotel brands and travel websites, including OTAs, meta search sites, and review sites, have developed their mobile presence and are using one or all the mobile web interface approaches.

There are numerous concepts to consider when developing or refining your mobile strategy.

Optimization v. Compatibility

You often hear people refer to the concepts of "mobile optimization" and "mobile compatibility" interchangeably. However, that isn't accurate. Just because your website is compatible with a smartphone doesn't mean it is optimized.

A website that is optimized for mobile will render properly on desktop and mobile alike. Text and images will display clearly, and users will easily be able to navigate the site with fingers and thumbs. It will take advantage of the device attributes and utilize features like pinch, zoom, portrait/landscape, and swiping. Contrast that with a website that's merely mobile compatible – the site will render on a smartphone, but without the proper device navigation features

or appropriate use of the screen size, will make it virtually impossible to read and/or navigate.

Choosing the Appropriate Website Build

There are several approaches to creating a mobile experience based on marketing objectives and budget. Ultimately, the goal is a consistent experience, designed for usability, with features appropriate for each device.

mDot or Mobile Website

One approach still commonly in use is referred to as an "mDot," or mobile website. This is a separate site with a separate URL, specifically designed for display on a mobile device. When visitors open your website on their smartphone, they have the option to a visit a different URL, which is set up specifically to deliver an experience for your mobile interface. Adaptive design is a similar strategy, except in this case, the site automatically detects device information and redirects traffic accordingly to either a desktop, tablet, or mobile version of your site.

Creating an mDot site requires maintaining and updating an additional website, and likely will add more load time to the user experience. In addition, the SEO benefits from visitors to the mobile site do not carry over to the desktop. Also, when someone shares your content on social media, they may be sharing the mobile version or the desktop version, but social media visitors could be on either platform, and might end up with a poor experience if they click through the shared link.

Responsive Website

A responsive website approach simply optimizes your one URL so that it functions well across multiple platforms. When a user visits the site, their screen size will determine the order and size at which each element will be displayed. In many cases, developers will take a "mobile-first" approach, which ensures that the best web experience will take place on mobile, while the desktop or tablet performance might suffer some.

Responsive doesn't provide full flexibility in optimizing across each device, but it can still create excellent user experiences on both desktop and mobile. And as of 2016, Forrester Research says that 87 percent of experience-makers approve of this approach. [7] Google has typically recommended responsive design in the past, particularly because of its advantages in SEO. Because Google's "mobile-first" index is set to begin rolling out over the coming months, web developers are encouraged to migrate their mDot sites over to responsive as soon as possible to avoid any penalties.[8]

Adaptive Design

Adaptive design is a potentially faster and cleaner solution than responsive design, in that visitors do not have to download the entire site – only the assets they will need to view the version that matches their device. However, this method requires significantly more server power and resources than responsive design.

Progressive Mobile Web

Progressive Mobile Web is a relatively new approach, emerging in the last couple of years as a more flexible, powerful alternative. Progressive integrates app-like functionality such as push notifications, full-screen mode, or offline mode into your site's mobile performance. Not only does it create better usability on mobile than mDot or responsive, it also typically delivers much faster speed,[9] since responsive design sites require the mobile user to download all the site assets, even the ones not used on the mobile version of the site.

Ultimately, your best approach is to contact an experienced, qualified web developer which is up-to-date on current web best practices. Because the digital space continues to evolve at an amazing speed, in-house teams may be behind the curve in terms of creating the most optimal experience for users who are flowing back and forth across multiple devices.

Make sure that you have clearly thought out what you want to accomplish with your marketing efforts, so that you can create a clear, simple pathway for your customers. Always look for ways to test and tweak your site, looking for adjustments which may bring in an increased number of conversions or simply provide a better experience.

Best Practices: Think about interface and screen size

Since most smartphones and tablets are touch-screen devices, the user's fingertip will be the primary input device when navigating your site. Clearly marked, reasonably large buttons are generally far better than tiny hotspots, clickable images, or embedded text links. In addition, minimize the amount of typing and data entry required. Use location services to learn where they are, and use cookies to recall previously-entered data. Make items "fingertip-friendly" – ensure links are easy to tap, allow swiping to move through tabs or photos, offer dropdown menus for selections, and include "Previous" and "Next" buttons to help guide users through the booking process.

Small and simple is necessary for smartphones. Although smartphones are generally trending upward in size, they are still pocket-sized devices. That small screen demands a different approach to user design, with a focus on clean, simple navigation. Display information in a single column (so users can avoid scrolling horizontally), and avoid cluttering pages with too much information.

Tablets offer a lot more room to play with than smartphones, so you can afford to take the experience up a notch. You can add tabs and more buttons to navigate deeper into your site. You can also include larger visuals to tell your story. However, keep in mind that these screens are still not as large as desktop screens. As such, it's important to clearly indicate what each tab or button does. Ensure links and calls-to-action are easy to tap, keeping in mind that "hover states" and mouse-over actions (that indicate where a link goes on a desktop) do not exist on a tablet. If buttons aren't appropriate, use clear contrasting colors or underlines in text links.

Keep your fonts large and crisp, and ensure a decent amount of padding around different elements (buttons, links, text, paragraphs) to avoid clutter. Increased "white space" can help give your site a clean, visually pleasing look.

Best Practices: Add eye-pleasing visuals

Watching video is one of the most popular things people do on their mobile devices: more than half of all mobile web traffic since 2012 was video content[10] and one-quarter of all smartphone data consumed is from watching videos.

Since 89% of leisure travelers (and 93% of business travelers) use online video in their travel planning,[11] the value of adding video to your mobile site is clear. Options to consider include everything from promotional videos of your property to videos of events and things to do around town.

Don't stop at just video, though. Add virtual tours of your rooms and facilities, and provide tablet-optimized photographs showing off your property and the surrounding area. In other words, take advantage of the tablet screen's size and clarity to show off your property!

Best Practices: Don't skimp on speed

While rich video and imagery will work just fine on mobile devices, you must properly optimize it, because the mobile experience requires speed. In a recent survey of U.S. smartphone users, 64% said they wanted a site to load within four seconds, with 16% of respondents saying they would abandon a site completely and never return if it didn't load promptly.[12]

This makes optimization critical to your smartphone or tablet site. While you want to tell your story with great videos and beautiful photographs, you don't want those larger files bogging down the mobile experience to the point where visitors abandon your content. With this in mind, ensure that animation, video, and high-resolution photographs are properly sized and optimized.

There are many web tools available that can provide insight, such as Hubspot's Website Grader or Google PageSpeed Insights. These can highlight areas where your site may not be performing well across each device, and offer suggestions to improve performance.

Best Practices: Make booking easy

As mentioned before, short-notice traffic has blossomed in the mobile environment. With that in mind, keep your "Book Now" button clearly visible on all pages of your optimized site, and make sure the check-out process is as simple and streamlined as possible. Always include a "Click to call" button, as there are always people who would prefer to ask questions or simply talk to a person when booking.

Your booking engine should be smartphone-optimized, because a visitor in a rush won't have time or patience to enter a great deal of text or mull over a lot of options. The booking path

– picking dates, rooms, and options — should be straightforward, with drop-down menus and easy-to-tap buttons for selections. And of course, your booking process needs to be safe and secure, including confirmation screens to maintain the purchaser's confidence in the process.

Best Practices: Take advantage of the platform

Smartphones and tablets are incredibly powerful multifunction devices, so it makes sense for your mobile-optimized site to take advantage of those functions as much as possible.

Leverage the smartphone's telephone capabilities – which are easy to forget in the rush to optimize the touchscreen experience. Sometimes, simply making a call is the best way to go, and some users will always prefer to transact by phone. Don't make your users copy and paste your phone number – they should be able to call directly from your app just by tapping your number. Or better yet, implement a "Call Now" button on your site, placed prominently on each screen.

Make use of maps and more. Mobile users shouldn't have to copy your address into their navigation app to find you or check out the surrounding area. Make sure you integrate mapping functionality on your "Location" page, letting visitors one-tap to open their default app and immediately show your location in context. You can also take advantage of calendar, email, and camera app integration where applicable. Many phones also offer integration to social media apps.

Best Practices: Make your mobile site "social-ready"

Transform your visitors into brand ambassadors through social sharing features. Travelers like to share their vacation plans and activities with their followers: 55% of travelers "like" Facebook pages specific to their vacation, with 70% updating their Facebook status while on vacation.[13] Additionally, Facebook recently revealed that 78% of all U.S. social activity takes place on mobile devices.

Whereas tablet users tend to share from their couch, smartphone users like to share on the go. Make sure you're encouraging them to share that they're staying with you when they check in, when they're by the pool, or when they're in the bar. And don't make them work hard to do it!

Regardless of device, word-of-mouth remains as important as ever in the travel sector, and social media allows that word to travel farther and further than ever before. Adding Twitter, Facebook, and "share-by-email" buttons to your mobile site is an easy way to encourage visitors to share their travel plans and to build digital advocacy for your property.

Best Practices: Display redeemable special offers

Everyone loves a good deal – and mobile shoppers are no different. In 2017, 33% of millennials, 25% of Gen Xers and 17% of Baby Boomers had used a mobile coupon in the past year, and 90 percent of mobile device users have at least one subscription to a service which offers coupons, promotions, or special discounts.[14] Promoting value-added special offers on smartphones and tablets not only grabs consumer interest and attention, but it also encourages them to book.

To appeal to smartphone and tablet users during each period of their buying cycle — early research, booking, on-property time, and post-vacation — ensure you have offers that will appeal to them at each distinct point in the journey. Not only can special offers entice booking, but they can create a more enjoyable stay, prompting more "wow" moments to share on social media.

Feature promotions that add value such as free parking, complimentary breakfast, bonus loyalty points, or happy hour specials at your restaurant, as well as special offers for tickets to local attractions and upcoming events.

- Ensure offers are easy to redeem by linking directly to your mobile booking engine with the appropriate offer code populated.
- Make offers easy to find and click on your homepage or landing page.
- Enhance the way your offers are displayed by using large and relevant visuals.
- Leverage data you've collected on your visitors throughout the buying process to customize offers while they're on property. Learn their interests, travel preferences, and potential activities, and make sure

you're offering relevant deals to make their stay more enjoyable.

Best Practices: Connect with your global customer through mobile

In many countries, the use of mobile devices has surpassed the use of desktop computers. But across various locales, people use mobile devices in notably different ways.

What's more, through a recent page ranking update, Google has begun moving to a mobile-first index. Eventually, all sites – mobile and desktop – will be indexed in this format, although currently, Google is utilizing a mobile and desktop index.

This means that Google's crawler will scan your mobile site as a mobile user, and your desktop as a desktop user. So it's vital to make sure that your site is clearly signaling to Google that your site either is mobile optimized or has a mobile equivalent.

The diversity of mobile trends across the globe and the significance of mobile for search show the importance of integrating your global and mobile strategies.

- Consider doing a mobile check of your existing website using Google's Mobile-Friendly Test.
- Test all aspects of your localized mobile site: booking, purchasing, scrolling, etc., on different mobile devices and browser types.
- Remember that not all countries have fast mobile internet, so optimize your mobile sites for slower internet connections.
- Keep in mind that there can be many languages spoken within a single country. Determine your language strategy carefully to reach your target audience in their own language.
- If you have – or are considering – a mobile app, plan to localize that application for your international markets.

Mobile Marketing Techniques

Since mobile is both a channel and a device,[15] what is true for traditional website marketing can and should be extended to mobile to complement your overall campaign. At the heart of any great advertising strategy are clear objectives for the campaign, a framework for measurement, and a detailed understanding of the user you wish to engage. This approach will give you the foundation to budget by channel and device while including geo-targeting as an added feature of your campaign.

- Segment and target your strategy and messaging for mobile devices.
- Run mobile-specific campaigns that have ads, landing pages, and content targeted to the needs and behaviors of the mobile user.
- Use Mobile Banner Advertising on mobile websites and within apps that are consistent with and a part of the overall hotel marketing strategy. Know that they do require some optimization in terms of the size of ads, the creative, and of course, mobile landing pages.
- Mobile Pay-Per-Click (PPC) is available via the major ad networks and can be run in conjunction with your regular PPC campaigns. The ad networks provide the ability to target (or not) mobile users. Think about focusing on keywords inherently used by a mobile consumer, and apply your knowledge to ad copy and mobile landing pages. Additional targeting may be available by leveraging geolocation (the physical location of the user).
- Geolocation and location based marketing can be further extended by "pushing" ads or offers to consumers via SMS (requires opt-in) as well as through geolocation specific applications like Swarm (Foursquare), Facebook, Google+, and Yelp. These applications allow a user to "check in" at a physical location and broadcast their proximity, allowing you to target a specific offer to them through that platform. Also, the distribution of Beacon sensors provided by Apple (iBeacons), Facebook (Bluetooth Beacons), and Google (Eddystone Beacons) is growing. In addition to being able to 'push' offers when a customer is within proximity (active engagement), beacons also are used to gather data (passive engagement) for refining other marketing efforts.
- Many location or proximity based mobile applications are leveraging local directories such as Google My Business to derive the profiles or listings of businesses, including hotels. It is critical to maintain these directories to take full advantage of the applications consumers use to conduct local and location-based search. Some applications also leverage smartphone cameras to create Augmented Reality experiences, superimposing listings from local directories along with consumer reviews on the physical world as viewed through the phone camera lens.
- Combine the concepts of SoLoMo (Social, Local, Mobile) around your product or brand on mobile devices by using local or proximity tools (e.g., GPS) with social networking efforts to drive conversation and engagement. QR (Quick Response) codes are another way to connect the physical and online worlds via mobile devices. The camera on a mobile phone is used to scan a QR code just like a bar code, which prompts the phone to open the designated website. QR codes have both advertising (e.g., QR code in a print ad scanned to see more info on the mobile phone) and on-property customer service applications. Use QR codes to connect your guests to TripAdvisor so they can easily write a review or access a "mobile only" special.

Last But Not Least: Measure!

Before you put your mobile strategy into action, it's important to determine the business objectives you'd like to accomplish (e.g., branding, awareness, loyalty) so that you can determine the right metrics to target (e.g., clickthroughs, average length of engagement). Additionally, the type of content that you choose for your mobile engagement has a big impact on your results. Remember, you can't manage what you can't measure.

In addition, make sure you can test toward those results. Perform A-B testing or multivariate testing on your site's booking functions and promotional pages, and see what performs well. Never assume that a page that looks more visually appealing to you is going to convert more visitors. Take subjective decisions out of the equation whenever possible!

One of the leading indicators of whether a mobile strategy is working is the level of engagement that's being achieved with your target audience. If customers are increasing their interaction with your property via their mobile device, and with certain pieces of content, then they're seeing value in the mobile experience. Although sales are typically the ultimate measure of success, it's important for marketers to recognize that the impact of mobile marketing may not be realized immediately. Getting consumers to engage more often and more deeply with your hotel can lead to long-term success.

There are several digital tracking solutions in the marketplace such as Google Analytics, Adobe Analytics, Piwik, and Etracker. Choose one that works best for your objectives and then ensure you enlist an analytics professional (e.g., your digital agency) to set up your tracking, as this requires very specific knowledge to ensure credible results. Any click of a button can be tracked if you properly configure events and define goals to measure conversion success.

Some key performance metrics for consideration include:

- total traffic across all platforms (mobile + desktop)
- percentage of traffic on mobile (tablet + smartphone)
- bookings by platform and device type (desktop v. mobile)
- media (photos, videos, virtual tours) consumption by platform and mobile device type
- length of time on mobile site/page

- What elements are visitors clicking on? Social widgets? Click to call? Mapping? Check Rates?

Mobile Internet usage is increasing faster than adoption of all previous technologies, including radio, TV, PC, and social media. This phenomenon gives hotel marketers a staggering opportunity to engage with guests and potential customers though mobile communications in an unprecedented way.

To compete, hoteliers must provide content that's relevant, distinguishing, genuine, and fun. People treat mobile devices as extensions of themselves, enabling communication with friends, family, companies, and brands whenever and however they choose. Mobile is hot and the time to act is now. Consumers are tied to their mobile devices and are innovative in finding new ways to use them. Hotels that approach this new frontier from a customer-centric position will gain competitive advantage and build stronger relationships with their guests.

Mobile is the new normal.

Chapter 6 Endnotes

[1] "Mobile Drives Growth of Online Travel Bookings." eMarketer. June 21, 2017. https://www.emarketer.com/Article/Mobile-Drives-Growth-of-Online-Travel-Bookings/1016053. January 10, 2018.

[2] Destinations on Google Data, U.S., Jan 2016.

[3] "The Role of Mobile for the 2012 Traveler." Google. January 2012. November 18, 2013. http://www.google.com/think/research-studies/insights-of-mobile-2012-traveler.html

[4] http://www.slideshare.net/Leonardo/how-mobile-devices-are-changing-the-way-we-market-to-todays-travel-shopper

[5] "Nearly All Mobile Video Viewers Are Mobile Video Sharers." eMarketer. January 7, 2013. November 18, 2013. http://www.emarketer.com/Article/Nearly-All-Mobile-Video-Viewers-Mobile-Video-Sharers/1009586

[6] Abramovich, Giselle. "15 Stats Brands Should Know About OnlineVideo." Digiday. April 3, 2013. November 18, 2013. http://digiday.com/brands/celtra-15-must-know-stats-for-online-video/

[7] "Progressive Web is the New Responsive." Mobify. January 24, 2017. https://www.mobify.com/insights/progressive-web-is-the-new-responsive/. January 10, 2018.

[8] "Google advice: Switch your m-dot domain to responsive before the mobile-first index rollout." Search Engine Land. June 20, 2017. https://searchengineland.com/google-advice-switch-m-dot-domain-responsive-mobile-first-index-rollout-277446. January 10, 2018.

[9] "M.dot vs. Responsive vs. Progressive: What's the Right Solution for Your Company?" Mobify. May 7, 2015. https://www.mobify.com/insights/m-dot-responsive-progressive-whats-the-right-solution/. January 10, 2018.

[10] "Cisco Visual Networking Index: Forecast and Methodology, 2012–2017." Cisco. May 29, 2013. November 18, 2013. http://www.cisco.com/en/US/solutions/collateral/ns341/ns525/ns537/ns705/ns827/white_paper_c11-481360.pdf

[11] Think Insights with Google, August 2012

[12] "Techie Traveler." Lab42 Blog. March 23, 2012. http://blog.lab42.com/techie-traveler. November 18, 2013.

[13] "Social Media, Mobile and Travel: Like, Tweet, and Share Your Across the Globe." WebFX Blog. http://www.webfx.com/blog/social-media-mobile-travel/. May 28, 2019.

[14] "2017 Coupon Statistics." Access. May 24, 2017. https://blog.accessdevelopment.com/2017-coupon-statistics. January 10, 2018.

[15] Parrish, Melissa. "Mobile for Marketing: Is It a Channel or a Device?" Forrester Blogs. March 4, 2011.

CHAPTER 7
Search Engine Optimization (SEO) for Hotels

KEY POINTS

- SEO defined
- Creating an SEO strategy
- Key factors for both onsite and offsite optimization
- The importance of local search
- White hat vs. black hat tactics

SUMMARY

Search engine optimization (SEO) means having your site appear higher in the search engine results pages. Accomplishing this goal is highly competitive in the hospitality/ travel industry due to individual hotel sites, brand sites, destination sites, review sites, and OTAs competing for the top lines. This chapter identifies the best practices for hospitality within the world of SEO.

SEO is the process of improving website visibility in unpaid web search engine results, which are also called "natural" or "organic" search results. The higher a website appears in search results, the more visitors it receives. Part 4 will cover Paid Media, including search and display advertising, which increases your presence in the paid, non-organic spots on search engines.

The differences between SEO and paid advertising need to be evaluated in your overall digital marketing strategy. SEO takes more effort than running an AdWords campaign, and the results take longer to achieve typically. If you optimize your website today, you may not see results for one, two, or even three months whereas with SEM, you will appear in the top spots as long as you are willing to pay. However, once you achieve a top spot organically, you won't likely lose it as quickly as the end of a campaign will eliminate your paid results. The ideal situation is to have both a well-optimized website and smart, targeted search marketing campaigns.

Good SEO is Key for a Successful Website

SEO is one of the most important components to driving revenue to your independent website's booking engine. The most beautiful website is rendered virtually useless if it has not been properly optimized.

Proper optimization techniques can help you quickly rank high in search engine results for terms that target your ideal guest, whereas poorly performed optimization can harm your hotel's online presence, and even remove it from popular search engines altogether. Gaining a firm grasp of all the complexities of SEO practices and learning to use trusted tools are the first steps to a successful SEO campaign, and will ensure your continued success in a competitive online marketplace.

How Search Engines Work

Search engines, including Google, Yahoo, and Bing, use programs called "web crawlers" or "spiders" that scan websites to build an index of information. Search engines use mathematical algorithms to determine the relevance of the information the spiders find, based on a myriad of over 200 major factors, including keywords, new content, page speed, domain authority, reviews, backlinks, personalization, and social signals. When a user enters a phrase into the search engine, the search engine displays results based on the index of information it has compiled.

The Evolution of Search Engines

The 1990s

The earliest search algorithms depended on meta data – information about a webpage that exists behind the scenes and describes what is on the page. Webmasters provided this information in the form of meta keyword tags, title tags, and meta description tags, and spiders used this information to index data for search engine results.

Because meta data could contain keywords that inaccurately represented the site's actual content, using meta data to index pages was found to be unreliable. Inaccurate meta data caused pages to show up in irrelevant searches.

By 2004

Because the success of a search engine depends on the quality and relevance of its results, search engines developed a number of more complex algorithms that took a variety of undisclosed factors into account to prevent system manipulation. For instance, Google said it used more than 200 different factors to determine relevance.

2009

Google added its users' web search history as a factor in search results, and also introduced Google Instant, which allowed new content to rank quickly. Historically, it could take months or years for sites to increase in search rankings, but the growth of social media and blogs created demand for more timely results.

2011

Before 2011, copying content from one site to another helped sites rank faster. Then, in 2011, Google began penalizing websites for containing content duplicated from other websites.

2012

In 2012, social media sites were playing an increasingly important role in search engine results and rankings. And the evolution continues.

2013

In 2013, Google released its Hummingbird algorithm which promises to change SEO fairly dramatically over the course of the next few years from being keyword-driven to dynamic content-driven. Keeping fresh and interesting content is what Google is looking for, and those sites that deliver this relevant content will simply rank higher because Google understands the importance of the best user experience.

2014

Panda's 4.0 and following updates continue to make it harder for sites with poor content to appear on Google's search results.

The Pigeon update also impacted local search, Google saying it was now more closely aligned with traditional web ranking. It also improved location and distance signals.

2015

Mobile Update (aka Mobilegeddon): Google announced this update in advance, and it centered around improving results for mobile-friendly websites. While the digital world braced for extreme changes in results, the reality ended up being a much slower and more subtle change. Additionally in 2015 there was a "phantom" change that many dubbed a "quality update" which Google later acknowledged as impacting its core algorithms.

The focus in 2014 and 2015 was also on semantic search, allowing Google to return results based on how you naturally speak. This means the difference between typing "beach hotels, Avalon, NJ" vs. "where can I find a great beach hotel in Avalon, NJ?"

Semantic search will likely continue to play a larger role, but what is it? According to Wikipedia (and Google), "Semantic search seeks to improve search accuracy by understanding searcher intent and the contextual meaning of terms as they appear in the searchable dataspace, whether on the Web or within a closed system, to generate more relevant results." According to Techopedia, "Semantic search is a data searching technique in a which a search query aims to not only find keywords, but to determine the intent and contextual meaning of the words a person is using for search."

Google uses a machine-learning artificial intelligence system called "RankBrain" to help sort through its search results.

For a history of all of Google's updates: https://moz.com/google-algorithm-change.

For further reading, Searchmetrics released a whitepaper in 2015 which compared changes in SEO based on results. You can find a detailed account of their findings here: http://www.searchmetrics.com/wp-content/uploads/Ranking-Factors-2015-Whitepaper-US.pdf

2017
Google deploys AMP pages for all websites. With the goal to find the most relevant site with the best user experience, AMP sites with Google hosted caching significantly improve your website's load time, which in turn will result in better ranking and lower bounce rates.

Best Practices: Determine what traffic you want to target
A hotel's target market will determine what keywords will have the most value and will pull in the most relevant travel shoppers. For instance, resorts in Orlando have a different target market than Orlando airport hotels, and will use different keywords to attract this market.

Increasing the amount of traffic to a site creates instant awareness and branding, but converting visitors is the ultimate goal. Choosing keywords that most accurately describe your property and also have a high value – meaning there are a lot of people querying for those keywords – will attract the highest converting traffic.

Best Practices: Do the research
Conduct keyword research to find the words and phrases of highest value for your property. There are a number of sources available to help you discover which terms are searched more frequently than others. Google Insights can be a help – while it is primarily used for pay per click, the valuable terms are the most coveted. Wordtracker is another software tool that can help. Wordtracker, like Google, will show the number of times a keyword or phrase shows up in a search. It also shows the number of websites that are optimized for that keyword – meaning they are using that keyword in any of their anchor texts. This gives you an idea of how competitive the keyword is. In an ideal world you would find a keyword or phrase that has a high amount of use, but very little competition. (See the following graphic for a sample Wordtracker report.)

Consider what sets your property apart from your competitors – are you pet-friendly or family-friendly?

Do you have suites, a variety of business amenities, or a large meeting space? Are weddings your target – traditional? same sex? Compile a potential list of your true targeted markets during the research phase.

Look at your competitors' websites to see which words and phrases they use. You can view source code to see the meta tags and descriptions they are using – though keep in mind they can also look at yours! Simply Googling potential phrases can help as well, to see if keywords are worth targeting, to look for competition for the term, and to see what iterations of the term appear in search results.

Keyword (?) (301)	Searches ▼ (?) (N/A)	Competition (IAAT) (?)	KEI (?)	KEI3 (?)
1 ☑ new york (search)	83,100,000	354,000,000	51,900,000	0.235
2 ☑ new york city (search)	9,140,000	35,800,000	1,350,000	0.256
3 ☑ hotel in new york (search)	1,830,000	161,000	43,700,000	11.3
4 ☑ the hotel new york (search)	1,830,000	639	9,130,000,000	2,860
5 ☑ hotel new york new york (search)	1,830,000	15,500,000	209,000,000	0.118
6 ☑ new york new york hotels (search)	1,220,000	37,800,000	225,000,000	0.032
7 ☑ hotels new york new york (search)	1,220,000	-	-	-
8 ☑ hotels in new york new york (search)	1,220,000	16,100	518,000,000	75.5
9 ☑ new hotels new york (search)	1,220,000	-	-	-
10 ☑ new york hotels (search)	1,220,000	61,100,000	5,710,000	0.020
11 ☑ hotels in new york (search)	1,220,000	212,000	5,730,000	5.75
12 ☑ hotels in new york ny (search)	823,000	23,500	439,000,000	35.0
13 ☑ new york ny hotels (search)	823,000	-	-	-
14 ☑ hotels new york ny (search)	823,000	17,600	293,000,000	46.6
15 ☑ accommodation new york (search)	450,000	12,700	62,200,000	35.4
16 ☑ new york city restaurants (search)	301,000	168,000	4,720,000	1.79
17 ☑ hotel new york city (search)	301,000	229,000	937,000	1.31

Best Practices: Optimize for brand and location

Your own site, not third-party sites, should come up first in a search for your brand terms. Visitors and bookings to your direct website are ideal, because you avoid paying third-party fees for bookings. After brand, the next most important set of terms to optimize relate to your location. Focus on the location by using words like hotels, lodging, suites, cabins, or resorts, and pairing them with the location, such as:

- Resorts in Orlando,
- Suites in Miami,
- Boston lodging,
- Hotels in downtown Chicago.

To the location terms, add more targeted niche terms, such as "Miami beach hotels with conference rooms" or "Miami beach resorts for weddings." These terms are very specific, relevant terms to your property and are quite valuable. Though the volume of searches will be lower for the more specific terms, the visitors you will attract will likely convert more often because they are looking for your product.

Best Practices: Optimize for demand generators

In addition to brand, location, and niche terms, consider demand generators — local business and leisure attractions — that bring guests to your area, such as:

- corporate offices
- hospitals
- theme parks
- beaches
- museums
- historic districts
- convention centers
- shopping, dining, and entertainment districts
- popular annual events

Pair these with lodging and niche terms, for example:

- family-friendly resorts near Disney World
- beachfront suites in Miami
- Boston Marathon lodging
- pet-friendly hotels near Magnificent Mile

Once you have done your research and optimized for demand generators, brand, and location, there are a few additional actions you can take to improve your SEO.

- INDEXING: If it is new, submit your site so it can be indexed on all search engines.

- COPYWRITING: Text must be crawlable (so avoid and/or account for flash), keyword rich (to help reinforce what customers are looking for), and each page should have its own set of unique keywords to increase the odds of your website being seen. If a page contains an image (which is not crawlable), it is advisable to put descriptive text below the fold.

- KEYWORDS AND TAGS: Keyword selection is the heart of an SEO campaign and should be checked for relevance and competitiveness at least every six months. The right keywords will allow for more relevant searches and therefore more qualified leads, in addition to a higher ranking. It is also important to include keywords in the page title and meta description tags in the HTML code for each page. This is especially important for search engines.

- LINK BUILDING: Inbound links are a vote of confidence and build credibility of the site. The greater the number of links from other sites pointing to a website, the more popular it is and therefore the higher the quality of the resource for search engines. However, it is also important that the websites linking to yours are reputable and not "spam." Unfortunately, even if the correct SEO techniques are used, you are still at the mercy of search engines. The web ranking on organic listings changes constantly since recent web crawls by a search engine may have uncovered more relevant sites, according to their algorithm.

Long & Short Tail Keywords

Long tail keywords are phrases that contain four or more words that are very targeted to your property. They receive fewer searches, but are very targeted, and result in a higher conversion rate. Examples of long tail keywords include: "pet-friendly hotels near Magnificent Mile" and "Houston hotels with indoor pool."

Short tail keywords are broad phrases that receive a lot of searches, but result in a lower conversion rate because they are so broad. Examples of short tail keywords include: "Chicago hotels" and "Orlando lodging."

Rules of Thumb for Long and Short Tail Value

- Location: Many low-value searches
- Location + hotel: More value, slightly fewer searches
- Property name: Even more value, even fewer searches
- Specific amenities or niche terms: Very few searches but very high value

Strategies to Ensure Website Optimization

Web users typically only visit the websites that appear on the first page of search engine results. At the same time, search engines try to establish the most relevant search results. The algorithms created by search engines are not put in place for trickery, but merely to ensure the most relevant results are returned to the searcher. How else would Google know that you really are a pet friendly hotel near the beach in Orlando unless you have keywords stating that, content describing that, and links from other beachfront attractions linking to you? You can help Google determine this by having schemas on your site. To do so, structured data is added directly to a page's HTML markup. Search engines use structured data to generate rich snippets, which are small pieces of information that will then appear in search results.

Best Practices: On-Site Optimization

On-site optimization is where you make changes to your website to tell search engines and users what your site is about, and make your site as relevant to your target market as possible. On-site optimization includes:

- creating title tags, meta descriptions, and heading tags with relevant keywords
- updating site with fresh, targeted content to keep search engine spiders coming back
- adding internal links from relevant keywords to the pages in your site that are associated with those keywords (internal cross linking)
- XML site maps
- image optimization and sitemap — adding relevant ALT and title tags for images (this is a particularly helpful traffic-building

technique for hotels and resorts, because travel shoppers want to see images of where they're going)

- URL normalization of webpages
- exciting, dynamic content – make sure that you have considerable relevant content that is consistently updated. Outdated content will harm your ranking as will stale or generic content

Best Practices: Off-Site Optimization

Off-site optimization is where you make your site more relevant in search engines by methods that don't involve your making changes to your site. The most important aspect of off-site optimization is link building – increasing the number of quality inbound links, or back links, to your site.

Each time another website links to your site for a particular phrase, it is a vote for your site for that phrase. If your site has a history of people visiting your site for that phrase, search engines will consider your content more relevant for that phrase, and your site will move up in search results. In addition, pages linked from other pages indexed by search engines are found automatically by spiders. The quality of the sites linking back to you are also relevant for your off-site optimization.

There seems to be a hierarchy in the value of off-site links. Links from .gov, .edu, and .org sites seem to help a hotel's SEO more so than .com sites. However, keep in mind that you only want links back to your site that help you prove some relevancy for that area. If you are nowhere near the White House, getting a link from the White House will not likely help you.

Having a number of irrelevant links or links from low quality sites can actually harm your web SEO. Paying $100 to a "link farm" that simply creates sites with nothing but links will not help you appear more relevant to the search engines.

Also be sure to link back to your site from any social sites you may have. If you have a Facebook page, be sure to post periodically and provide a link back to a specific area on your site. Blogs are a great way to help SEO because it enables you to frequently change and update content as well as encourage others to link to you if they are interested in what you have to say.

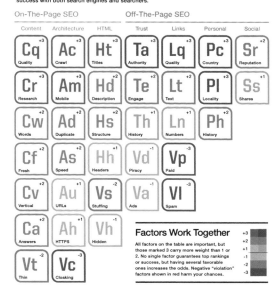

The Periodic Table of SEO Success Factors [1]

Search engine optimization (SEO) seems like alchemy to the uninitiated. But there's a science to it. Below are some important "ranking factors" and best practices that can lead to success with both search engines and searchers.

The Importance of Local Listings in Search Engines

With nearly 60% of searches coming from mobile devices, optimizing your site for local searches becomes more important. For hoteliers, the most important step to optimize your site for local listings is to claim your business listings in Google, Yahoo, and Bing. This is important in particular for Google+ Local because these listings are among the first results on a Google search results page.

In addition to local listings, there are also "social local" listings, which use signals from social networks like Facebook to move local listings up in local search results.

Best practices for optimizing your site for local returns include ensuring that you have consistent UNAP (URL, Name, Address, and phone numbers) in text, not graphics, on your website; including maps on your site that are interactive, not static; and updating your profile on social channels linking back to your site.

Software Tools to Improve Optimization

There are a variety of tools that can help evaluate and improve website optimization, but as with any software, these tools should be used in conjunction with common sense and thoughtful strategy. Some particularly helpful tools include:

- Google Webmaster Tools
- Raven Tools
- SEOmoz PRO Tools
- AWR (Advanced Web Ranking)
- BrightEdge
- Wordtracker

White Hat vs. Black Hat Optimization

White hat optimization is any optimization technique that is recommended and approved by search engines, and that does not involve any form of deception. A basic guideline for producing an optimized site that search engines will approve of is that the content a search engine uses to index and rank your site should be the same content users can see.

Black hat optimization is any optimization technique of which search engines do not approve. Black hat optimization is designed to trick search engine algorithms by manipulating content so that what the spiders see is different from what users can see.

Examples of black hat optimization include:

- Using text that is hidden, either by making the text a similar color to the background, hiding text behind an image, or positioning text off screen.
- Offering a different page to the search engine than to a user (a technique called "cloaking").
- Keyword stuffing – using a word in the content so much that the content loses its meaning.

White hat optimization naturally produces long-term positive results, but black hat optimization only works as long as a site can get away with it. When a search engine discovers deceptive optimization techniques, it either temporarily or permanently bans the site from its search engine.

Best Practices: Connect with your global customer through SEO for your website

Competition in travel and hospitality is fierce. To keep up with competitors, your customers must be able to find your website—regardless of the language they speak, the search engine they use, or the device they choose. So to meet this need, you'll have to implement a strong global SEO strategy.

If global prospects can't find you on the web, they can't become customers through digital channels. If they don't find relevant and interesting localized content once they reach your website, they'll soon leave—and your brand can suffer. And if your competition ranks higher in local search engines, potential customers are even less likely to buy from your site.

Ease these challenges and ensure global SEO success with the following tips:

- Don't just translate your website—optimize your content for local search engines and common local search phrases (keywords).
- Understand that your international customers use a variety of search engines. For instance, Chinese visitors may use Baidu's Qunar.com, but South Koreans will likely use Naver.
- Perform global SEO during the website translation process so translators can translate and customize content using the right SEO keywords.
- Create localized landing pages with compelling, original content to engage your website visitors.
- Ensure that your "meta content" (content about the content) is localized correctly. This includes meta descriptions, a key element that informs search engines—and more importantly, your visitors—what the page is about.
- Optimize your site for mobile use. Google recently updated their search algorithm to rank mobile-optimized pages higher. This should be part of your SEO strategy, if it isn't already.

Chapter 7 Endnotes
[1] *"The Periodic Table of SEO Success Factors." Search Engine Land.* https://searchengineland.com/seotable. *January 7, 2018.*

KEY POINTS

- Rich media has significant value in a digital marketing toolbox.
- The targeted use of rich media can increase bookings.
- Storytelling by visual methods impacts online shopping behaviors.
- Understand the best practices for using rich media across multiple channels of your digital marketing strategy.

SUMMARY

Rich media for hotels includes photos, full motion video, 360° virtual tours, digital slideshows, interactive schematics, and audio. Storytelling comes to life with rich media, and the better the story, the stronger the connection made between hotel and consumer. Travelers rely on rich media to inform themselves, help plan itineraries, and give them confidence to make their lodging purchases.

The power of visual merchandising should not be undervalued. It can be used to inform, inspire, and differentiate your hotel to drive awareness, sales, and guest loyalty.

In 2016, eighty-five percent of the U.S. internet audience watched video online and over half of that is viewed on mobile. Fifty-one percent of marketing professionals worldwide named video content as having the best ROI.[1] Additionally, 4.8% is the average conversion rate for websites using video compared to 2.9% for those that don't. [2]

Specific to hospitality, according to a 2013 Google and Ipsos MediaCT study, 62% of travelers have watched videos from hotels, airlines, cruises, or tour companies. Fifty-one percent of leisure and 69% of business travel-ers watch online travel videos, and over half do so to help make accommodations decisions. In 2012, two major websites, TripAdvisor and Facebook, redesigned their websites to capitalize on the value of rich media. An article by CMO.com

in May 2017 furthers the importance showing that travelers spent an average of 53 days visiting 28 different websites over a period of 76 online sessions. [3] With these statistics, differentiating your ho-tel's website becomes even more important.

Today's rich media options are extensive, addressing the needs of all types of properties and for every budget. A typical portfolio of rich media production includes full motion video, 360° virtual tours, interactive floor plans, 3D schematics, digital photo slideshows, and most recently virtual reality. The type of media chosen depends on your hotel's marketing objective and budget.

Full Motion Video

- Videos tell stories and bring your hotel to life by creating emotional connections with guests. Video:
- Helps a property stand out in a crowded online environment.
- Inspires and creates desire, and as consumers are drawn into a property or brand story, they become emotionally engaged and inspired to book.
- Encourages consumers' confidence in their selection because they have a better understanding of what to expect from the hotel and/or surrounding areas.
- More effectively communicates key selling points than through text or photos alone.
- Increases look-to-book conversion rates.

Hotels can take advantage of the sight, sound, and motion of the medium to tell their story in new and creative ways. Whether it's a guided tour of the hotel narrated by the general manager, a "day in the life" story, or a series of videos showcasing different areas or behind-the-scenes takes of your hotel, video is your way to be creative, set your hotel apart, and inspire lookers to become bookers.

According to comScore, exposure to online video can lead to a 40 percent increase in buying. "For people who are wondering whether they should book a room, video will be that final little tap that will say, absolutely the place is awesome," says Susan Shields, General Manager of the Kimber Modern in Austin, Texas. According to Google, half of leisure travelers (and even more business travelers) are encouraged to visit the website of an advertiser after viewing their online video.

360° Virtual Tours
Virtual tours are becoming the de facto standard for basic rich media production due to their versatility and low cost of production. Virtual tours:

- Give consumers more complete and engaging visual information compared to static photos.
- Transform the photographic image from a flat two-dimensional world to a 360° virtual reality experience, allowing the consumer to explore a property as if they were physically there.
- Provide confidence and help set expectations among guests.
- Improve look-to-book ratios compared to just photos alone.

Virtual tours showcase rooms and amenities from every angle and provide a realistic idea of what the hotel is like – what equipment is in the fitness center, how much storage space is available in the guestrooms, or even what types of amenities are available in the room or on property. Providing this information is important because travelers come from different generations, demographics, and behavioral groups. Some travel alone, others with spouses or families. Some are leisure travelers; some are business travelers. Today's guests have different needs and expectations in travel; virtual tours can help guests easily evaluate whether your hotel may be a good fit for their needs.

Digital Photo Slideshows
A digital photo slideshow, sometimes referred to as "photo video" or "photomontage," is built to balance function with budget for any type of hotel that has good quality digital photos. Digital slide shows:

- Scale efforts that are economical and effective.
- Combine photography and traveler engagement with movement, music, and voice-overs.
- Combat commoditization by differentiating what a hotel has to offer above standard price comparisons.

- Increase consumer confidence.
- Inspire booking.

The Impact of Online Shopping Behavior
Like all online shoppers, those shopping for travel are looking for rich visual experiences that educate and help them better understand and feel comfortable about the purchase they are considering.

Travelers visit many different websites in what is a non-linear and very complex online shopping journey from inspiration to research, comparison, purchase, post purchase, and sharing stages. A typical guest will use more than two dozen touch points to research a trip. This means that there are multiple opportunities to grab their attention and make a great impression; alternatively brands need to ensure that they are differentiating their value propositions in order to stay top-of-mind.

Consumers are going to different sites for different reasons and at different stages of the travel shopping journey. According to Atmosphere Research Group, the top three websites that consumers cite as particularly helpful in the planning stage are travel supplier websites, online travel agencies (OTAs), and travel-focused ratings/review websites. Eighty-four percent of travelers will visit brand.com or several different brand.coms to get the hotel's direct perspective. Eighty-three percent will also visit an OTA, such as Orbitz, to see what hotels are available in the market. Similarly, 83% will go to a traveler review site like TripAdvisor to read what others are saying, and 81% will check out a meta search engine like Kayak to compare the prices.[4]

What consumers see about an individual hotel across these various sites must be consistent, relevant, and interesting; otherwise, hoteliers risk not being in the traveler's consideration set.

Another trend that should not be ignored is the increasingly blurred lines between business and leisure travel. Both travel shopping segments want immersive, visually-rich presentations. While there is a misconception that business travelers are not interested in researching their stay, 93% of business travelers watched travel related video online last year (versus 89% of leisure travelers). At the same time, 56% say that they plan to spend more time shopping around and researching before booking business travel in order to find good value for their money.[5]

Consumers are Visual

Pinterest and Instagram, among other websites and apps, led the breakout trend of visual marketing in 2012 - 2013. When we look back (not that long ago) blogs were one of our earliest forms of social networking with people writing 1000 word posts, according to Dr. William Ward, social media professor at Syracuse University. When we moved to status updates on Facebook, our posts became shorter. Then "microblogs" like Twitter came along and chopped our updates down to 140 characters. Today, we're leaving out words altogether and moving towards more visual communication with sites like Pinterest.

On Pinterest, for example, when you type in the keyword "hotels," the wide range of visuals being pinned, including both professional and non-professional photos and videos, is astonishing. The common thread is that the images create inspiring stories about design, location, people, and interaction. Not surprisingly, travel ranks in the top third of categories on Pinterest.

The Importance of Storytelling

Located near the National Zoo and its wildly popular pandas, the Best Western in Rockville, Maryland used a unique and touching storyline to appeal to travelers looking for a romantic getaway in the area. The special offer was enhanced with photos and videos of the pandas hugging. This successful campaign made an emotional, visual connection with consumers – making the property memorable.

Always begin the process of producing media for your hotel by answering one central question: what is your story? Explain what makes your hotel or brand uniquely compelling to the travelers you wish to attract. Rich Media is simply the medium through which you will show and tell this story – whether it is video, a virtual tour, audio, or something else.

Hotel marketing teams can develop a story that will attract more online travel shoppers – and more guests in general – by answering a few questions[6]:

- Who are your guests?
- What are guests saying about your hotel?
- What makes your hotel unique?
- What are your competitors' value propositions?
- What would excite and inspire you if you were a travel shopper?

Much of this information can found by reading online reviews about your hotel. Reviews are a good place to start because guests will tell you what makes your hotel unique and compelling and what doesn't.

Through this process, you'll know what sets your property apart and you'll become much more skilled at conveying this message. You will then be in a better position to tell your story, and provide resources for new initiatives to do so in the near future.

Best Practices: Make it authentic

When everything is available at the click of a mouse, having a clean and comfortable hotel product is not always enough to drive action. Creating authentic videos that capture the human element of your brand allows travel shoppers to connect on a personal level. This connection builds trust and drives action. Do not be afraid to go on camera and welcome your guests in the same way you would welcome them when they arrive at your hotel.

Best Practices: Make it relevant

With customers in control, irrelevant video is at best ignored and at worst will create a negative impression when viewers feel their time is wasted. Video that works shares compelling stories that resonate with the audience. Respect viewers' time and provide them with actionable content. If you cater to young families on leisure travel, show them how their stay at your hotel will enhance their vacation. If you cater to business travelers, show them how their stay at your hotel will add to the success of their business trip. A good gut check could be: if you were the customer, would you find your video interesting and compelling enough to prompt action?

Best Practices: Make it engaging

With thousands of sites providing similar services and information, your online video has to stand out from the competition. Entertainment goes hand-in-hand with engagement. Video must deliver content in a format that interests and excites users. This is why a story is so important and why just walking around the hotel with a video camera is not enough.

Best Practices: Make it short
Online shoppers have short attention spans. As such, considerable effort and thought must be put into developing the story that you want to tell and how you will do it. Short videos (best practices suggest 1 minute or less) force you to think creatively and distill your value proposition down to its very essence. Is it engaging from the start?

Best Practices: Make it available
Your ability to distribute and show your video through search engines, destination sites, online travel agencies, and thousands of other specialty sites will enable you to welcome the travel shopper through your digital front door in a way that differentiates your brand.

Best Practices: Make it shareable
YouTube taught everyone that video is portable and starts conversations between friends. Videos that fail to meet this new expectation limit their own effectiveness. Sharing is an easy action that viewers can take to promote your business. By enabling conversations to spread, you're giving yourself an easy opportunity to gain viewership. To promote sharing, make sure your video can be embedded, emailed, and posted to the different social media sites.

Best Practices: Make it on your budget
As mentioned earlier, questions about production costs always come up quickly when the issue is video. The good news is that you can produce persuasive video in a way that matches your objectives and your budget. Hotels can produce enticing photo slideshows for as low as one hundred dollars. For those with very limited budgets, another option is to leverage user-generated content. A quick search on YouTube can yield some valuable content, and if repurposed appropriately with the owners' permission, user-generated content may even seem more authentic to future customers.

Best Practices: Socialize it
There are some very good reasons why social media is critical to your success. Thirty-two percent of surveyed travelers chose a different hotel based on the impact social media had on them[7]; and according to research by Atmosphere Research Group, 62% of leisure travelers find travel brands' Facebook pages helpful. Consider using Twitter to tweet links that drive consumers right to your hotel's media. For example: @MadisonHotel: Take an online tour of our hotel! Link (don't forget to use bitly.com to make your links shorter). Post links on Facebook that lead people to your hotel media and use the suite of Facebook apps to create a multimedia gallery right on your Facebook page.

Best Practices: Optimize it for Mobile
See Chapter 6 for a complete overview of the mobile topic. Mobile is complex, but more and more travelers are replicating their desktop activities across all devices. Ensuring that the consumer receives the information they are looking for on the platform, device, and operating system they are using is going to have a direct reflection on the success of your mobile marketing strategy.

Incorporating Rich Media Across Marketing Initiatives[8]
In addition to ensuring that your hotel's story is being maximized across all the relevant websites and screens, there are additional opportunities to increase the size of the audience that your media is reaching by simply incorporating your visually rich story into marketing initiatives you're likely already doing.

Email Signatures
Add a button that says, "Take a Tour" to your email signature and link it to the gallery section of your website. This way everyone you email can easily explore your hotel and become immersed in a rich visual experience. Get all of the employees at your hotel to do the same to further its reach.

Sales Proposals
If you have a great multimedia presentation that you can easily share, it can act as a sales proposal in itself. Send prospects a link that includes photos, floor plans, written descriptions, videos, and tours that are relevant to them. For example, a meeting planner wants to see your event facilities and learn about their features and capacities. Why send a long, written proposal when you can send them to visuals with accompanying descriptions? This is far more effective than any written sales proposal, and hotels can vouch for that. Further,

meeting and event planners who book their events at your hotel can then share a multi-media tour with their registrants and attendees so they know what to expect when they arrive.

Online Advertising

Add relevant visual media to the landing pages from your online banner ads and PPC (pay per click) programs, or any of your other digital advertising campaigns. Studies show that online shoppers who watch video spend an additional two minutes on the site and are 144% more likely to purchase. [9] Present your best and most influential marketing assets – your hotel's story – using rich visual media along with compelling matching descriptions that will turn lookers into bookers.

Email Newsletters and Promotions

When sending newsletters and promotions by email, add a "Take a Tour" button that directs readers to your hotel's rich media. After reading your newsletter and hearing about what your hotel has to offer, prospective guests who have never stayed before will be able to see visuals of your hotel and envision what the experience would be like, while past guests will be reminded of how great their experience was. Rich visuals give travel shoppers confidence to book, so in both scenarios the visuals make them more likely to book or book again.

Attribution

As with all marketing initiatives, it is critical to remember that there is not a single silver bullet answer regarding how much to invest in each marketing medium or channel. A common best practice, however, is to not limit your perspective in only valuing the "last thing" that a consumer does before completing a booking.

Rather, consider all of your marketing programs when evaluating your return on investment (ROI) for rich media and know that oftentimes, a booking can be influenced by multiple sources, interactions, and touch points.

Measurement

Measuring the effectiveness of your rich media can be as specific as an ROI on your email campaign. The following are potential measurements based on the specific media.

Audio
- subscriptions
- listening audience size
- duration of attention
- forwards
- evoked action solicited by the content

Video
- subscriptions
- views
- duration of attention
- forwards
- evoked action solicited by the content

Rich Media
- action count
- views
- frequency of use
- forwards
- evoked action solicited by the content

As you can see, similarities abound concerning the types of metrics related to media measurement. The following reflects a simple formula you can use to evaluate the ROI potential of your online visual marketing efforts. [10]

Highway Property
- Average 200 views per month
- 1% conversion rate
- 200 x .01 = 2 bookings per month
- Sample ADR $80
- LOS = 1.2
- Incremental Revenue = $192
- Cost per month: $100
- 2 x ROI

Resort Property
- Average 1000 views per month
- 1% conversion rate
- 1000 x .01 = 10 bookings per month
- Sample ADR $115
- LOS = 2.4
- Incremental Revenue = $2760
- Cost per month: $200
- 14 x ROI

Downtown Property
- Average 2000 views per month
- 1% conversion rate
- 2000 x .01 = 20 bookings per month
- Sample ADR $210
- LOS = 1.9
- Incremental Revenue = $7980
- Cost per month: $300
- 27 x ROI

A partial list of other general metric considerations includes:

- increase in bookings
- increase in ADR before/after
- views of media
- site traffic
- time spent on website
- number of likes
- number of pins

Conclusion

Start by figuring out what your story is. Think about location, style of property, staff, guests, experience, and positioning. Once your story is developed, ensure you're using all of the visual merchandising tools available to you. SHOW it, don't just tell it, in a way that compels people to take action. Optimize the experience for the consumer to ensure that they don't disregard your offering because of a bad visual experience. Use visual content on your hotel website, social media sites, and on all the channels where the property is represented to increase engagement, inspire sharing, and boost sales.

Chapter 8 Endnotes

[1] "37 Staggering Video Marketing Statistics for 2017." WordStream. December 18, 2017. https://www.wordstream.com/blog/ws/2017/03/08/video-marketing-statistics. January 7, 2018.

[2] "The Top 16 Video Marketing Stats for 2016."Adelie Studio. http://www.adeliestudios.com/top-16-video-marketing-statistics-2016/. January 7, 2018.

[3] Abramovich, Giselle. "15 Mind-Blowing Stats About Digital Trends in Travel and Hospitality." CMO. June 2, 2017. http://www.cmo.com/features/articles/2017/5/5/15-mind-blowing-stats-about-digital-trends-in-travel-hospitality-tlp-ddm.html#gs.QDoQsCY. January 7, 2018.

[4] Atmosphere Research Group US Online Leisure Travel Benchmark Survey, October 2011

[5] "Traveler's Road to Decision 2011." Think with Google. October 24, 2012 http://www.thinkwithgoogle.com/insights/library/studies/travelers-road-to-decision-2011/

[6] A portion of this section was adapted with permission from Paolo Boni from an original article by Paolo Boni titled "Want to Attract More Online Travel Shoppers? Tell Your Hotel's Story with Video," originally published on HotelExecutive.com

[7] "Infographic: Social and Mobile Make Summer Travel a Breeze." Column Five Media for Rasmussen College. October 24, 2012. http://www.rasmussen.edu/student-life/blogs/main/socialand-mobile-make-summer-travel-a-breeze/

[8] Reused with permission. "6 Creative Ways to Use Your Existing Hotel Media." Leonardo. October 24, 2012. http://blog.leonardo.com/6-creative-way-to-use-your-existing-hotel-media/

[9] "Video Best Practices Guide for Marketers." Marketing Profs and Thomson Reuters Multimedia Solutions. January 15, 2012. http://thomsonreuters.com/content/news_ideas/white_papers/financial/video_best_practices_guide_for_marketers

[10] Used by permission from Leonardo.

KEY POINTS

- Consumers are increasingly employing multiple devices and search channels – including voice search – throughout all stages of travel.

- Voice search and chatbots offer automated ways for consumers to get answers about and communicate with your hotel – quickly and without human interaction.

- Driven by advances in artificial intelligence (AI), the uses for and use of voice search and chatbots in hotel marketing are expected to increase significantly.

SUMMARY

Focusing your website (or parts of it) towards influencing featured snippets is an SEO technique that's been around for some time now, but the emergence of hands-free voice search devices brings a new importance to this strategy. If you are successful, you'll not only increase the influence of your content, but you'll also limit the influence of your competition and third-party sites by claiming the top spot, or in the case of hands-free devices, the only spot. Invest in local search and SEO, but a bit differently – to deliver schema-rich content in your answers to customers' questions, not links.

At the same time, even though we are in the initial phase for chatbots, with the significant push from Google and Facebook on artificial intelligence (AI), these are likely to become widely used in the next 5 years. Now is a good time to become familiar with how the digital interface with your consumers will continue to transform over the next several years.

A Multi-Device World is Driving Voice Search

According to ComScore, the average consumer owns almost 4 connected devices. In such a fragmented, multi-device world, in order to create a plan to effectively engage and inspire consumers it is critical that marketers understand where and how their target consumers are using different devices and search channels. Mobile devices started the revolution in search – all the way back to the original iPhone – but a new generation of "headless" devices, devices powered by AI engines like Alexa, Google Home, and Siri, are poised to further change how people search and find information. The increasing reliance on voice search has already changed the landscape of search engines – 20% of searches are already being conducted via voice assistants. ComScore predicts that this trend will only grow, with more than 50% of search becoming voice-based by the year 2020 – that's only 2 years away!

Digital Personal Assistants and How They Work

This year, some of the hottest devices are hands-free assistants, such as the Amazon Echo and the Google Home. In an article on business2community.com author Brad Keys explains how SEO is affected by the key differentiators between Google Home and Amazon Echo, which is Google Home's robust updated software, a tool called "Google Assistant." Apart from being able to play music, edit your calendar, or create notes on your behalf, the biggest selling point of Google Home is its ability to quickly answer your questions in a conversational format. Due to the screen-less nature of these types of devices, the inherent difference between asking Google Assistant a question or running the same search query on your phone is that Google Assistant is going to provide you with a simple conversational answer to your question, and there will be no opportunity to explore a results page, as you would on your screened device. So, where does Google Assistant get its answers from, and how can you use them to your advantage?

Google Assistant relies heavily on Google's featured snippets to answer questions. Featured snippets (also known as rich answers) are the brief explanations that appear at the top of the search engine results page when you ask a question that Google thinks it can answer. These are also called "Zero Position" in Google search. In simple terms, if you asked Google Assistant a question and then you ran the same search query on your desktop or mobile browser, you would likely see the same answer that Google Assistant gives you at the top of your results page as one of Google's featured snippets.

Voice Search is About Answers

In this new world of voice-powered smart phones, speakers, home assistants, and bluetooth enabled automobiles, consumers are increasingly relying more on search to provide answers, not lists of results. While a user might type "hotels San Francisco downtown," that same user is more likely to ask, "five-star hotels with spa near downtown San Francisco?" Users are far more comfortable asking long, more complex, and more specific questions using voice than when typing. The improvements in voice-based assistants is driving this even further. Systems like Google are now beginning to provide conversational queries – questions that are related to earlier answers. For example, our same user might follow up the "five-star hotels" question with something like "which ones have a pool?" Obviously, with this conversational approach to search, the technology necessary to stay ahead is changing.

Best Practices: Get Your Hotels to Feature in Voice Search

The biggest opportunity, and threat, for the hotels is that Google and Apple will take the answers to queries from any website that provides relevant answers. All major OTAs are making a significant push to dominate the organic rankings in voice search and featured snippets. It is imperative for hoteliers to ensure that the answers in featured snippets come from your website and not any third-party site. If you want to turn your content from the hotel website into a featured snippet and claim this coveted top spot, there are some general steps you can follow.

1. Identify what question(s) your content is trying to answer. It should be something relevant to your market area. It is important that the question literally appears (as it would in a search query) on your page within a header tag (e.g., h2, h3, etc.). Beneath that header, provide the content as you want it to appear in the featured snippet box. This content should be within a <p> paragraph tag.
2. Add valuable supporting information or content beyond the direct answer.

3. Make it as easy as possible for Google to find your content by adding structured data, which allows Google to better understand what type of content you have on your site.

Structured data is "a standardized format for providing information about a page and classifying the page content."[1] Further, a group effort by Google, Microsoft, Yahoo, and Yandex has created Schema.org which provides a shared vocabulary that allows website content providers to more easily communicate the specific content contained on the site with search engines. By providing industry specific content labels, content is more easily categorized for the most relevant returns.

To understand the critical importance of structured data and schemas, we must look at how search engines use them. Take the question "How many five-star hotels near downtown San Francisco have a pool?" From a search engine's perspective, that question has 4 key elements to it:

- Business category: hotel
- Rating: 5 stars
- Address: located near geolocation 37.773972, -122.431297
- Hotel amenities: pool

Google uses your website's structured data to understand the content on the page, and to enable special search result features and enhancements like graphical search and voice search. Because the structured data labels each individual element describing the hotel, consumers can search for your hotel by rating, location, amenities, and more.[2] A current listing of data labels for hotels is at http://schema.org/docs/hotels.html.

The point? To be successful when it comes to voice search, you need to present as much of your content as possible as structured data.

Best Practices: FAQs are Your Answers for Google

Schemas can help you with voice-based searches that are non-branded. But how does a hotel respond to voice searches that are highly specific, and branded? For example, how do you ensure that your website answers the question: "Does the Hotel Nikko have a pool?"

Once again, part of the answer lies in schemas in your meta data, but another critical piece to the puzzle is having dynamic and properly formatted content on your site that supports what your schema is presenting. One approach that appears to be successful is the concept of Frequently Asked Questions, or FAQs. Follow this link to see how the Hotel Nikko has approached the FAQ challenge: www.hotelnik-kosf.com/faq.aspx.

Chatbots Defined

People want to communicate anytime, anywhere, and they want relevant and useful answers, quickly. Facebook Messenger campaigns have seen 88% open rates, and click-through rate of 56%. In 2018, inbound marketing will expand to handle messaging from multiple channels seamlessly including internal and external messaging (from Messenger, WhatsApp, message, etc.), website chat, and social channels like Twitter, Facebook, LinkedIn, and Instagram.

Chatbots are an automated way for a consumer to communicate with your hotel and get the answers to their queries quickly without human interaction. Although this may sound counterintuitive to the hospitality personal touch that most hotels are striving for, the younger generation prefers to communicate via type-written messages on their phone screens versus actually calling the hotel. Facebook launched their chatbot platform for businesses, and several major hospitality players such as Booking.com and Expedia are in the process of creating chatbot platform for their websites. Additionally, chatbots may be able to help hotels engage in customer delight by answering their queries immediately and also offer the opportunity to realign resources that were previously used to answer questions in order to further enhance customer service and interactions.

The opportunity that exists for hotels with chatbots is best summarized by this quote from Robert Cole, a hospitality social media consultant and founder of Rock Cheetah. "Facebook has 1.6 billion unique active users per month," he said. "A large number of travelers are already on Facebook and already on Messenger. If you can [communicate] through Messenger, you have access to this massive audience, and if you have a relevant audience within that massive user base, that's an interesting [outlet for the industry.]"

How Chatbots Work

Chatbots are essentially an automated way for a hotel to answer the questions that consumers ask them. To start off, the hotel would have to input their most frequently asked questions in the chatbot engine. If the chatbot engine is built with smart tools (artificial intelligence), it is able to interpret different variations of the natural speech language and provide answers to similar queries even if they are not asked exactly the same way. When the chatbot is not able to answer the question, the hotel will need to guide the consumer to a live attendant or a phone. However, each time the chatbot is not able to answer the question, it learns questions that it was not able to answer and keeps getting smarter through use of artificial intelligence. A well-executed chatbot can enhance the consumer experience for the increasingly sophisticated younger generation that prefers to type on their phones instead of calling the hotel.

From the hotelier perspective, the first decision needs to be around what function they want the chatbot to perform. There are two main types of chatbots:

1. Conversational
2. Transactional

Conversational Chatbots

Conversational chatbots can provide information about the amenities at the hotel, hours of operations of outlets, information about attractions close to the hotel, dining facilities, and similar kinds of queries. Essentially, the chatbot acts as an online concierge. We believe that these will be the first implementations of chatbot technology, and the main function is to enhance the consumer experience. Consumers don't have to wait on the phone or in the concierge line to get some simple answers. Often this information is already available on the hotel website and can easily be programmed into the chatbots.

When building a conversational engine, start with the most popular or frequently asked questions, or conversational topics, that customers regularly raise. Cover at least 80% of the conversations by providing answers to the top 20% of questions. Create a system that can seamlessly engages live agents when the conversational bot cannot answer. Leverage the human interactions to capture these "non-supported" questions and train the engine by feeding answers to questions that were not answered automatically.

Transactional Chatbots

This is the holy grain of chatbots. With this, you could potentially see a scenario where consumers book a room at your hotel or inquire about the prices at your hotel through the chatbots. This type of chatbot will need an integration with your booking engine. This is the direction major OTAs and brands are likely heading – being able to provide a booking through a chatbot query – "book me a hotel room at Hotel Elite in Boston on the 29th of January at the lowest available rate."

Marketing Through Chatbots

Chatbots can also facilitate message-based marketing campaigns and become an essential solution for businesses wishing to serve their customers in a smarter and more cost-effective way.

Chapter 9 Endnotes

[1] *"Introduction to Structured Data." Google Search.* https://developers.google.com/search/docs/guides/intro-structured-data. January 25, 2018.

[2] *"Introduction to Structured Data." Google Search.* https://developers.google.com/search/docs/guides/intro-structured-data. January 25, 2018.

KEY POINTS

- Three primary categories of email – Transactional, Promotional, and Relational
- Six steps of the customer journey as it applies to email marketing
- Using email marketing to entice new customers through lead nurturing
- Six critical factors for every email campaign
- Email marketing analytics

SUMMARY

Email marketing is often referred to as the workhorse of digital tools available to marketers. But like any tool, it needs to be used for the appropriate job. There are a number of important elements to consider when planning email marketing and we will cover each in this chapter.

The primary goals of email marketing today include moving the guest along their digital journey from awareness through the booking process and after the stay by encouraging brand advocacy.

Email marketing is an integral part of the hotel's direct online channel strategy and marketing mix, and is crucial to digital customer relationship management (eCRM). Hoteliers must always be searching for new guests, communicating with current guests, and maintaining contact with past customers as they are the most likely to book the hotel again since they are already familiar with the product. Email marketing serves a lot of different functions, and it is critical to identify the right time to send the right messaging your guests. This means the creation and segmenting of customer lists, crafting compelling messaging and making offers based on what is appealing to that customer at that time.

There are three primary categories of email today – transactional, relational, and promotional. Where your customer can be found along the journey to purchase and beyond will drive the type of email that should be utilized. In the world of email marketing, these are the steps of your customer's journey.

1. Awareness

Your customer is in the dream phase or in the very early planning stages of the hotel visit. They may be thinking of planning a wedding or a business meeting on the group side. For transients, this might mean they are planning a vacation, taking the kids on a tour of colleges, or moving across country. This is the very beginning of the journey and more likely than not, asking for a hotel booking at this juncture would be premature.

2. Engage

Once you have been able to make a prospective guest aware of your property or brand, the next step on the email journey is to engage them. Entice them by sharing what is unique about your destination, brand, or property.

3. Subscribe

In email terms this is the point in the guest's journey where they are willing to share some information with you because they are both aware of your property and engaged enough to want to know more. A typical email at this phase might include an invitation to join a brand loyalty club or subscribe to your blog or newsletter service.

4. Convert

At this point your prospect may have visited your website, or even done a site inspection of your property with your group sales managers. Your goal in this step is to move them to purchase.

5. Excite

Post-purchase, pre-stay is the stage where your future guest is most likely to read and respond to any email they receive. It will be critical to use this time to further educate and create enthusiasm on the part of your guest about your property or brand.

6. Stay

The guest is onsite, and the role of any email during this phase will be to further educate and engage your guest.

7. Advocate

The guest has left your property and your goal in this phase is to invite the guest to share their experiences (assuming they were positive!).

8. Promote

Invite your guest to return to your property or brand, or to invite their friends or business associates to try your property or brand.

It is critical at each step of the journey to apply the type of email that is appropriate. For example, in the awareness and engage phase, you will likely use promotional emails because you don't have an existing relationship with the guest, so both transactional and relational would be inappropriate and not likely to result in moving that guest to the next step.

The subscribe, convert, excite, and stay phases may be a mix of relational and transactional. The advocate and promote stages will likely be a mix of relational and promotional. We have broken down each of the email categories into the likely roles they would play along the journey.

Transactional Email Examples
- reservation confirmation
- confirming loyalty membership
- sending receipts post stay
- loyalty account creation
- newsletter subscription confirmation
- support tickets
- password reminders
- unsubscribe confirmations

Relational Email Examples
- new subscriber (to loyalty club or newsletter) welcome
- gated content delivery
- newsletter/blog
- confirmation
- survey/review
- social updates
- contest announcements
- referral requests

Promotional Email Examples
- promotional content
- new gated content
- flash sale announcement
- new product announcements – renovations, new services, etc.
- loyalty program updates
- event announcements
- trial offer
- upgrade offer

Best Practices: Lead Nurturing

The focus of lead nurturing is on the ongoing relationship you have with a past or future guest, cultivating it not only through their experience at your property but also through their interaction with your hotel digitally.

Lead nurturing should have a large role in your digital marketing strategy. It begins with what is vital to your email marketing efforts: focusing on the collection of new email addresses as needed to grow your email marketing database. This collection can then be expanded and built on to foster a prosperous relationship with these new leads. It is important to remember that what you do once you have those addresses is just as important to the potential revenue-generating relationship as it is just to gather them initially and amass a larger audience.

Bought or purchased lists do not constitute valid leads, as those recipients are not necessarily interested in your property, product, or offer and will likely either opt-out or their email address will be invalid. It is better to invest your time and resources in growing your database organically with leads that can be nurtured into a prosperous relationship.

Best Practices: Growing Your Email List

Consider the following best practices for gathering new email addresses and maintaining your relationships with your fresh, new leads:

- Opt-in via a collection form on your website: Make sure you provide leads with a place to indicate what they are interested in receiving (e.g., golf specials, dining offers, etc.) so that you can cater to those interests with your marketing materials later.

- Upon making a reservation: Whether a new reservation comes in through a phone call or a reservation request online, make sure those guests' email addresses are being collected (you can make it a required field on your booking engines or reservation pages).
- Upon check-in: If a guest is part of a group or booked through an OTA, you may not have had a chance to collect their email prior to their stay and can certainly do so when they check in at the front desk.
- Upon check-out: If the guest's email address still hasn't been secured by the time a guest checks out, make sure that you request a valid email address so that they can be sent a follow-up email after their stay.
- At various outlets on property (restaurants, spas, etc.): Email addresses captured to reserve dining or appointment times can also be used when sending interest-based marketing pieces.
- The sales team: Email addresses collected by your sales teams at conferences and conventions are also a great lead to begin nurturing with digital marketing.

Best Practices: Nurturing New Email Addresses through Digital Marketing Efforts

Obtaining email addresses at any point in the reservation process allows you to not only secure those leads for future marketing purposes, but it allows you to start nurturing those guests and providing them with a higher level of service before they even step on property.

Prior to their stay you should be sending them reservation confirmations and pre-arrival pieces with options to upgrade or sign-up for specific requests. This allows you to paint a vivid picture of the high level of service they can expect from you while on property through communications methods such as request submission forms. While on property, present them, via email, with an opportunity to take advantage of a special offer at an on-property outlet or just inquire about their stay. You'll enhance your presence and start to build a dialogue with your guests. After their stay, send a follow-up survey allowing them to provide feedback concerning their time spent at your property, continuing the dialogue after their stay, and helping increase the quality of future stays. To increase repeat business, you can then send automatically triggered offers throughout the year, based on learned stay and booking behavior.

An email service provider (ESP) that directly interfaces into your property management system or customer marketing database will be able to provide you with customized, triggered emails, as well as the ability to send targeted marketing messages based on other opted-in email addresses. If you are not using an ESP that directly interfaces with your property management system, it may be time to incorporate that into your marketing budget. The hospitality industry has a huge advantage over other industries in that there is so much information about our past and loyal customers (guests) at our finger tips waiting to be extracted from the property management system or customer database. Combined with our opted-in leads, you can target them with specific messages in the future.

Digital marketing to any lead, whether it came from an opt-in system or a reservations system, should focus on and adhere to the best practices of email marketing. See the first page of this chapter regarding "Six Critical Factors for Email Marketing Campaigns."

Best Practices: Email Marketing

A number of factors need to be considered prior to launching any email campaign.

- TARGETING: To whom will you mail? Past customers tend to be most responsive (assuming a generally positive past stay experience). It is better to have a smaller well targeted list. Determining where you will obtain your list should be your first step. Does your list comply with opt-in compliance?
- COPYWRITING: What will your subject line say to entice your targeted list? What will you be selling primarily? What will your offer be?
- DESIGN: Visually, how will you support your message? Is there a photograph that showcases the element of your property that would be particularly appealing to your targeted audience?
- DELIVERY AND DEPLOYMENT: How will you send the email? Will you use a software company like Constant Contact

or ExactTarget? What links will you have back to your website? What action will you be asking your audience to take? Are the links working and landing pages operational?

- MEASUREMENT: Start with a goal – opens, clicks, revenue produces – and then measure your results to that goal. If you fell short, at what point along the way did you miss the target? Was it the wrong list? Was it the wrong offer?

- TESTING: Each element of your email can have a dramatic impact on your success, so always test and verify results. Try new subject lines, change your offers, or change the visuals. Repeat successes and learn from failures.

Additional best practices include the following:

- Plan your email marketing campaigns the same way you plan any other quarterly or yearly marketing schedule. Start with a purpose, and make sure your emails are purpose-driven and will support your other marketing efforts to attain specific goals.

- Every email should be planned in advance so that timing is taken into consideration on a large scale, with each email having a goal or specific purpose behind it. Do not send emails just to send emails. It will end up decreasing your response rates for future campaigns when you actually have something of value to offer or mention.

- Segment your email lists by market and customer type (meeting planner, leisure traveler, business traveler, etc.) and tailor your marketing messages to target consumers strategically.

- Consolidate past guest email addresses from your Property Management System, booking engine, and past customer relationship management databases.

- Segment the data you have from your Property Management System not only to target customers by market or customer type but also by their past purchasing behavior (booking date, stay dates, amount spent, rooms stayed in, etc.) to even better tailor your messages.

- Each message should present a concrete offer, available only for a limited time to create urgency. Include a direct and easy-to-follow booking link or instructions.

- Ensure the landing page you are driving your customers to is congruent with the creative, the message, and the call to action that is in your email to provide the best customer experience.

- Design your pieces so that they are responsive to whichever device, email software, or browser they are viewed in, automatically optimizing the piece to be viewed and responded to from any device.

- Strong and short subject lines are key.

- Create clean, enticing designs, in line with other branding and marketing efforts, so that the guests are able to associate the offer with your property.

- Be concise. In email marketing less is more, driving deliverability rates upward as well as increasing the likelihood of response and action on your offer/message.

- Comply with the CAN-SPAM Act and respect customers' privacy and the frequency with which they desire to receive marketing messages.

- After a campaign has been sent, analyze the reporting statistics to see the response to different aspects of the email: day of week it was sent, time it was sent, how many links/materials were included, and bookings generated. Adjust aspects of your future emails based on the information learned from previous campaigns. It is all part of the process to determine what works best for your specific audiences and property.

- On property, request guests' business cards or contact information upon check-in or via in-room questionnaires to build your email databases.

- On the hotel's website, an email sign-up widget should be present on the Home page so that email addresses can be collected from people who have an interest in receiving your email. Also, have a dedicated Stay Connected page.

- Your Facebook page should also have a Stay Connected widget which will allow people to submit their email addresses directly to your database.

Best Practices: Functionality Requirements for Email Marketing Systems

Your email marketing systems should not only be able to launch time-sensitive newsletters, but also:

- Resend bounces.
- Support multiple IP addresses.
- Allow for bounce/media domains.
- Perform A/B testing.
- Send automated Welcome & Goodbye letters to guests.

Best Practices: Email Template Design

As photos sell a destination and hotel, hotel email template designs should support multiple images. Templates should also allow for multiple sections of copy to appeal to various customer segments. Include social media icons (Facebook, Twitter, YouTube, Flickr, Pinterest, TripAdvisor, etc.). If the hotel has won any awards, the icons or logos of each award should be present (e.g., Small Luxury Hotels, AAA Diamond Hotel, etc.).

Though each email you send will have a slightly different purpose, all should include links to the hotel website's Home, Special Offers, and Contact Us pages. Leisure-focused newsletters should link to the hotel's Reservations, Calendar of Events, and Visual Gallery pages. When targeting business travelers, be sure to call out to the Services & Amenities pages, particularly if they highlight complimentary WiFi or airport shuttles. For meeting and event planners, the newsletter should call out to relevant RFPs and Meetings Services pages.

Best Practices: Email Analytics

Traditional email metrics include bounce, delivery, open, and read rates. For hotels that use campaign performance analytics tracking, they can further quantify the value of email marketing. Track clicks that lead to bookings or RFPs initiated and further to bookings and RFPs completed. Hoteliers should also review reservations made via the voice channel, pass-alongs, and sharing across social media. See Chapter 28 for more information on analytics.

Best Practices: Audit, Optimize, and Test Email Marketing Campaigns

Similar to testing for search engine marketing, using A/B testing, remarking, and strategic variations of emails each month, hotel marketers can audit past campaigns and optimize future ones for the best results. Headlines can be tested, as can specific offers and specific calls to action (e.g., book now, request more information, have someone contact me, etc.).

Best Practices: Connecting with your global customer through email campaigns

Global email campaigns can reach and connect with customers effectively. But with 182 billion emails sent daily (according to a Radicati Group survey) and a human tendency to have a short attention span, crafting emails that stand out is a challenge.

So how do you compete in today's noisy international markets? Include some language and locale-specific adaptation so your emails resonate with customers. You'll drive a stronger campaign return on investment and stand out from competitors.

Some useful suggestions for effective global email campaigns are:

- Above all, be aware and respectful of local opt-in laws and privacy regulations. They constantly evolve, and they differ from country to country. For instance, in Germany, Switzerland, and Austria, there are specific regulations around opt-in, consent, and legal notices.
- Segment your audience by language and locale preferences. This helps you target the right audience with the right content.
- Localize your emails so they are both in the reader's language and relevant to their culture. For instance, be aware of current local events (e.g., Singles Day in China, religious holidays, etc.).
- Use culturally appropriate imagery and colors that resonate with your audience.
- Be sure to craft your email greetings correctly. Email best practices recommend you use personalized greetings because they have a 6x higher transaction rate and 41% higher click rates. But remember that in many languages, the gender of the addressee changes the structure of the greeting.
- Optimize your emails so they 'respond' well to a smartphone email application and browser. They're likely to be viewed on mobile devices.

CHAPTER 11
Customer Relationship Management (CRM)

KEY POINTS

- Hotels have so much data about their guests at their fingertips. It's important to use the data hotels already have about their guests and use that data to improve the guest experience before, during, and post-stay.

- A strong CRM strategy helps hotels to close the loop on the travel planning and booking journey and help hotels acquire, engage, and retain their best guests.

- CRM data can help fuel new guest acquisition. By using the data hotels have about their own guests, they can build look-alike and act-alike audiences to reach future guests. By using this strategy, marketing dollars go farther and deliver higher ROIs.

SUMMARY

Today's hotel planning and booking customer journey is becoming increasingly complex in this multi-device, multi-channel, and multi-touch point digital landscape. In fact, according to Google, the average consumer engages in 38,983 digital micro-moments in just under two months. That's over 38,000 digital moments in a 60-day booking window. As consumers are living their lives digitally connected throughout these digital micro-moments, when they embark on the travel planning journey, which on average includes 19 different touchpoints before making a booking (Google research), each one of these touchpoints presents an opportunity for a hotel to build a brand connection, influence intent, and be there for every step of the journey.

In light of this complex digital landscape, hotel marketers should engage online travel consumers throughout their complex "digital journey," and can no longer afford to have a fragmented customer engagement and acquisition approach. CRM can break this fragmentation and help hoteliers develop a single view of their guest, which they can use to deliver more targeted and personalized messaging within the guest journey, and ultimately drive higher loyalty and guest conversion through direct booking channels.

What is CRM?

CRM (Customer Relationship Management) means using data to develop a 360° view of each guest, and ensuring they receive the most targeted, dynamic, and relevant communication throughout the entire guest journey. CRM also allows hotels to know who their best guests are (and treat them as such on property by recognizing and tailoring the experience to their preferences), in terms of how often they stay at the property, how recent their last stay was, as well as how much revenue the hotel extracts from each guest.

A good CRM technology platform must integrate into a hotel's existing IT landscape and connect with PMS, CRS, ORM, RMS, & other data sources.

Fundamentals of a CRM Strategy

One Central View of the Guest
A Guest Data Management Platform (DMP) should be cloud based, able to store data profiles, and provide one clean view of the hotel guest. This DMP should serve as the "smart" data layer incorporating past guest data extracted from the PMS, CRS, and other guest data sources, and be continuously updating, cleansing, and enriching customer profiles to serve as the main "guest knowledge depository" for ongoing guest engagement and retention, as well as new guest acquisition efforts. This platform should be able to dedupe and combine several guest profiles if they belong to one guest (i.e., one guest may have different profiles because they have provided different email addresses in the past). This allows the hotel to recognize their loyal guests on property, as well as on the hotel website and throughout digital marketing initiatives.

Follow is an example of how a hotel's Guest Data Management Platform should be able to extract data from several different sources, cleanse and then enrich the profiles.

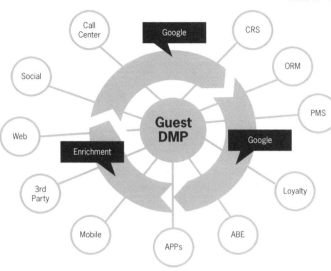

Guest Communications
Automated transactional emails engage customers with personalized guest communications, such as pre-stay, in-stay, and post-stay emails, cancellation emails, guest surveys, and more.

Guest Marketing Automation
Marketing automation tied to CRM data allows a hotel property to initiate or schedule targeted and highly personalized email marketing campaigns and "drip" campaigns to smart customer lists with unlimited targeting options.

Loyalty/Guest Recognition
Mid-size and smaller hotel chain, luxury, or boutique hotel brands or even independent hotels and resorts must be able to recognize and reward repeat guests through either a comprehensive Reward/Loyalty Program (points or perks) or through a Guest Recognition & Appreciation Program (based on number of room nights).

Today's Fragmented Approach to Hotel Data
One glaring example of today's highly fragmented approach is keeping past guest engagement efforts (CRM) in a silo from new customer acquisition and marketing efforts. Less than a third of hotel guests on any given night are repeat guests, while two-thirds are first-time guests. This means the reality that General Managers and DOSMs face every day is having to secure about 70% of occupancy on any given night with brand new guests that they know very little about while trying to ensure they have a pleasant and meaningful stay. Furthermore, once the property has acquired this new guest, when the guest walks out the door, there is no guarantee they will ever stay again, resulting in a vicious cycle that affects the bottom line.

Following are examples of how hoteliers are operating in a fragmented world.

- HOTEL WEBSITE: The property knows their guests intimately: their home address, credit card number, what they ate or how many drinks they had last night, and more. Yet, when these same guests visit the hotel website, they are treated as complete strangers.

- DATA ISLANDS: For most hotels, guest data lives on multiple "data islands" that do not talk to each other: PMS, CRM, CRS, Social Media, Web Analytics, Marketing Data, BI, etc. In other words, past guest data (CRM Data) is not being utilized to engage and retain past guests, as well as target new guests and sharpen the focus and reach of digital marketing campaigns, in order to acquire new guests that are similar to past "best guests."

- TECHNOLOGY & DIGITAL MARKETING SILOS: Hotels tend to use a myriad of vendors that do not "talk to each other," and in many cases do not even know each other: one for CRM, one for the property website, a third for SEO, a fourth for SEM, a fifth for online media, another one for social media marketing, etc. Digital marketing campaigns are not taking into consideration who past guests are, who are "best" guests (e.g., highest RFM Value: Recency, Frequency, and Monetary), their preferences, stay and booking behavior, and are failing to capitalize on these insights to fuel campaigns to reach the right guest.

- CRM DATA NOT "TALKING" TO INTENT DATA: Knowledge from past "best" guests is not being used to identify "Marketing Personas" and target look-alike audiences thus significantly expanding the marketing reach to acquire new guests that are similar to a hotels' "best" past guests and are "in market," (i.e., planning to travel to the property's destination).

By tying a CRM strategy into the property website, technology, and marketing strategies, hotels can do a better job of engaging, retaining, and acquiring guests throughout the customer journey. This is not only more efficient and more effective at driving direct bookings, but it is incomparable in growing the bond with customers and their lifetime value.

How Can CRM Go a Step Further?

Through the use of CRM data, hotels can acquire new guests by capitalizing on the knowledge of past guests. Everything should function in one seamless ecosystem to "close the loop" in a hotel's past and future guest engagement, retention, and acquisition. This includes:

- PERSONALIZATION: Fully integrated with the Guest DMP, hotel websites should be able to deliver dynamically personalized content and promotions on the hotel website based on users' past booking history, guest preferences, loyalty program affiliation, demographics, geo location, website behavior, or market segment affiliation.

- SMART DATA MARKETING: Smart data marketing takes full advantage of "owned data" (past guest data, demographics, website data, etc.) and then layers on real-time travel planning insights and intent data points to target in-market potential guests during the travel planning process to a property's destination. Smart data marketing should utilize programmatic advertising and dynamic rate marketing (DRM).

- ACQUISITION MARKETING: This type of marketing should utilize knowledge from past guests to target and acquire new guests through direct response and evergreen digital marketing initiatives such as SEM, SEO, GDN, online media, programmatic display, and dynamic rate marketing. Acquisition Marketing also includes seasonal and targeted multichannel campaigns with one cohesive message across channels to answer occupancy needs, target current and new segments, capitalize on events and holidays, and more.

Conclusion

When a hotel CRM strategy is incorporated into their overall strategy of acquiring guests, they can truly engage a travel consumer at every touchpoint in their travel planning journey. Here is a snapshot of what this journey looks like, and how hoteliers can be there every step of the way.

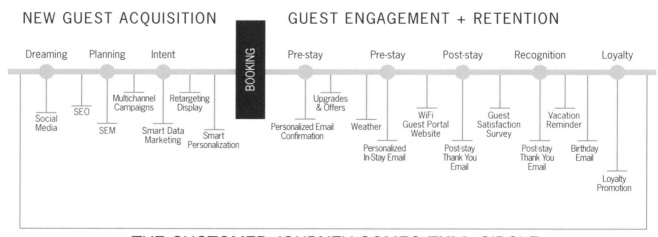

THE CUSTOMER JOURNEY COMES **FULL** CIRCLE

KEY POINTS

- Loyalty programs reward customers when they continue to engage in desired behaviors and build stronger brand ties.

- Loyalty programs are not limited to points but can include leveraging deep knowledge of personal preferences to customize service, and surprise, delight, and enrich the traveler journey with content.

- A new category of loyalty engagement is emerging fueled by mobile technology: Guest Experience Management.

- Loyalty Marketing is emerging as a potential differentiator by the brands to direct their bookings to the brand.com sites.

SUMMARY

Loyalty programs have become a core offering for larger hotel chains, many online travel agencies, and increasingly, independent hotels. Large branded point-based programs provide participants with a number of benefits including room upgrades, check-in amenities, preferred room availability, and the most sought after reward – free nights.

Increasingly, however, independent hotels and small groups are leveraging the same program fundamentals and technologies to develop subtle, "behind the scenes" loyalty programs with guest recognition and preference management at their cores. The objective of these programs is to differentiate by providing customized service, and to "surprise and delight.".

These programs can be complex to manage and costly to offer, but many brands see them as necessary components of their marketing mix. Loyalty programs offer the digital marketer a treasure trove of data, as well as the holy grail of web analytics – multichannel customer tracking.

The hotel industry is using interesting technology, and some would say mobile technology fueled the evolution in loyalty program fundamentals. A whole new category is emerging around Guest Experience Management with technology at its core, with mobile devices as the point of engagement between the hotel and the guest, loyalty technology as the facilitator, and the fundamentals of loyalty programs as described above as the outcomes. The digital marketer now has additional opportunities to leverage loyalty and build a relationship with the guest throughout the lifecycle: research (website, travel agent), booking (website, call center, travel agent, OTA), pre-arrival (e-concierge, mobile app, mobile check in, and using mobile as the room key), on property (PMS, mobile concierge app), check out(PMS, Online, mobile app), and post stay (loyalty program app).

A bit of history: Although it was not the first loyalty program, American Airlines launched the first frequent flier program in 1981. Two important environmental changes set the stage: deregulation, and computerization of reservation systems. Prior to deregulation, airlines' advertising and marketing efforts were largely image based, and used to differentiate commodity products from one another. Loyalty programs as we know them today would not be possible without data storage and data-mining systems.

Holiday Inn and Marriott were the first hotel brands to enter the loyalty program arena, with both launching programs in 1983. At first, these programs simply fed into the airline programs as additional ways to earn points/miles toward free flights. It didn't take long, however, for the hotels to get into the business of redeeming loyalty currency for free room nights and other perks.

Goals of Loyalty Marketing

- Retain the best and most profitable customers.

- Make good customers better.

- Acquire customers with potential to be best customers.

- Reconnect with customers who left the brand.
- Build strong brand ties by engaging with customers through the guest lifecycle with personalized content.
- Prevent customers from switching to competitors.
- Provide insights into customer behavior and preferences.
- Make each customer feel valued and appreciated.

Loyalty programs, when well executed, reward the best customers who continue to engage in desired behaviors. These programs are more than a "buy 3 get 1 free" promotion, but rather an ongoing conversation with a customer. They can entice customers to stretch beyond their normal behavior with aspirational elite tiers. In the airline world, for example, so called "mileage runs" are common among travelers looking to get to the next elite status. Similarly, hotel guests may book additional stays to qualify for elite perks in the next year.

By partnering with credit card companies, loyalty programs can also target customers who will potentially be among their best. These partnerships typically include extensive direct marketing and customer segmentation opportunities so the message can be customized and made appealing to various target markets.

Loyalty marketing offers a way for brands to reconnect with customers who may have left the brand. As with customer relationship management, loyalty programs offer a number of metrics and vehicles to identify customers who are likely to, or have already left the brand. The digital marketer, then, can create and deliver a rich offer to re-engage the customer. Retaining a customer is much cheaper than acquiring a new one.

Hotel loyalty programs are no longer just about accruing and redeeming points – it's about providing an enhanced, personalized experience for every member. Loyalty programs allow companies to gather data and insights on customers that they can turn around and use to provide a personalized experience. Digital technology and the mobile app allow companies to further personalize the experience and give customers more choice and control over their travel.

Taking back their customers

Brands began seeing their loyalty members as a way to attract customers to "book direct" on their websites vs. the OTAs in order to decrease distribution costs and create a stronger bond with their loyalty members. Some offer discounts for loyalty members to book direct on the brand.com site while others are beginning to offer upgraded services or perks. While the jury is out on whether or not discounting for loyalty members is more profitable than losing the booking to the OTA sites, the brands focusing on continuing to enhance the loyalty experience once on site and post stay will likely be the winners in the battle for the customer.

There are five common characteristics of loyalty programs: accrual, redemption, elite tiers, partners, and acting on personal preferences.

Accrual

All loyalty programs are based on repeat activity. Loyalty programs develop their own currency, which members can earn by engaging in specified activities, such as staying a night in a hotel. For online marketers, loyalty programs offer the ability to streamline the booking path and reduce friction by pre-populating form fields with customer name and address information, all provided by the customer upon registering for the program. Accrual can also be non-point based or what are known as Soft Benefits. Much the same way as room nights or stays can be counted and converted into points, soft benefits like upgrades can be accrued based on a repeated activity and redeemed from an accrual account. Most loyalty program management technology can accommodate this type of program.

Redemption

The "what's-in-it-for-me" element of loyalty programs, redemption involves exchanging the loyalty program's currency for something of value. Gamification has expanded the definition of "something of value" to include digital badges, access to exclusive online content (extra game levels), and "power-ups," items that have no value in the real world, but enhance the digital experience for the customer.

Elite Tiers

Many programs offer members additional benefits when they reach certain thresholds of activity in a given time period. These additional benefits are often combined into tiers, or status levels. Benefits vary widely by brand, but may include accrual bonuses, late check-out, special reservations line, free wifi, room upgrades, etc. These higher levels within the program serve as aspirational targets, designed to drive more activity.

Partners
Nearly all loyalty programs offer some cross-promotional opportunities by incorporating partners. From the beginning, American Airlines partnered with Hertz and Hyatt to offer AAdvantage members access to additional travel benefits, or to allow members to accrue miles for activity with these partners.

Acting on Personal Preferences
By tracking and building comprehensive profiles of customers, personalized service can be structured building loyalty. Also deep insights into guest preferences and actions can be gleaned pre-stay, on property, or after stay, and content customization (see content marketing) can be leveraged to build loyalty and brand ties.

One of the fundamentals of all Loyalty Programs is a robust Profile Management System that can provide a single guest identifier and "single source of truth." Sometimes referred to as a "gold guest profile," it is the profile system of record that ties or updates all other systems involved in the guest experience.

Digital marketers have in loyalty programs the holy grail of analytics: a unique identifier. When joining loyalty programs, members are assigned a number, login, member name, or some other unique identifier that is attached to all activity. By encouraging loyalty program members to login to the brand's website early in the visit, marketers can track the member across the site. This ID also solves the issue of how to track an individual across devices. In today's multi-screen world, customers may research on a laptop, transact on a tablet, and further engage on a smartphone. Cookies are not yet cross-device, but a unique ID that a customer voluntarily offers allows marketers to connect the dots across devices.

Loyalty & Recognition and the Independent Hotel/Brand
While loyalty programs have mostly been the domain of the big brands, smaller brands and independent hotels have developed approaches to try to get the benefits associated with these programs and to help better compete with the big brands. Approaches include building out their own unique programs, like Kimpton Karma (prior to the IHG acquisition of Kimpton), joining a coalition like Global Hotel Alliance, being part of a soft brand like Preferred Hotels, choosing an "off the shelf" program like Stash Rewards, or looking at new entrants in the space like Stay Wonderful. Independent brands and hotels need to carefully weigh the costs and benefits of any of these approaches.

Incorporating Loyalty Programs into a Digital Marketing Strategy

Best Practices: Call to Action.
Always include a "join now" prompt in any digital communication; this serves for lead generation, as well as providing a secondary way to interact with the business for consumers who may not be ready to purchase.

Best Practices: Customize, Customize, Customize.
Through loyalty programs, marketers learn a lot about individuals. Use that information to customize the experience for that guest. Loyalty member data can also be used to customize content for non-members by establishing a "looks like" approach.

Best Practices: Connect the Dots.
A unique identifier, such as a member number, can connect the dots across various programs and platforms, not only for the marketer but for the consumer as well. Providing a common experience in new media, such as logging into a loyalty program, extends the connection the consumer already has with the brand, and makes the new engagement more comfortable for the consumer.

Best Practices: Incorporate Experience.
Personalize content and promote soft benefits (non-point related rewards like upgrades). Leveraging all you know about a guest can be a great way to deliver personalized content during all phases of the guest experience. Leverage all the touch points in the guest experience (see guest lifecycle) to message the guest with relevant content and messaging.

CHAPTER 13
Digital for Pre-Stay, On Site, and Post-Stay

KEY POINTS
- Digital provides the opportunity to establish a stronger relationship directly with guests through pre-stay, on site, and post-stay communication.
- Communicating the right message at the right time is key to creating more loyal guests.
- Creating customer marketing advocates is more likely through digital.

SUMMARY

The last few years have seen the beginning of a revolution for guest communication. Historically, the only communication our guests would receive pre-check in might be a reservation confirmation. Communication on site was limited to a welcome letter in the guest room and then various front desk interactions. Once the guest checked out, we might send them a survey or an email asking how their stay was but that was often the extent of our planned guest communications.

Today, we are recognizing a multitude of reasons and opportunities to increase the amount of communications we are having with guests – and the delivery systems we are using are equally varied. Eventually there will likely be widespread use of a single platform that follows your guests from their first interaction of searching online all the way to sharing information about your property with their friends and family via their own social networks long after they have checked out. Currently, most properties and brands are taking a little bit more of a piece-meal approach.

Reasons for More Frequent Communication

The first thing we should look at is why we are communicating more with our guests – what are the benefits to them and to us? For the purposes of this section we are going to look at the steps from the instant of booking all the way through the post-stay experience.

Of course, the primary reason is to develop a stronger relationship with the guest. The more you know about them, and the more they know about you, the more loyal the relationship. But in growing that relationship, there are several reasons for interacting along the way:

1. Upselling
The first reason for reaching out to a guest in advance of their arrival is to let them know how they might be able to enhance their stay. This time period — between booking and arrival — is a time when guests are most likely to open and read your correspondence so hotels should use this opportunity wisely. The guest will benefit from knowing what opportunities there are to have a better stay – is there a suite they can have instead of a room, do you have a spa that you want them to visit, or a golf course, or restaurant?

2. Education and Excitement Generation
Apart from upselling, informing future guests of all that the property — and surrounding area — has to offer is of value to the guests — helping them to plan their itinerary, or even helping them understand what kind of clothes to pack based on weather forecasts or activities that are available either on site or nearby. Enhancing the experience for the guest beyond the hotel room may prevent last minute rate shopping that today's guest is often encouraged to do. If they have formed a stronger relationship with the hotel through information sharing, they are less likely to cancel and book elsewhere to save $5.

3. Preventative
Are there restaurants or attractions in your area that fill up so quickly that advance reservations are required? This would be good information to pass along to your future guests to build a relationship. Is the parking facility your guests normally use closed so other recommendations might be suggested? Is your pool closed for renovation? All of these items can be communicated in advance to your guests to ensure their check in is seamless. Something as simple as communicating the weather forecast for

their stay might be an opportunity to make a unique connection with your guest in advance of their arrival.

4. Data Gathering

By communicating about the likes or interests of your future guests, you are able to continually add to the data you collect about them. How responsive are they to offers? What types of offers do they find most appealing, what information are they clicking on to read more about, what special requests might they have for their stay? This is all potentially valuable data that you can begin to collect that will allow you to not only maximize their spend once on site, but also allow you to make future targeted offers that will be of genuine interest to them and solidify their attachment to your brand or property.

5. Social Network Sharing

This is a concept that is rapidly gaining ground. Is there an opportunity for you to help your future guests share the excitement about their upcoming trip with their social networks? Providing enticing "out of office" visuals of your property or resort is an opportunity for your guests to let others know how they will be spending their upcoming vacation or trip.

Some hotels are even beginning to gamify this experience – offering perks or points if the guest shares their information prior to their arrival.

Onsite communication options have changed.

Once the guest arrives on site, the reasons, opportunities, and delivery systems continue for ongoing guest communication.

Geofencing allows you to determine when a guest is approaching your property and you can send them an instant message welcoming them. Mobile check in is another reason for contact – allowing them to skip the long check in interaction at the front desk and instead select their own room and use their mobile phone as the key.

Some hotels have begun to utilize what is often referred to as a virtual concierge. Several companies have developed software or apps that allow guests to communicate with hotel staff in every area of the hotel – from inquiring about

spa reservations to ordering room service or requesting an extra towel.

Most companies in this space are creating platforms – so your guests can be connected with your hotel before, during, and after their stay. Two of the most prevalent currently are KeyPR and the Alice App.

KeyPR has both a mobile app that allows guests the ability to access their reservation prior to arriving, as well as checking in remotely – bypassing the front desk and then using the app as their key to their room. Once on property, they can order room service and book future reservations. When the guest checks into the room, KeyPR provides a tablet in each guest room which allows the guest to link to city guides, order room service, and request any guest services such as extra towels or pillows. Additionally, they can report any maintenance problems through the tablet. From a staff standpoint, all of these requests are tracked and so repeat maintenance issue trends can be spotted, peak guest request times can be identified, and any other operational KPIs can be easily analyzed.

The Alice App offers the guest request elements but also adds the concierge interactivity and allows guests to easily contact staff outside of the app via text if that is the guest preference.

The goal of these platforms is to help to automate the guest experience in order to improve it by allowing guests the choice to interact with the staff online, via the phone, or in person.

Another trend is for hotels to provide in room virtual assistants like Alexa, Cortana, and Siri. As the population becomes more dependent on the voice activated assistants in their home, their expectation will be to also find it in their hotel rooms. Several hotel brands are experimenting with these in room assistants and this practice is likely to grow over the next few years.

Post-Stay

Probably the largest realization in guest marketing is the opportunity to create customer advocates once the guest has left the property. Historically we might have sent a post-stay survey and then included the guest, segmented by stay type, for future emailers inviting them back but, outside of loyalty membership, that was probably the extent of our post-stay conversation with our guests. Today, that focus has shifted a bit. We still send surveys and include the guest in future emailers based on their interests and history with us, but we are also trying to work our way into their social networks.

Many hotels have found that running ongoing photo contests is a great way to engage guests post-stay. The guest is invited to share a photo taken during their visit and enter it into a contest to win a future free stay. Once the photo is entered, they are encouraged to invite their friends to vote for their photo. The goal is to encourage the guest to share information about the property on all of their social network connections.

One company, Flip.to, has elevated this concept and created an opportunity for guests to really advocate for properties by writing about their experiences at the hotel, and include photographs. They are incentivized to do this and their friends will also receive some incentives to be involved. The result is more social sharing but also many focused, positive, experience based stories on the property website.

Another concept in this space is gamifying the guest experience. Once a guest is involved, they are offered points for different activities – like sharing a photo of the hotel, or writing a review, or even sharing a blog post that the hotel has written with their friends and family. Points can be redeemed for future stays or other items. The leader in this space currently is probably Influitive but other concepts are now developing.

Critical to most of these pre, during, and post activities is a strong customer relationship management (CRM) component. There is more information on CRM in chapter 11.

Conclusion

Digital continues to evolve around increased opportunities to communicate with guests before and after their hotel stay. The benefits of engaging more with guests are the antidote to the commoditization of hotel rooms. The more unique the experience of your guest, the more they feel loyal to your brand or property, the more likely they are to spend more on site, return to your property, and share their experience of your property with their own networks.

CHAPTER 14
Social Media

KEY POINTS
- Social: All About Sharing
- 2017 State of Social
- Why Social?
- Visual Storytelling
- Best Practices
- Measuring/Metrics

SUMMARY

The media environment has shifted. Where once marketers created a message that told consumers what we wanted them to know — and then put it in front of as many eyeballs as economically possible — today it's not how many people SEE our message but who ENGAGES with it. Once a static milieu, advertising has become a dynamic enterprise — both online and in-house — that's all about dialogue. Social media creates an incredible opportunity for interaction between consumers and brands, transforming conventional messaging into a two-way conversation. Anyone can create and share content — and almost everyone does. Social marketing makes the most of all this user-generated content via consistent participation on networking platforms, publishing sites (blogs), micropublishing sites, review sites, message boards, and groups.

As social beings, we are drawn to interesting stories. When we find a compelling story we instinctively want to share it. In traditional marketing, hotels fed stories to consumers. It went one way. Today, consumers share stories with hotels and with other consumers. In lauding all the statistics about users and uploads, it's sometimes easy to forget the "social" part of social media — the sharing and connecting between individuals, businesses, brands, and more, worldwide.

People share because we like feeling connected. Whether it's with our friends on Facebook or the expanse of the "Twittersphere," social media is a 21st-century expression of human interaction: social media drives word-of-mouth in a far greater way than anything seen before. Whereas word-of-mouth was previously limited to people you spoke to directly, social media has no such limitation — you can communicate with anyone, anywhere, about anything. Word-of-mouth has always been an important factor in a traveler's decision-making process, and that's certainly still true today.

People want to share — what they're doing, whom they're following, the news they're reading, or the latest viral video. According to the 2017 State of Social by tracx, there are 2.8 bil-

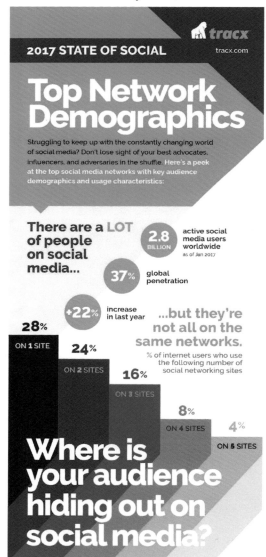

chart continues next page

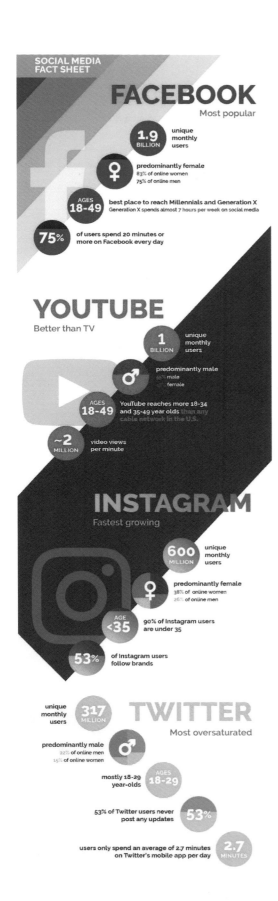

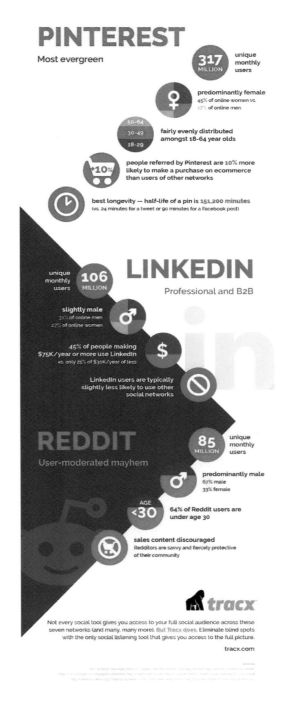

Source: SocialMediaToday

lion active social media users worldwide. Facebook has more than 1.9 billion active unique users every month; YouTube has 1 billion; Instagram, 600 million; Twitter, 317 million; Pinterest, 150 million.[1] Snapchat has 166 million daily users[2] — mostly between the ages of 18-24 — and this fast-growing channel ranks as the most popular social media site[3] among teenagers and young adults in the United States.

These numbers change constantly, but one thing is for certain: social is a powerful force.

Facebook users like to "like" — indeed, they generate more than 4 million likes per minute. Twitter users send more than 500 million Tweets per day and 3/4 of them retweet information from businesses and brands. Inspiring ideas are sought — and shared — on Pinterest; an average 95 million photos and videos per day are posted on Instagram. Over 400 million snaps are shared on Snapchat per day[4].

Video is definitely king. Facebook users rack up 100 million hours of daily video watch time[5]. YouTube reaches more 18-34 and 18-49 year-olds than any cable network in the U.S.[6] — and the fact that "viral video" has entered our lexicon is proof of YouTube's shareability!

By 2019, 80% of all internet traffic is predicted to be to video[7], dominated by in-the-moment updates via live video from platforms including Facebook, Instagram, and Snapchat. Facebook Live, for example, had businesses streaming six times the amount of live videos on their pages in June 2016 than they were in January 2016.

Why Social Media?

If using visuals is a great method of storytelling, using social media is a great platform for your hotel's story. Taken as a whole, today's social networks create a storytelling "ecosystem" wherein you can tell your story in your own words — and pictures — and your guests in turn can share their own experiences with you and with other consumers.

In fact, social media has become one of the common ways that society connects in the 21st century. While we can debate the meaningfulness of those connections, the power of social media to attract users can't be denied. Social media is no longer new, but social networks are still experiencing steady — and in some cases rapid — growth. The amount of time people spend on social media is constantly increasing. Teens now spend up to nine hours a day on social platforms, while 30% of all time spent online is now allocated to social media interaction.[8]

A big part of that growth has been driven by the proliferation of mobile devices. People love to use social media on the go and the growth of mobile apps is unprecedented. Compared to 2015, overall app usage grew by 11% and time-spent in apps grew by 69% in 2016. U.S. consumers now spend some 5 hours per day on their mobile devices.[9] A 2016 mobile insight study showed 52% of all non-map travel searches start on mobile with 48% starting on search engines, with19% of that time being spent on Facebook.[10]

While marketing in the traditional sense is very much about brand and product awareness, social media goes beyond that to actual engagement with consumers. Creating community members based on deep contact and one-on-one relationships, where they have a voice, can turn consumers into loyalists and even brand evangelists. As consumers rely more and more on their peers for endorsements and word-of-mouth referrals to make online decisions, it is this type of engagement that creates powerful relationships that are more likely generate sales in the long term.

At the same time, consumers are interested in rich visuals on social networks like Facebook, TripAdvisor, and Google — all of which have been redesigned to be more visual.

The advantages of using social media as part of your marketing strategy are many.

- Social media is an incredible source of content. Think of it as a worldwide pool of photographers and writers creating content for your hotel. You just need to curate it into snackable chunks and re-amplify it into the community.

- As a research tool, you can use social media to spot trends, see where people are spending their time, what they're looking at and talking about, and learn what they are using at any time. In fact, the reviews they write and the photos they take give you great insight into what your audience values. They literally show you why they've chosen your hotel over the competition.

- From a marketing and brand-building perspective, social media is a way to generate awareness and credibility, maximize conversion and traffic, establish yourself as an expert in your market, and increase organic search engine rankings.

- From a public relations point of view, releasing optimized, sharable, and media-rich news and information ensures staying top of mind with the media, while at the same time heightening your search engine optimization (SEO).

- Through revenue management, social media is the ideal channel for driving special rates, offers, promotions, and packages. By monitoring reviews, you can elevate guest relations and increase loyalty with customers like never before.

- As a customer service tool, social media allows you to monitor and positively influence the way potential and existing customers perceive your brand. By paying attention to all comments and reviews, and providing feedback or action when needed, the right response can turn a negative into a positive.

It is important to be mindful of the generational differences of today's travelers. There are those who thrive on being part of communities, and those who opt for the more traditional approach. To balance those needs, social media should be a part of your marketing efforts, not all there is.

The "Conversation Prism" is an excellent illustration of the global social media ecosystem and clearly defines the scope of this media.

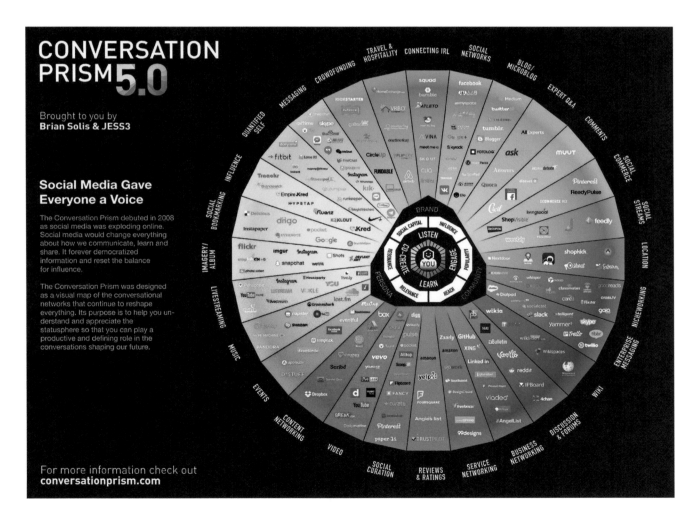

Source: https://conversationprism.com/

Visual Storytelling

The following checklist, reprinted in its entirety with permission from Leonardo, will help hotel marketers use the basics of visual storytelling to help tell a hotel's story on social networking channels. This is particularly applicable for the five most popular channels — Facebook, YouTube, Twitter, Pinterest, and Instagram.

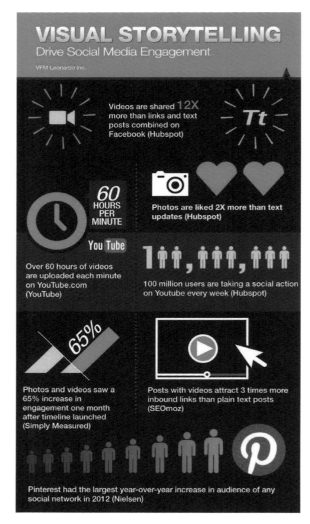

Source: Leonardo

Profiles

Your social profiles need to be visually compelling and help convey your hotel's story and brand. Consider McDonald's Golden Arches, Nike's Swoosh, or Tide bottles and the vibrant orange we connect to their brand. Each of these is an example of easy-to-recognize images associated with a brand's profile.

- Ensure your profile images represent your hotel and make it easy to identify.
- Update the visual appearance of your social profiles often.
- Describe your hotel and its story in the "about" section on each site.
- Include multi-media apps on Facebook to drive interaction.

Posting

The more interesting and relevant your posts are the better. One way to get interesting visual content is to photograph events at your hotel — post to Instagram, tweet them out, post on Facebook, and create an events board on Pinterest. This shows real people and real events at your hotel, which helps tell your story.

- Post interesting images that appeal to your fans and followers.
- Create and post videos that visually showcase the unique aspects of your hotel.
- Post regularly on each social platform.
- Share content posted by others that may be of interest to your audience. Do NOT share copyrighted content without first asking permission.
- Post content that encourages fans and followers to engage with you.
- Boosting posts for a fee in some platforms will help with engagement by bringing more eyes to your post.

Engagement

Add a personal touch to your social presence by sharing pictures and videos of travelers while they are staying at your hotel. Host photo contests that encourage travelers to share pictures of their favorite meals, or places in and around your hotel.

- Constantly monitor for consumer engagement and respond promptly.
- Host special campaigns such as contests that focus on creating social interaction.
- Involve guests in your posts and photos.
- Monitor your interactions and use that knowledge to improve.

General Visual Storytelling Practices

Ensure your social platforms are easy to recognize through the profile picture, the type of content posted, and a constant presence of posting and engagement to build up consumer confidence and trust.

- Include social media widgets wherever possible and appropriate, like email campaigns and landing pages.
- Ensure your content is always visual, interesting, and relevant to your current and target guests.
- Encourage consumers to connect and interact with you.
- Maintain a consistent image and appearance across all platforms.

Best Practices for the Most Popular Platforms

As social media channels have matured, they've become increasingly driven by visuals. YouTube, with its millions of videos, has always been visually driven, but Facebook, which was once mostly text-driven, has evolved to include ever more photo and video sharing features. While Twitter remains mostly the province of 140-character info-bites, it now fosters more photo and video sharing. In fact, re-tweeting links to videos is one of the most popular activities on the site.

Best practices for the hospitality industry have emerged for several of the most commonly used social media platforms. Use them to tell your hotel's story, and attract and engage potential guests.

Best Practices: Facebook

Facebook is the largest and most well-known of the social networks. More than 50 million businesses use Facebook pages[11] and one-third of Facebook users engage with brands regularly[12]. Consider the following when building and maintaining your property's page.

- Make use of the cover photo feature. Your cover photo is a great way to establish your brand in a big, bold way. And given its prominence on your page — and the simplicity of updating it — you can change it regularly to tie in to promotions or to give seasonal views of your property.
- Take advantage of the Facebook app infrastructure. There are more than 7

million apps and websites that integrate with Facebook. Using apps is a great way for you to leverage the Facebook platform while telling your story the way you want to tell it — and the way that engages your customers most effectively. With apps, you can customize your Facebook experience to your hotel's brand, display multi-media, promote loyalty programs and offers, enable booking, and more.

- Be responsive. More and more, people are using social media as a support platform. If you have guests and prospects asking questions on your wall, write back promptly — and politely!
- Study your community. Analyze and better understand your Facebook audience and their interests — align Facebook content to better resonate with your community.
- Be human and authentic. Be approachable and honest, and personalize the page so it is consistent with your brand/property.
- Get existing customers and prospects to be fans by emailing to your opt-in list, blogging about your page, sending out Tweets, linking it to your email signature, and posting a link or badge on your website.
- There are advertising options that target specific demographics. Facebook Polls can be used to get input and opinions, and Facebook's built-in analytics lets you track valuable metrics such as page views, wall posts, discussion threads, and photo views.
- DO NOT…constantly change your "profile" picture. This is the image users see in their news feed every time you're active on Facebook — it should be something recognizable and familiar, so that everyone knows right away who you are.

Best Practices: YouTube

YouTube revolutionized online video sharing with its introduction in 2005. Quickly bought by Google, YouTube now sees more than 1 billion unique users — watching more than 6 billion hours of video — every month.

Ensure hotel videos are posted on channels that make sense for your personality, style, features, and amenities. Some brands are successfully creating YouTube channels to syndicate their content for the benefit of the grander marketing objectives.

- Consider the global audience. YouTube is localized in 56 countries and 61 languages worldwide, and 70% of the site's traffic comes from outside of the U.S. Include videos that have global appeal to attract worldwide travelers. The beautiful thing about imagery is that it requires no language translation.

- Share videos other than your own. You might not have the resources to create new videos every week, but that doesn't mean your YouTube channel page should sit idle. Consider the types of videos your guests and followers might like; showcase local events and other travel videos.

- Listen, monitoring all mentions of topics relevant to your brand/property to better understand customer sentiment. Use YouTube Insights and comment/discussion sections to monitor customer concerns or misconceptions of the brand/property.

- Link channel videos on other social mediums. Integrate other social media properties, for instance adding your YouTube content to your Facebook fan page, to better unite social media efforts and raise the relevancy of your content in search.

- Maximize SEO opportunities. Title and tag videos and channel appropriately to maximize their SEO value for consumer searches. Be sure to brand yourself by displaying brand/property information, URL, email, and phone number in every video and post links to your videos on social networks.

- Tag videos with relevant keywords.

- DO NOT…share completely unrelated videos. While it's tempting to share the latest hilarious video you see making its way through social media, be careful not to dilute your message: stay on brand and give your visitors only the videos that relate to your property's image and identity.

Best Practices: Twitter

Twitter launched its mobile photo filters feature on iPhone and Android in December 2012. Twitter's quick bursts of information are ideally suited to our time-crunched, on-the-go, increasingly mobile society. They've recently embraced more visual storytelling features as well, including header photos, photo streaming/swiping on mobile apps, and new photo filters for mobile uploads.

- Use your background. Use an image that says something about your property, or that shows off what you have to offer. Consider the way your background image "splits," with your timeline in the middle. Why not have a photo of your hotel on the left and photos of your pool, business center, and restaurant on the right?

- Re-tweet. As with other social sites, sharing is a huge part of Twitter. Follow local businesses and other Twitter users that may be relevant to your guests, and re-tweet anything you think has value.

- Add photos to your tweets. To engage visually, augment your tweets with photos — of your property, of your guests enjoying themselves, of your chef's latest creation. And while Twitter no longer supports Instagram, the company's new mobile filters allow you to add a similar retro-like feel to your images.

- Use hashtags. Hashtags are used before a relevant keyword or phrase to categorize tweets and help them show more easily in search. They are a great way to join an existing conversation or even start your own. A great example of hashtag use and success is #discoverIHG hashtag. It's also important not to overuse them. Hashtags are intended to add value to your tweets, so use them sparingly and respectfully. A good rule of thumb is to use no more than two per tweet.

- Keep tweets short to allow room for your followers to give you credit when they "retweet" and share with their friends. Always include a link within the message, ideally at the beginning, since it will increase the likelihood that followers will click on it. Twitter also allows an image to be added to each tweet.

- DO NOT…worry if your tweets don't get a response. Avoid focusing on measuring retweets; instead, focus on making your content engaging and relevant to your followers.

- #dontmakeyourhashtagafullsentence. They are simply too hard to read and no one will ever hashtag that again, and therefore no conversation will happen.

Best Practices: Pinterest

Pinterest is a perfect platform for visual storytelling.

- Stay organized. Pinterest makes "pinning" cool photos a breeze, but your board can quickly become cluttered. Keep your pins neat and streamlined by creating different boards for different aspects of your property, such as rooms, guests, the grounds, local attractions, and events. Since sharing food ideas and recipes is one of the more popular activities on Pinterest, consider a board showcasing your property's restaurant or bar offerings, or local restaurants.

- Be a content curator. Remember that social media is a two-way conversation and be sure to upload and repin relevant images that others post about your hotel and surrounding area to contribute to your hotel's story through the eyes of guests.

- Draw people to your content. Put a "Follow Me on Pinterest" button on your website and periodically post Pinterest content to your other social networks to create awareness and interest. You can link to specific boards which gives you an opportunity to segment your followers in ways relevant to your business.

- DO NOT…ignore the past. If you have old photos lying around, put them to use. Nostalgia drives many pin boards. Your guests might enjoy seeing what your property looked like over the years, before and after renovations, or seeing how the neighborhood around you has changed.

Best Practices: Instagram

With its retro filters and snap-and-upload simplicity, the mobile photo-sharing phenomenon Instagram has proven extremely popular with users. Originally launched on Apple's iOS, Instagram has expanded to the Android platform and continues to grow rapidly.

- Show visitors the human side of your property. While you never want to make your marketing all about you, it never hurts to show off the faces behind your business. It can help humanize your hotel and remind potential guests that it is more than just a brand.

- Show off the surrounding area. Unless you're an inclusive resort, your visitors want to know what else your neighborhood offers beyond the hotel doors. Using Instagram's filters and special effects, you can convey how much your local restaurants and attractions have to offer.

- Take lots of photos. While you want to keep your Facebook albums tight and focused, Instagram is all about photos. Your followers will expect regular updates, or they'll quickly forget why they follow you.

- DO NOT…get too personal. While it's great to show your staff hard at work and your guests enjoying your property, you never want to embarrass anyone. Awkward and embarrassing photos will create a negative image of your property in a consumer's mind that you may not be able to shake.

Best Practices: Snapchat

Snapchat, a mobile app that's all about pictures and videos, is wildly popular amongst teens and young adults. Snapchat is inherently ephemeral — Snaps are viewable for about 10 seconds before they disappear; Snapchat Stories, about 24 hours. With some 150 million daily users creating 9,000 Snaps every second, now is a good time for brands to get on board.

- Make your profile public and make "everyone" your friend.

- Create original geofilters for your hotel and/or for special events there.

- Make it snappy. Snaps should be brief and easy to read in about 10 seconds.

- Link individual Snaps together to create a Snapchat Story.

- Stories should last only 1-2 minutes.

- Go vertical. Snapchat is used via mobile phone, so vertical content is easiest to view.

- Fill your space. Make sure images take up the whole frame.

- Go for contrast — white text on a dark background, for example.

- Make liberal use of emojis.

- Engage followers with Snaps about contests, coupon codes, employee bios.

- Be responsive. Reply to snaps and connect with influencers.

- Don't play solo — allow employees, influencers, even guests to "take over" your account or host a snap-based Q&A.

- Selfies were made for Snapchat.

- You cannot share links on Snapchat but you CAN cross-promote on other social channels.

Best Practices: Connect with your global customer through social media

Before booking hotels, reserving restaurants, or choosing attractions to visit, most consumers take to the web. They've become accustomed to reading travel reviews and recommendations on portals such as TripAdvisor, Expedia, and Kayak. This familiarity with portals has accelerated consumers' use of social networks — like Facebook, Twitter, Sina Weibo, Wechat (China), and VK (Russia) — to get destination information and peer recommendations.

There's an important difference between portals and social networks, however. Through recommendations, photos, and travel experiences posted directly by friends and family, social networks offer a greater level of trust. In fact, *Social Media Today* noted that "84% of Facebook users admitted in a PRSA Travel & Tourism poll that viewing their friends' post actually influenced their own future travel plans."

This trend holds true for global social network users. So what should you do to join and influence conversations? And when those conversations span many social networks and include multiple languages, how do you stay connected?

The following are helpful tips on where to start:

- Recognize that not all social networks are the same, and develop a global social media strategy accordingly. For instance, if your audience is primarily in China, use Sina Weibo or Wechat to reach those customers.
- As with any conversation, there are two parts: listening and engaging.
- Use social listening to gain an understanding of your consumers' sentiment.
- Support social engagement with a local community engagement manager to answer questions, defuse issues, and be a trusted part of the conversation in real-time. Customers increasingly expect customer service on social networks.
- Once you've tracked conversations and gained insights, plan to deliver localized and targeted content, promotions, and information around popular topics.
- If you're using a social network's advertising platform, be sure to localize ads accordingly so they stand out to your targeted consumer.

Best Practices: Measuring Social Media

There are a variety of social media marketing tools and an almost infinite stream of data available. Remember though, there's no magic potion to turn your social media activities into dollars. The social sphere is and always will be a rapidly evolving marketplace. Understand the role of social media in the shopping journey so that you can keep your eye on how it's helping you achieve your larger marketing objectives. So, what should you measure and why? Following are nine time-honored metrics[13].

1. Share of Voice

The number of mentions of your brand versus competing brands on the social web. Your Share of Voice can be a good indicator of the consumer awareness of your brand as compared to your competitive set. It essentially shows how much of the social conversation your brand has earned or is currently earning.

2. Brand Volume

The total number of brand mentions over a given period of time. If this number isn't growing, your campaign probably isn't working. Tracking brand volume week-over-week and month-over-month can be a good way to measure the overall health of your social presence.

3. Engagement

The overall number of times a user talks to your brand on social sites. You can push out all the content in the world, but if no one cares to reply or discuss it, what's the point? Social media is a conversation, after all. The more highly engaged your followers and fans are, the more likely they are to be brand-loyalists, or become influencers and evangelize your products or services on their own personal networks.

4. Interaction Per Post

The number of replies or comments you receive on a given post, tweet, or update. Similar to the engagement metric, the more times a user makes the effort to comment or reply, the more likely it is that they will grow to care about your brand and what you have to say.

5. Sentiment Analysis

The process of determining how the people

who talk about your brand on social media actually feel about your brand, products, or company. Although P.T. Barnum famously said, "All publicity is good publicity," it's an obvious problem if your hotel is consistently being trashed on social media. Also, if the sentiment is mostly neutral, that could be a sign your marketing is not making a big enough impact, and no one cares enough to have a strong opinion either positively or negatively.

6. Social Click-Through Rate

The number of times a user clicks on a link to one of your owned web properties (e.g., your hotel's website) shared via social media. Typically, one of the goals of a social media campaign is to drive traffic to a brand's website, microsite, or other owned media, thereby creating consumer awareness and subsequently bookings. The growth in the number of click throughs can be one of the indicators of a successful, engaging campaign.

7. Key Influencer Mentions

The number of mentions by users you've designated as "key influencers" due to their substantial and loyal social media following. Having influencers discuss your brand and serve as a brand ambassador is an extremely powerful way to organically extend your reach within key communities. While having anyone mention your brand on social media can be proof your tactics are working, mentions by key influencers are considered more valuable since they have a deeper reach or more pull/influence with your target demographic or communities.

8. Platform Reach

The number of social platforms that your hotel appears on, or the social "reach" across various online networks. Your brand might be a hot topic of discussion on various forums, but your Twitter mentions are low. Whether this is a problem depends on the social networks your targets actually use. After all, having a popular Pinterest page, which has a predominantly female user-base, doesn't really help if your brand is trying to target teenage males.

9. Mobile Mentions

The number of mentions of your hotel on mobile social sites. Social media is an increasingly mobile form of communication, and posting updates while on the go is quickly becoming part of nearly everyone's lifestyle, thanks to smartphones and tablets. If consumers aren't bringing your brand with them via mobile apps, this could be a sign you are getting left behind. It is especially important if your campaign involves mobile coupons, QR codes, or anything else that's tied into the Android, iPhone, or Windows phone operating systems.

Conclusion

Many social sites have some sort of forum or group component — a gathering area for like minds. The single largest mistake is to target quantity of a network on any social site; instead, strategically align your product with your target audience on the sites that most closely match your targeted demographic.

Turn enthusiastic customers into a powerful marketing force, recruit loyal customers to become evangelists, and encourage sales through their recommendations. The biggest reason people turn to friends and family for recommendations is because of trust, according to Clout. The best marketers and salespeople can be found among your most loyal, engaged, enthusiastic, and valuable customers.

For hotel marketers, it is extremely important that — no matter where you focus your marketing efforts — you make your activities shareable on social media, and make your activities interesting enough for people to want to share them. In addition — since sharing is by its nature a two-way street — it is important for you to share interesting items that others have produced that are relevant to your hotel's story and your customers.

The age of social media has given rise to hyper-aware consumers. No longer limited to what we can see and experience directly in front of us, we can now virtually tap in to a worldwide network of fellow consumers to gather information, thoughts, reviews, details, and more. We're also more aware of ads and sponsor-driven content; we've developed better "filters" to weed out the content we don't want, and we're better equipped to search out the relevant, engaging content we do want. And — coming full circle — we want to share that content on social networks.

For hotels, visual storytelling on social media is an ideal way to connect with potential guests in a very real, personal way. More than just a TV ad or a "brochureware" website, social media gives you the chance to tell your hotel's story in a visually compelling manner, and show off your rooms and amenities, as well as your people and your guests, with impactful visuals, quickly and easily, across multiple channels.

By connecting with guests and allowing them to help you tell your story, you're allowing future guests the chance to see, first hand, the true experience of staying at your property. You are also inspiring confidence that their visit to your hotel will match what they see online, not just what they've read online.

Chapter 14 Endnotes

1   "Top Social Network Demographics 2017." SocialMediaToday. March 21, 2017. https://www.socialmediatoday.com/social-networks/top-social-network-demographics-2017-infographic. January 9, 2018.

2   Number of daily active Snapchat users from 1st quarter 2014 to 3rd quarter 2017 (in millions). Statista. https://www.statista.com/statistics/545967/snapchat-app-dau/. January 9, 2018.

3   Reach of leading social media and networking sites used by teenagers and young adults in the United States as of February 2017. Statista. https://www.statista.com/statistics/199242/social-media-and-networking-sites-used-by-us-teenagers/. January 9, 2018.

4   Morrison, Kimberlee. "Snapchat Is the Fastest Growing Social Network." ADWEEK. July 28, 2015. http://www.adweek.com/digital/snapchat-is-the-fastest-growing-social-network-infographic/. January 9, 2018.

5   Constone, Josh. "Facebook Hits 100M Hours Of Video Watched A Day, 1B Users On Groups, 80M On Fb Lite." TechCrunch. January 27, 2016. https://techcrunch.com/2016/01/27/facebook-grows/. January 9, 2018.

6   "YouTube by the numbers." YouTube. https://www.youtube.com/yt/about/press/. January 9, 2018.

7   Osman, Karen. "ATM 2016 in Review — Social Media and Blogging Trends." WTM. http://news.wtm.com/atm-2016-in-review-social-media-and-blogging-trends/. January 9, 2018.

8   Asano, Evan. "How Much Time Do People Spend on Social Media?" SocialMediaToday. January 4, 2017. https://www.socialmediatoday.com/marketing/how-much-time-do-people-spend-social-media-infographic. January 9, 2018.

9   Khalaf, Simon. "On Their Tenth Anniversary, Mobile Apps Start Eating Their Own." Flurry Analytics. http://flurrymobile.tumblr.com/post/155761509355/on-their-tenth-anniversary-mobile-apps-start. January 9, 2018.

10   Fetto, John. "Mobile Search: Topics and Themes." Hitwise. http://hitwise.connexity.com/rs/371-PLE-119/images/hitwise-mobile-search-report-us.pdf. January 9, 2018.

11   Chaykowski, Kathleen. "Number Of Facebook Business Pages Climbs To 50 Million With New Messaging Tools." Forbes. December 8, 2015. https://www.forbes.com/sites/kathleenchaykowski/2015/12/08/facebook-business-pages-climb-to-50-million-with-new-messaging-tools/#171436de6991. January 10, 2018.

12   "Why Brands Should Embrace Instagram Instead of Facebook." selfstartr. https://selfstartr.com/why-brands-should-embrace-instagram-instead-of-facebook/. January 10, 2018.

13   Zenn, Jacqueline. "9 Ways to Measure Your Brand's Social Media Health." Mashable. June 11, 2012. http://mashable.com/2012/06/11/social-media-brand-data/#qL895kx0TqqJ. January 10, 2018.

KEY POINTS

- Definition of public relations.
- Distribution methods for press releases.
- Public relations topics that are relevant for hoteliers.
- Case study showcasing the new interactive public relations model.

SUMMARY

Like most marketing tools in the digital age, public relations has evolved beyond a one-way communication process into an interactive tool that allows — and, in fact, encourages — ongoing feedback. Once targeted only toward media outlets, public relations now has multiple audiences, often dealing directly with customers rather than through an intermediary source.

When the Public Relations Society of America (PRSA) gathered international opinion on what constitutes the modern concept of public relations (PR), the crowd-sourced response defined it as "a strategic communication process that builds mutually beneficial relationships between organizations and their publics."

In short, public relations — as it specifically relates to hoteliers — is about managing the perception of your company via the flow of information between a property and its audiences.

In today's times, two primary types of PR exist: the traditional model and the interactive model. The traditional model relates more directly to relationship building — developing beneficial connections with the media in order to successfully pitch well-crafted, relevant stories about your property to the local press and other publishers who may be interested in sharing your content. Tools used in traditional PR include press releases and press kits, which are distributed to the media to generate coverage.

The interactive model incorporates traditional tools while adding new outlets to the mix, including social media, blogs, and influencers. Social media is at the forefront, fostering a direct conversation between a business and its audience, unlike the traditional tools that allow only one-way communications. With the advent of digital and social outlets, conversation and engagement are now more vital than ever.

See the Adrian Awards case studies at the end of this chapter for three award-winning examples of how using traditional public relations can contribute to your overall marketing strategy.

Press Release Distribution

Technology is increasingly important in the aggregation and distribution of content. Properties both large and small can easily increase online visibility and generate publicity through digital press release distribution, also known as wire services. Wire services charge variable fees depending on the size of the distribution and formatting options. This distribution method provides more online exposure and links (hyperlinks embedded in your press release copy) pointing to your website, Facebook, Twitter, and other social channels. Valid links give your website and social platforms credibility, thus fostering search engine optimization (SEO).

Wire services such as Business Wire and PRWeb help properties boost online visibility and generate publicity by engaging journalists and social networks. These tools make it easier to identify key influencers, monitor program effectiveness, and protect and promote your property's brand. More than 30,000 organizations use PRWeb for its extensive reach through a variety of distribution partners. Press release distribution outlets that pick up wire service releases specific to the travel and hospitality industry — sites such as Hotel-Online and Hotel News Resource — help hotels reach industry-specific media that could have business-to-business benefits.

Simply selling the commodity of a bed and a bath means you will always ride the wave of ups and downs in your local market's occupancy and average rate. But breaking through the pack — distinguishing your guest experience and your brand identity as uniquely desirable — is the way to ensure that travelers choose your property over competitors', even if it means paying a little bit more, just to have the pleasure of enjoying the special experience you offer. For this reason, and many more, a good public relations campaign is critical. There may be no better investment than a creative public relations agency that understands your business needs in terms of increasing website traffic that results in sales. Even if you lack the budget to hire a major agency, you can utilize the principles of public relations to gain brand awareness.

The first step is identifying your hotel's unique selling points and then creating programs, special offers, and events to showcase its distinctive features. What would you like writers to say about you? Create that experience. Do a semantic analysis of your reviews and see what your customers say is important to them. Then, think about your target audience. Take the time to identify your most enthusiastic fans. What do you think they are reading? Where is the best place to reach that market with a unique message?

Designing a Story
The key to great press is understanding what's newsworthy and staying abreast of the latest trends. A good way to do this is to read current publications and see what is inspiring writers now.

It is fabulous to be the very first one to have a fresh idea, but in the reality of public relations, the big winners are often those who did not think of something first, but rather saw a trend or potential trend and ran with that, making it their own with a fresh spin.

What words do you find popping up again and again? *Design, local, organic, yoga, spa, sustainable, rooftop, artisanal, authentic experiences, customized experiences, pet-friendly, eco-friendly, gay-friendly, human-friendly, tech-friendly*? How about *bleisure* and *glamping*? *Glamour, love,* and *romance* are always current but finding a fresh way to express that can be powerful.

A wise woman once said, "Launching a fall menu is not press worthy. But if a head-of-state came in to try that menu, now, that's press worthy." That wise woman is Florence Quinn, founder of Quinn, who has been recognized by HSMAI with the Winthrop W. Grice Award for Lifetime Achievement in Hospitality Public Relations. Even though you need to create and identify a hook for your story, take a look at what you want to discuss, based on your business needs.

Topics Relevant to the Traveler/Hotel Guest
All the topics below (and many others not mentioned) are potential avenues for public relations. When key members of your staff understand the principles of PR, positive publicity more easily comes your way. Technology plays a huge role — especially with social media — but old-fashioned people skills are still important when it comes to forging relationships with members of the press. And, of course, it's necessary to have in-demand news.

Good PR serves as free advertising for your property, something that is increasingly important in today's competitive hotel industry. Here are a few examples to help you start generating ideas:

Business Meetings
- Did your property host a large, successful conference? What about that conference exemplifies an up-and-coming trend? Did the event tie in any kind of fundraising or community outreach?
- Did a high-profile company and/or guest stay at your hotel? Did they enjoy something at your hotel that speaks to a current trend?

Unique Use of Event Space
- Have you noticed any business or cultural trends in weddings? Does your hotel specialize in a particular type of wedding or event?
- Did you have a famous speaker in a conference room?
- Have you provided space as an in-kind donation to a local charity or community organization?

Property
- Have you renovated and updated your property to provide a more modern experience for your guests?
- Do you meet any "green" certifications or standards of excellence?
- Have you recently added a major amenity such as a new restaurant, spa, or business center?

Promotions & Packages
- What special rates or promotions are you offering for an upcoming holiday, noteworthy concert/sporting event, or a local festival?
- Do you offer a military discount?
- Has your property been featured by any credible sources — travel magazines (print or digital), TripAdvisor Certificate of Excellence, any "Best of …" lists, etc.? If so, "recycle" this information with your local media.

Creative Contests and Angles
- Create a program specifically designed to garner media attention and brand engagement, such as a contest, giveaway, or stunt.

PR, Social Media, and SEO

It is becoming more difficult to draw a distinct line between social media and public relations. When travel writers blog about their stay at your property, or publish a printed article, the publicity increases exponentially when they also tweet about their visit and/or post photos on Facebook and Instagram. In some instances, a tweet or post *about* an article draws more visitors that the article itself.

Even if a travel writer's blog does not have a huge following, it can still create SEO value by providing links back to the hotel's website, which helps rankings on Google. Leveraging available rooms to attract influencers to blog about your hotel and/or share about it on their social media channels is an effective way to achieve public relations goals without spending a lot of money — this can be particularly beneficial for hotels that do not have a budget for full-time PR representation.

While travel bloggers specifically target people interested in learning about hotels, destinations, restaurants, and attractions, bloggers who influence other interests such as fashion, design, lifestyle, music, and art can also draw attention to your hotel if it caters to those audiences. Encouraging influencers to communicate what they love about your guest experience can be much more effective — and less expensive — than trying to communicate that message directly.

According to Nielsen, only 33% of consumers trust ads, while 90% of them trust peer recommendations — indeed, influencers can be a powerful force.

See the article "Blurred lines: hotel public relations in the age of social media"[1] by Daniel Craig for additional insights.

Best Practices: Evaluating the Value of an Influencer

When partnering with an influencer, be specific in your agreement about a complimentary stay and clearly outline your expectations.

When in doubt, work with a company to help you select, attract, and verify the best influencers for you. BuzzAndGo.com provides a service which connects hotels and influencers; Buzz Sumo and Followerwonk are effective as well.

- Determine how many followers an influencer has on his or her blog, Twitter, Instagram, Facebook, Pinterest, and/or other digital platforms.
- Monitor the influencer's posts to ensure they are relevant to your brand and appropriate for your target audience. Attracting the wrong audience can have a negative impact on your online reputation, while consistently reaching the right audience greatly and economically improves awareness just where it can help your business the most.
- Is the look and feel of the writing and graphics a good fit for your company's identity? Does the influencer already share content similar to your brand? How have past travel articles been executed?
- Does this influencer have a travel section? If not, how will people find articles about your hotel?

CASE STUDY
Bermuda: Finding an Island's Adventurous Side

This Adrian Award Best in Show winner uses a story-driven public relations strategy to revitalize a destination's image and attract a younger demographic.

SITUATION

For decades, Bermuda has been known for its pink sand beaches, Dark 'n' Stormy cocktails, and world-class golf courses — and for decades, it's been attracting the same, aging demographic. The destination was seeing a decline in tourism and needed to find a way to draw a younger crowd to the island's wide array of lesser-known adventure travel offerings: incredible cliff diving, deep water solo rock climbing, a historic-railway-turned-bike-trail, and more than 200 explorable shipwrecks.

OBJECTIVES

- Position Bermuda as the perfect destination for young, affluent travelers who like a few thrills on their vacations.
- Get the island's extensive-but-under-publicized offerings in front of an untapped audience.
- Create a new brand persona via narratives and media outreach featuring the most adventurous options on the island.
- Develop a new narrative for the destination as a top adventure option.

STRATEGY

- Pinpoint all the adventure offerings on the island and develop rich narratives to reach a millennial audience.
- Develop rich press materials and extensive story angles speaking to the new narratives.
- Develop adventure-rich press trips and host a targeted list of media on the island to experience Bermuda first hand.

- Target major publications with a proactive travel public relations pitching campaign that highlights not only Bermuda's outdoor adventures, but also the historic attractions that come along with those adventures: historic forts, hidden caves used by the British military, and sunken treasure waiting beneath the waves. Adding the historic element distinguishes Bermuda from competing destinations, giving writers an extra angle to highlight.

RESULTS

- Media coverage of Bermuda's adventurous side ranged from consumer and travel outlets like Virtuoso Life and Islands to endemic publications like *Climbing* and *Triathlete*.
- *Outside* Magazine named Bermuda as "Best Island" in its Best of Travel issue.
- *Men's Journal* included Bermuda in the "20 Most Adventurous Beaches in the World."
- *The Wall Street Journal* touted the island as "the new destination for adrenaline junkies."
- Broadcast coverage included CNN and The Weather Channel.
- As a result of the campaign, Bermuda is attracting a younger demographic: 78% visitor growth for Jan-Jun 2016 is from travelers under 45 years old. Vacation air arrivals were up 10% through Jan-Jun 2016; 68,462 leisure air passengers landed in the first half of 2016: the largest volume of air vacationers since 2008. Leisure visitor spending is up 12% YOY through June 30, 2016 (up $10 million in the first six months of 2016).

CASE STUDY
ABC Nightline News Goes Glamping

This Adrian Award Gold winner uses a traditional PR pitch to re-establish a destination's reputation as a niche leader.

SITUATION

The Resort at Paws Up, a luxury ranch in Montana, has established itself over the past ten years as the leader in "glamping" — the niche travel category of glamorous camping. While the resort garnered numerous media hits for its glamping product, this also increased the media spotlight for competitors. The destination needed to legitimize glamping as a still-newsworthy trend after all these years and remind glampers that Paws Up is the resort that "started it all."

OBJECTIVES

- Position the Resort at Paws Up as the luxury leader in the well-established glamping travel trend.
- Secure a national broadcast segment on glamping at Paws Up.
- Reach a wide national consumer audience consisting of the affluent, sophisticated traveler who enjoys the outdoors but will not compromise any of the luxury services found at a five-star resort.

STRATEGY

- Target national broadcast outlets for a glamping (luxury) lifestyle/trend piece.
- Pitch with a specially filmed glamping B-roll + original content.
- Upon discovering that an ABC Nightline crew was already on assignment for a news story in Montana, pitch the producer to come over to Paws Up as well for a lifestyle piece on glamping.
- Provide producer with all background info and stats on glamping, including competitive resort examples.
- Lock in an on-location shoot (in the midst of the resort's busiest season) to showcase the best of what Paws Up has to offer.
- Secure interviews with staff and guests to provide insight on the glamping experience at Paws Up.

RESULTS

- 2+ minute segment on ABC Nightline News specifically on glamping at the Resort at Paws Up.
- "Inside the Ranch Where Glamping Can Cost at Least $10,000 a Week" reaching 1.6 million viewers.
- Segment highlights include:
    - A spotlight on the accommodations using a mix of original B-roll and resort B-roll.
    - An interview with a Paws Up Camping Butler.
    - Highlight on the variety of activities available at the resort.
- Segment was syndicated to ABC World News Now reaching an additional 663,854 viewers.
- Total PR value over $500K.

CASE STUDY
Tapping the Philadelphia Market for the Ocean House

This Adrian Award Silver winner uses a traditional media outreach approach to turn on off-season bookings.

SITUATION

The Ocean House in Watch Hill, Rhode Island, is the quintessential summer "Americana" beach destination — perfect white sand beach, pristine croquet lawn, ice-cold cocktails, and an evening fire pit. This luxury resort consistently sells out June through August but, when the temperatures fall, there's a corresponding drop in demand. Already popular in its key drive markets in Connecticut, Massachusetts, and New York, the Ocean House wanted to expand to other northeast markets to drive off-season bookings — particularly the affluent suburbs of Philadelphia — and promote winter travel messaging.

OBJECTIVES

- Generate off-season messaging, particularly highlighting the Ocean House's world-class farm-to-table B&F program and promoting the resort as an ideal destination for a culinary-focused getaway.
- Promote Coastal Rhode Island's easy proximity to the Philadelphia area (one-hour flight or four-hour drive).
- Highlight the Ocean House's sister property Weekapaug Inn, which complements the resort.
- Secure a multi-page feature story on the Ocean House in a top Philadelphia-area lifestyle magazine in order to reach affluent leisure travelers based in the Philadelphia area.
- Increase annual bookings from the Philadelphia area by 20%.

STRATEGY

- Research media outlets with affluent readership.
- Upon identifying *MAINLINE* and *BUCKS Life* magazines* as top targets (both under the same publishing umbrella), pitch the maga-

zines' editor on the charm of the Ocean House in the off-season; highlight the fall/winter activities available; point out non-stop flights on both American Airlines and US Airways (often under $200 round-trip).

- Invite the editor for a media visit to experience the destination first hand in the fall.
- Design an itinerary for the visiting editor to particularly spotlight the outstanding culinary elements of the two hotels, despite any inclement weather (a definite possibility during that timeframe).

RESULTS

- A four-page feature story filled with images ran in the winter travel issue of both *MAINLINE* and *BUCKS Life* magazines.
- The story highlights the cozy and romantic atmospheres of the Ocean House and Weekapaug Inn in the cooler months, with descriptions of impeccable dining experiences and the hotels' restorative natures. The article ends with booking details for both hotels.
- *MAINLINE* has a circulation of 30,000 and *BUCKS Life* has a circulation of 25,000 targeted readers. The two stories had a combined PR value of $81,000.
- Following the publication of this story, the Ocean House reported a 36% increase in stays from the Philadelphia area, and a 46% increase in room nights to date.

* Mainline's audience is comprised of residents of the wealthy "Main Line" suburbs of Philadelphia, and BUCKS Life reaches the community that stretches from New York to Philadelphia, with Bucks County at its heart. These sister magazines reach Ocean House's targeted audience, with an average household income of over $250,000 and an average home price of more than $850,000.

Chapter 15 Endnotes

[1] *Article is available online at* http://bit.ly/DanielCraigArticle

CHAPTER 16
Reviews & Reputation Management

KEY POINTS

- The advent of guest reviews.
- What components drive review ratings and ranking.
- Best practices for responding to reviews.
- The benefits of review aggregators.
- Adding a review feed directly to hotel websites.

SUMMARY

Online reviews drive business because consumers trust each other as much, if not more, than they trust hotel marketing. Positive reviews, management responses, up-to-date content, and photos are the primary factors that contribute to an online review strategy.

Prior to 2000, hotels capitalized on increasing demand on the internet by creating websites, taking advantage of third-party intermediary sites, and providing the content that they wanted the general public to see. The internet was often perceived as a digital brochure for a property. Hotels and brands controlled the content, photos, branding, and message on their websites. Several professional review sites did exist at that time — born from offline guide books such as *Frommers* and *Lonely Planet* — and while these could expose some less-than-brochure-perfect properties, generally the business owner had content control.

At the turn of the millennium, things began to change with the emergence of user-generated content. Hotels and other industries could no longer maintain total control over their digital presence, because users — guests — were now able to post their own perceptions online.

Initially, most user-generated reviews were presented as simple additional features on existing websites. Since the hotel or brand controlled the content, these reviews could be moderated, edited, or skewed to show a property in a pos-

itive light. Most third-party booking engines and Online Travel Agencies (OTAs) began to allow comments, and in some cases also created rating systems for properties.

Then came TripAdvisor. The site, which wasn't a booking engine, launched in 2000 and quickly became a popular venue where the general traveling public could become hotel reviewers by sharing their experiences and photos with anyone who was interested. Over the past 17 years, the site has amassed some 500 million — half a billion! — reviews and opinions; it now attracts an average of 390 million unique visitors every month.

Early on, as the practice of sharing details and opinions about hotel properties became increasingly widespread, there was cynicism surrounding anonymous reviews. What prevented disgruntled employees or competitors from writing negative reviews? What kept hotel owners from writing positive reviews about themselves? Such cynicism has lessened (though it's never completely gone away), and today statistics show consumers trust peer recommendations significantly more than traditional advertising.

It's a myth that people only post reviews when they have a bad experience — indeed, 80% of all reviews are 4- and 5-star reviews, while fewer than 3% are 1-star reviews.

It is important to monitor review sites as well as reviews on OTAs and search engines. The review landscape is in constant flux. Four main players have come to dominate a crowded field in recent years, with 78% of all reviews coming from Booking.com, TripAdvisor, Google, and Hotel.com. Booking has surpassed TripAdvisor, generating 39% of reviews compared to 24.6%.

In addition, it's become the common for hotel brands to include reviews on their hotel websites.

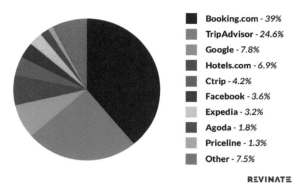

Booking.com - 39%
TripAdvisor - 24.6%
Google - 7.8%
Hotels.com - 6.9%
Ctrip - 4.2%
Facebook - 3.6%
Expedia - 3.2%
Agoda - 1.8%
Priceline - 1.3%
Other - 7.5%

REVINATE

Source: Revinate

Common Components of Review Sites

Most review sites are similar in approach. They list basic content — address, phone number, summary of property details, and photographs, often provided by the hotel owner/operator — and they provide an opportunity for visitors to write reviews and rate the hotel. Most review sites have some sort of popularity ranking of properties within a market and filtering capabilities for the user. Many sites default the display of reviews to the most recent ones, while others will show reviews more tailored to the user, e.g., reviews from friends on Facebook at the top of the sort. Lastly, most sites also allow a management response to a review.

How a property ranks in customer satisfaction on review sites can have a powerful impact on the number of visitors to the business profile page as well as to the hotel's own website. Ranking criteria is site specific, based on algorithms known only by the review site employees, but in general, success is built upon the Five Rs: Ratio, Rating, Recency, Relevancy, and Response.

- RATIO: Number of reviews relative to the size of the property.
- RATING: User-generated score/rating of the property.
- RECENCY: Number of recent reviews.
- RELEVANCY: The clout/authority of the person writing the reviews (usually determined by quantity of reviews).
- RESPONSE: Frequency and quality of management responses to reviews (on sites where applicable).

While these factors are important, TripAdvisor and other sites increasingly tailor the display sort to customer behavior or specific preference attributes, thus decreasing the importance of the actual "rank" in a market, but increasing the importance of focusing efforts on overall review management.

Fraudulent behavior on the part of the property harms its ranking. For example, if a hotel is influencing guests to write positive reviews by offering a financial incentive, or if an employee of one hotel is writing negative reviews about a competitor — and this behavior is reported and verified — your popularity will decrease.

If TripAdvisor determines there is cause to believe a business is manipulating the reviews, the site will red flag that business with a banner identifying the reviews as suspicious. To avoid damaging your business reputation in this way, it is a best practice to learn what constitutes manipulation on the review sites — and ensure everyone at your property is familiar with those rules as well. Not all the rules are obvious and they can change over time. For example, while many hospitality professionals understand that incentivizing guests is not allowed, they may not realize that selectively soliciting reviews from travelers who have written positive guest surveys is also considered manipulating the results. Be sure to periodically check the management center on each review site for information.

Search engines jumped on the review bandwagon once hotel mapping became prevalent. Search results on Google began returning local business results with an opportunity to read or write reviews; most search engines now allow reviews and provide some ranking and filtering capabilities. Location-based sites encourage visitors to check in to a property and then share tips to be viewed by others.

Guest surveys are similar to online reviews in that they collect the opinions of actual guests; however, there is generally a lag time in reporting. Review site postings are instant; feedback is often quick, giving a savvy manager real-time information that can be used to take immediate action. From a marketing standpoint, a survey response sent to the general manager does not have the same potential to attract new business compared to an online review that may be read by thousands of people.

A good rule of thumb is that if your guest surveys are not at least 90% positive, continue with private surveys while identifying any problems and creating opportunities for more positive feedback. Once you have 90% or higher in positive survey results, make them public and live on review sites where they can help pull revenue to your business.

ROI on Reviews

The exact attribution rate of any review site has not been determined, but a Cornell University study found that a larger number of positive reviews correlates with increased bookings and the ability to raise rates. Trends suggest that the following factors increase conversion and ADR:

- hotels ranked at the top of the market
- positive review scores
- appropriate management responses to reviews — both positive and negative
- multiple property photos showing the hotel in a positive and realistic light
- videos showing hotel in a positive light
- detailed hotel information provided

The benefit of increased conversion due to a strong reputation can be seen not only in electronic bookings, but also in bookings of groups and corporate accounts through traditional sales and marketing efforts.

Advertising is possible on review sites. Business listings, links directly to your brand.com or independent website, or display, graphic, or video ads are all available. Like any advertising decision, a strategy guiding the targeted ROI, measurability, and overall effectiveness should be determined beforehand. Best practices suggest that an easy link from a review site to a property website or booking engine shows a positive ROI; however, some review communities shun any traditional "marketing" approaches. If strengthening your direct business is important to your revenue strategy, then adding a business listing (with contact information and a link to your website) may help.

If your hotel is part of a major brand, check first with your brand representatives to see if there are any corporate relationships between sites such as TripAdvisor and the brand, and what is included in those agreements, such as business listings, metasearch, display advertising, etc.

Who is Responsible for Reviews?

Responding promptly and politely to reviews — especially negative reviews — can create a positive impact. How you respond to a negative review says more about your property than the review itself.

It's generally recommended that reviews be responded to at the hotel level. The hotel staff is in the best position to understand any situations or issues that may have occurred, and thus can best respond with appropriate context to a review. However, review management crosses disciplines and is often "touched" at both the property and above-property levels.

Review management also has a strong property operations component. Many issues, especially those that are recurring, need to be relayed to and handled by the operations team at the hotel for resolution, preventing these issues from occurring in the future.

Above-property ecommerce/digital or social media managers are often responsible for the overall coordination and accountability of reviews. Sites like TripAdvisor and the OTAs often fall in the realm of above-property team members from hotel information, listing, ranking, and advertising perspectives, and they may oversee an entire portfolio ensuring that all hotels are responding in an appropriate and timely fashion. These team members may also uncover recurring issues across numerous reviews and work with the hotels to resolve them.

The hotel's search engine optimization (SEO) lead — whether on property, above property, or a vendor — will also have an interest in the reviews and management responses because user-generated content can influence hotel rankings in the search engines.

Some brands now include responses and response times in their QA assessments. This shows that brands recognize the impact reviews and responses have on revenue, as well as the value of this process to the guest experience and future intent to return.

In the end, it is best to understand all impacts that reviews may have on the hotel and ensure accountability for all aspects of review management.

Best Practices: Responding to Reviews

It is first important to mention that not all sites displaying customer reviews allow management responses. But when you can, do — hotels that provide a management response to reviews are 21 percent more likely to receive a booking inquiry via that site. A 2016 Cornell study also found that hotels that respond to up to 40 percent of their reviews observe a 2.2x average lift in revenue.

Some of the major sites that allow public responses include:

- Booking.com: This large review (and booking) site recently added the public response feature; to respond, select "Guest Reviews" on the Extranet.
- TripAdvisor: The world's largest travel site. You must first register as the hotel owner in the Owners' Center.
- Yelp: Hotels must register first at Yelp Business Owners.
- Expedia & Hotels.com: Hotels must first log into Expedia Partners Central.
- Google+/Google My Business: To respond to reviews, hotels must first claim their listing.
- Travelocity: Hotels can add photos or videos to their responses.
- Facebook: Hotels must opt in to allow ratings and reviews on their pages.
- Ctrip: The largest OTA in China, which also has the largest share of online reviews.
- Wotif: The dominant review site in Australia and New Zealand, now owned by Expedia.
- And others…Trivago, Rakuten, Holiday-Check, HRS, etc.

When responding to reviews:

- Research the situation before responding to make sure you have the story straight and understand what action needs to be taken in the future to prevent recurrence.
- Make it a priority to respond to negative reviews — reply to all of them. If handled well, this can increase your esteem in the eyes of the readers. In fact, 84% of users surveyed by TripAdvisor agree that an appropriate management response to a bad review "improves my impression of the hotel."
- Thank the reviewer for their feedback.
- Be sincere and genuine. Do not use generic canned responses.
- Apologize for the negative guest experience.
- Explain steps you will take to prevent the negative experience from happening again.
- Do not offer compensation online. This can make readers believe that complaining can bring financial reward.
- Wrap up by acknowledging any positive comments and ask for an opportunity to show them the improved guest experience.
- Invite the guest to contact you offline.
- Have someone else read responses for tone and intent prior to posting.
- For every negative review that receives a response, also respond to a positive review.
- Per industry research, aim for a 40 percent response rate (data from a 2016 Cornell study indicate diminishing returns on response rates beyond this). It is not necessary to publicly respond to every positive review, but it is good form to privately thank all positive reviewers.
- Respond as quickly as possible, within 24 hours whenever possible; however, it is sometimes better to wait another day than to get the details wrong in your research of the events or planning your recovery. Some brands require a response within 48 hours.
- You can ask TripAdvisor to remove an old response and replace it with a new response when new information is available.
- You can even follow up months or years later if a renovation has removed the item of contention. This can be helpful to travelers who like to read the worst reviews first.

One study shows that potential guests visiting review sites read management responses more carefully than the actual online review. So when writing a response to a review, keep in mind that you aren't communicating only with the person who wrote the review — you are responding for the benefit of everyone else who may one day read that review. Indeed, a management response could be viewed by hundreds, or even thousands, of potential customers, so a response should be treated similarly to an advertisement. A responsible marketer would never place an ad without reviewing the content, and having it proofread for errors and messaging. The same is true for management responses to reviews. Each response may drive a potential guest to your hotel, or drive them away to a competitor.

The single biggest mistake made when responding to reviews is to be defensive and diminish what the customer is telling you about their experience. Criticizing the guest — or somehow holding them responsible for their poor experience — makes you look arrogant or uncaring, not only disappointing to the reviewer but also to other readers as well. According to a TripAdvisor survey, 64% of users say an aggressive/defensive management response to a bad review "makes me less likely to book that hotel."

While it may be unfair to book a Disney Resort and then complain that there are too many kids, pointing a finger at the guest for "not visiting the website before booking" runs the risk of turning other potential guests off. Being humble and kind yet authentic can help clarify for travelers if your hotel is the right match for them, so approach replies with caution. It can be a difficult task not to take negative reviews personally. Just keep in mind that the reward can be very high. You can make a powerful impact, generating demand for your hotel by harnessing the power of reviews to communicate your property's message to lessen any potential disappointment and increase satisfaction.

Best Practices: Generating More Positive and Fewer Negative Reviews

Every hotel has an underlying desire to make every guest happy. With the ubiquity of online reviews, that coincides with the goal of generating more positive reviews and fewer negative reviews.

Generating More Positive Reviews

Observe the behaviors that inspire positive comments at your hotel — and at your competitors'. Look for ways to consistently integrate similar experiences into every guest's stay.

Be authentic in the descriptions and depictions of your property so you only attract those who genuinely prefer your type of hotel.

Graciously request reviews in your post-stay email, giving a link to the review site(s) to make it easy for guests to respond.

Generating Fewer Negative Reviews

Immediately find creative solutions to problems mentioned in reviews. Do not wait until you have many complaints about the same issue.

Assure staff members that they will not get in trouble for looking for creative solutions to resolve problems and make guests happy.

Create the opportunity to resolve guests' issues. Have staff members in all positions ask guests how their stay is going.

Ensure feedback loops are in place at the hotel and follow up with unhappy guests while they are still in-house. Do not let a guest leave dissatisfied without efforts to make their stay a pleasant one.

Best Practices: Eliminating Past Reviews

The most frequently asked question about reviews is whether it's possible to remove negative review. The policies for different sites vary, but in general it's difficult to do. At TripAdvisor, for example, reviews will only be removed if:

- There is a change in the property's ownership.
- There is a change in the property's brand.
- The property has undergone major (not simply cosmetic) renovations.
- The review violates TripAdvisor guidelines and/or is proven to be fraudulent.
- The negative review is being used to "blackmail" a property into providing goods or services.
- The guest who wrote the review requests that it be removed.

In general, the best practice for downplaying a bad review is 1) to provide a management response promptly and politely, then 2) to ensure that many positive reviews are posted after it. The most recent reviews usually show up first and, in most cases, reviews on the third page or beyond will not be read. Keep in mind, as well, that a small number of older negative reviews may not hurt your overall business, especially if more recent reviews trend positive.

TripAdvisor's Certificate of Excellence

Since 2010, TripAdvisor has been awarding the TripAdvisor Certificate of Excellence to recognize businesses that are focused on delivering great service. In 2015, TripAdvisor also announced the Certificate of Excellence Hall of Fame to hotels that earn the award for five consecutive years.

TripAdvisor provides free Award "widgets" that hotels can place on their own websites, in email signatures, or for use on property on signage or collateral, letting guests know the hotel has been recognized. While this can be positive marketing for the hotel, do NOT link your Award widget from the hotel website back to the hotel's TripAdvisor listing. First, best practice dictates not "linking away" potential customers from your site to another site where they may become easily distracted with many other hotel choices. More importantly, this negatively impacts your hotel's website by providing TripAdvisor with potentially thousands of "inbound" links to their site, giving them additional SEO "juice" over your hotel's site in the search engine rankings.

Review Aggregators

There are thousands of hotel and travel review sites. Keeping up with the comments being broadcast about a hotel is a time challenge. As a result, there are several companies that will collect every review written about a single property and place them on a single dashboard. In addition to monitoring review sites, these aggregators will also collect comments about an individual hotel and competitors on blogs, YouTube, and other social media outlets.

Sentiment analysis helps make sense of the "noise" of many reviews — helping a hotelier truly understand the online conversations about their property. Aggregators, using sentiment analysis, can sort reviews into positive and negative around a single keyword. For example, "front desk" may show a 69% positive sentiment meaning that 69% of the guests who included a comment about the front desk had an overall favorable opinion of the property.

A single review may be complimentary or damaging, but should be taken for what it is, a single opinion. Hotels that do very well on review sites still tend to put importance on the individual perspective; however, the value of aggregators is that they also allow a property to recognize patterns. If one guest complains about noise, they might have loud neighbors.

That does not mean you can't have someone investigate if a solution exists. If 25 guests complain about noise, there is likely a larger problem. Aggregators can tabulate the number of reviews received from sites to give you a broader picture of your guest review landscape.

Alerts can also be set to notify management of a potentially negative or harmful review as soon as it is posted. Most aggregators will allow you to select certain keywords that will trigger an immediate email notification — "bed bugs," for example.

Generally, third-party aggregators charge a monthly fee for their services. A free alternative for aggregators is Google Alerts. Though far more cumbersome, alerts can be established, with daily or weekly emails sent to you based on keywords. You can select your property name in several variations, as well as competitors' names, and a daily collection of those keyword appearances can be collected. The analytics are missing, but for the budget conscious property this is a viable option. Many hotel brands already have an internal or proprietary review aggregation tool. First understand what such tools capture before purchasing additional third-party tools.

Hotel/Brand Websites and User-Generated Content

Allowing user-generated content on an individual hotel website is becoming more prevalent and most major brands now collect customer reviews to be published on their own hotel websites. Some brands are adding a feed from TripAdvisor directly to their websites as a testimonial source, along with a widget to collect more reviews, while others are allowing guests to create reviews directly on their hotel websites or through guest satisfaction survey portals.

Keep in mind in this case that both the third-party review sites as well as brand.com reviews need to be managed and acted upon. When weighing the pros and cons of each option, remember that reviews created directly on a hotel's website do not help increase your ranking on larger travel review sites, though they might be seen as more trustworthy if reviewers are verified as actual guests — something not every third-party site is able to do (Expedia and Booking.com can and do verify, but TripAdvisor does not). Remember, too, the reviews are appearing much lower in the conversion funnel (closer to the booking engine). On the flip side, using TripAdvisor sourced reviews on your website allows you to leverage the popularity of TripAdvisor to generate additional demand for your hotel.

Consumer reviews add credibility, so if your reviews are positive overall, adding them to a hotel website might make sense. The flip side is that a negative review on your own website also has credibility and will likely influence purchasing decisions. However, a single negative review in a sea of positive reviews can actually add legitimacy to the overall collection of reviews.

Another pro on the side of hosting user-generated content directly on the hotel website is the SEO value. Recent and relevant content is appealing for search engines and can have a positive impact on your search ranking.

Conclusion

Review sites continue to grow in relevance and can help or hinder conversion rates for hotels. In our digital world, hotels must have a robust review strategy that includes:

- A plan for reading, analyzing and sharing review results.
- Responding effectively to reviews in a timely manner.
- Reviewing and sharing competitor review information.
- Modifying behaviors, policies, and products based on guest feedback to lessen complaints and inspire positive reviews.
- Updating current and authentic information, as well as photos and video on top review sites and anywhere people may look for information about your hotel.
- Creating opportunities to increase the number of positive reviews received and minimize negative reviews.
- Leveraging technology to aggregate reviews, improving the efficiency of review responses, and more easily identifying trends through sentiment analysis.
- Analyzing and taking advantage of marketing opportunities available on review sites.

PART 4: PAID MEDIA

KEY POINTS

- Paid advertising has several elements that drive viewers to your desired destination, typically your website. Paid search, programmatic display media, metasearch, and social are the four primary forms of digital advertising options.

- All forms of media utilize various forms of keyword or data-based targeting methods and require extensive analytics to gauge results. This includes the ability to target a user based on their past and present behaviors, demographics, purchase history, and relationships with a hotel.

- Programmatic display media and social media add visual components to the delivery including photos, images, logos, animation, or videos.

- A hotel or brand can extend its reach to attract potential guests through affiliate marketing, creating partnerships with companies that offer complementary or non-competing services.

- Metasearch is a pay-per-click model designed to drive travel-intent visitors away from comparison hotel shopping sites to a supplier's site.

SUMMARY

Driving traffic to your website, blog, or any web destination will involve either organic optimization (covered in Chapter 7) or paid advertising. Paid advertising includes search engine marketing (SEM or paid search) and display advertising. Paid search works best at the bottom of the conversion funnel, capturing consumers at the moment of intent; standard display advertising works extremely well higher in the funnel to generate awareness; and display remarketing and data-driven display advertising are extremely effective at lower funnel conversions, especially when integrated with your SEM strategy.

Paid advertising, display advertising, or search engine marketing (SEM), sometimes referred to as pay-per-click (Paid Search) or search engine advertising (SEA), affects the promotion of websites in search engine results pages (SERPs) through advertising and bidding on keywords for paid placement. Depending on the context, paid advertising can be an umbrella term for various means of marketing a website through search engines including organic optimization (see Chapter 7 on SEO) and paid search. Ultimately paid search is a means for achieving first page SERP placement without organic optimization of the site. The overall process involves bidding on keywords for placement. Your paid search strategy can be directed to various levels (by keyword, keyword groups, etc.), while placement and rotation of your ad is based on your maximum bid amounts and allocated budget. Paid search listings allow for nearly complete control of the message and title in contrast to organic listings where these are determined by the search engine.

How Online Behavioral Advertising Works[1]

A basic premise in marketing is the more you understand your customers' preferences, the more effectively you can advertise and ultimately sell your product or service. Marketers are constantly trying to answer questions such as: What do customers like to see? What do they want to hear? What do they like to do? What prompts them to buy?

Recommending relevant advertising based on past browsing activity is commonly referred to as "Online Behavioral Advertising" (OBA). This practice is also called "Behavioral Targeting" or "Interest Based Advertising." Because online behavioral advertising is based on the users' inferred or declared interests from the cumulative browsing patterns across a variety of websites and pages, it differs from contextual advertising, which is based on the correlation between an advertisement and the content that directly surrounds it.

Let's look at an example of the distinction between online behavioral advertising and contextual advertising. Imagine you are an advertiser, trying to promote a French vacation package. Your best bet, then, is to advertise your vacation offer to users who display interest in travelling to France. You could try to reach them on a website that reviews and recommends vacations in France (contextual advertising). However, you may also want to display your vacation package to users who previously have visited sites that involved travel to France through advertising on a subsequent, unrelated website, for instance one about their favorite baseball team (Online Behavioral Advertising). For more information, please review the Interactive Advertising Bureau's "Self-Regulatory Principles for Online Behavioral Advertising": https://www.iab.com/news/self-regulatory-principles-for-online-behavioral-advertising/.

Part 4 Endnotes

1 *"Data Usage & Control Primer: best practices & definitions." Interactive Advertising Bureau. Web. November 15, 2013. http://iab.net/data_primer*

KEY POINTS

- Paid search, otherwise known as Search Engine Marketing, is part of the Google Ecosystem and should be a part of your digital marketing strategy.

- It is important to reach guests at every stage of the travel planning journey to influence and shape decisions that lead to a booking. Before you conduct keyword research and launch campaigns, think about your KPIs and how you will reach users throughout every step of their journey, from planning to booking.

- Consistently measure and test the effectiveness of your campaigns and fine tune them while considering your available budget.

- Avoid analyzing the performance of your paid search campaigns in a silo. Looking at the ROI of every keyword is not the right approach and can lead to pausing keywords and campaigns that reach users at the top of the funnel.

SUMMARY

Paid search, or Search Engine Marketing (SEM), should be an integral part of any digital marketing strategy. SEM is one of the highest revenue drivers for hotels, with more than 25% of direct online revenue coming as a result of SEM/paid search. Plan strategically, keep your goals in mind, research carefully in advance, and then measure and test to determine effectiveness.

SEM is a great way to increase market share within the SERP (Search Engine Results Page) and allows delivery of a concise marketing message to a highly relevant marketing segment with measurable results. A balanced strategy that includes paid search in addition to Search Engine Optimization, online media advertising, social media advertising, native advertising, meta search marketing and email marketing yields the best results over the long term. Paid search, due to the inherent immediacy of its results and control of the message, lends itself to the tactical promotion of specific rates, packages, and promotions.

With an understanding of booking lead times, paid search campaigns can be executed with precision and coordination with the revenue management strategy of your hotel. The strategic use of paid search can supplement a solid Search Engine Optimization program.

Differentiators of Paid Search

Paid Search advertising is popular because it is easy to measure the return-on-investment (ROI). If you spend $10, you know your ROI because you can likely track the transaction from the click through to the actual booking. How much you are willing to bid for a given search term directly affects how much you pay. The platforms utilized to manage Paid Search campaigns allow for adjustments to your bids, ads/messaging, keywords, and ad extensions that take immediate effect. Paid Search engines, like Google, factor a relevancy score into the process which impacts the cost to the advertiser, ultimately impacting your ranking, or placement, and the effectiveness of your ads.

Paid placement models beyond traditional search engines include those based on impressions or even Pay-Per-Acquisition. These models should be considered, from budget and campaign strategy perspectives, similar in nature to Paid Search.

Recent developments in the technology interfaces between search engines and central reservations systems (CRS) allow for dynamic content, such as specific rates, to be pulled directly from a hotel's CRS. This extends the capabilities of the CRS as a channel management tool and allows Paid Search to be even more tactically precise. This is best facilitated via the application programming interfaces (API), third-party Paid Search management tools, or web services being developed by technology providers on both sides of the equation.

Best Practices: Keyword Research & Analysis

Any marketing program or campaign should start with clearly outlined goals and objectives and should be complementary to the overall digital marketing strategy. By ensuring this at the outset, the results will be more quantifiable, and for Paid Search specifically, it is critical for the development of an appropriate keyword strategy and for writing ad copy.

Begin by making a list of words and phrases that describe your hotel by its location and unique selling points (USP). Where is your hotel located? What would the consumer have in mind when looking for a hotel in your location? Asking yourself why the consumer would be traveling to the destination can be helpful. Consider including modifying words like the city, state, or country, as well as the neighborhood and surrounding landmarks.

The major search engines have access to a huge amount of data about which keywords people search for every day. For instance, Google has a keyword tool within its AdWords interface that provides additional keyword suggestions based on a list of keywords you might enter. By leveraging the tool, you can understand not only the potential of your keywords but also related terms that you might want to use in your Paid Search campaign. This same tool can be utilized to estimate the required budget. Each keyword or keyword group will provide an estimate of the number of impressions you will receive, and from this you can anticipate the budget required to fund your campaign.

Include long and short tail keywords as part of your strategy. See Chapter 2 for additional information on these keyword types.

Organize your keywords into related or similarly themed groups. These will become "Ad Groups" in your final campaign setup. By approaching the keywords in this manner you can optimize the use of ad copy and descriptions. Many campaign management tools utilize this concept to organize the keywords and manage budget. Otherwise, you will need to identify a keyword, then a description, then a headline repeatedly. If you can group similar words, you can write less copy, and the smaller sample will enable you to test your headlines a little easier. Tightly themed ad groups also help to ensure that the most relevant ad copy is being served for all keywords within the group. As a rule of thumb, groups of 10 to 15 keywords work well.

Best Practices: Campaign Set-Up

The implementation of a successful paid search campaign involves several elements.

Ad Copy & Headline

Your ad copy and headline should be brief, and, in conjunction with the keyword utilized, provide a compelling reason to click through to the landing page. It must be succinct due to the character limitations imposed by the search engine. It should communicate your unique selling proposition (USP), what you are promoting, and encourage a call to action in a small amount of space. Think about these issues when you create your copy:

- Include keywords in your ad copy whenever possible as this will assist in continuity and relevance.

- Why should someone click on your ad? Consider your USP and use this as the ad headline or the call to action.

- Create a sense of urgency and a call to action (example: Book now!) to trigger the desired action (which is to click through).

- Include rate, percent off, or value adds if applicable as these are strong compelling messages.

- Consult search engine guidelines for rules about ads to ensure you don't violate any editorial policies, or experience ads being disapproved by the engines.

Keyword Group

Develop the ad copy to correspond with the ad groups created to ensure that the ad copy is relevant to what users may be searching for.

Consider the Competition

Some simple searches of your keywords should show you what your competition is doing and what you are competing against. The intent here is not to copy the competition, but to position your ads and messaging well. However, being aware that your ads will display alongside these is a key consideration. Knowing what your competition is doing can help you modify your ad copy to stand out, and help you decide whether to bid on certain keywords at all.

Keyword Matching

Keyword matching is a method the search engines use to serve ads based on keywords that might be similar to what you selected as targets or similar to what the consumer has utilized. Understanding this allows you to determine how broad or narrow you want to set your campaign. It is important to understand the difference between a "keyword" and a "search query." A keyword is the word or phrase you choose to bid on in paid search. A search query is a word or phrase that a consumer actually types into the search box of the search engine. Matching helps you refine your keyword list so you don't have to bid on and manage every possible keyword combination. While the details of use vary by search engine, there are some general concepts that apply to all of them.

- EXACT MATCH: Your ad will show when someone searches for your keyword or close variations of your keyword. This includes but is not limited to: misspellings, singular or plural forms, stemming, abbreviations and synonyms or paraphrases. Exact match now allows for you to show up for keyword variations you may not have thought to bid on.

- PHRASE MATCH: Your ad will appear on searches that include the words in your keyword phrase, in the same specific order, but the query can also include other words before or after the word or phrase you are bidding on.

- BROAD MATCH: Casts the widest net and is the most difficult to control. When using Broad Match, your ad is shown on queries containing similar phrases and relevant variations of the keyword. This will generate a lot of activity, some less relevant.

- MODIFIED BROAD MATCH: This match type is offered by most search engines and is a more targeted approach than simple Broad Match. By utilizing a plus sign (+) in front of a word within a Broad Match keyword, you ensure that your keyword will only match to queries that contain each word that you've marked with a plus sign. Searched keywords can be added before, after, and in between the search term you are bidding on

- NEGATIVE MATCH: Used to ensure that your ad does not show for any query that includes the terms you specify. Think about phrases containing words like "free," or "cheap," inappropriate content, customer reviews, news-related terms (like robbery, bedbugs, fraud, etc.), competitors' brand names, etc. Do you want to show up in these searches or not?

- DAILY CAMPAIGN BUDGETS: These are set for each individual campaign to determine how much on average you want to spend a day. It is possible to be charged slightly more or less each day on your set campaign budget. In the end you will never be charged more than your set budget in the month and in any given day you will not spend more the 2 times the daily budget.

- AD DISTRIBUTION: Allows you to control whether your ads appear only on Search Engine Result Pages (SERP), or also on display network sites like news and blogs, mobile apps, etc. You will want to consider that users on other websites may or may not be as likely to click as those directly searching on a search engine.

- AD ROTATION: The manner in which you would like your ads to be delivered on the Search Network and Display Network. You can have them rotate ads indefinitely, or in an optimized rotation.

- GEOGRAPHICAL AD DISTRIBUTION: Allows you to pinpoint where you want your ads to be displayed based on the physical location of the consumer, or the location that they are searching for. This can be particularly useful if you understand the major feeder markets for your hotel, or if a campaign is intended to focus on a specific market.

- LANGUAGE: Language settings allow you to target the consumer based on the language they have specified in their internet browser settings. This is a key consideration as your campaign can be more effective if you also have keywords translated into the preferred language of your target audience. It is important to also have translated ad copy as well as translated landing pages used in the ad copy.

Best Practices: Measuring your Campaign Performance

Paid search metrics for hotels include:

- CONVERSIONS: When a person who clicked your ad completes an action on your website, such as booking a room, buying something, signing up for an email list, or requesting more information.

- CONVERSION RATE: The percentage of clicks that resulted in a conversion.

- **COST PER CONVERSION:** Total conversions divided by total cost.
- **ROAS (RETURN ON AD SPEND):** Also called ROI (return on investment), this metric measures how profitable your advertising is.
- As well as revenue, ADR (Average Daily Rate), room nights, and market share.

Additional cross-industry metrics include:
- **IMPRESSIONS:** How often your ad is shown. Each appearance of your ad equals one impression.
- **IMPRESSION SHARE:** The percentage of impressions you received divided by the estimated number of impressions you were eligible to receive based on your targeting, bid, and other factors.
- **CLICKS:** The number of times a user interacts with your ad by clicking on it.
- **COST:** Total cost that you have spent with each search engine or campaign.
- **AVERAGE COST-PER-CLICK (CPC):** How much you paid for each click on your ad. Can be calculated by dividing cost by the number of clicks.
- **CLICK-THROUGH RATE:** Expressed as a percentage, this metric is the number of clicks divided by the number of impressions.
- **AVERAGE AD POSITION:** A statistic that describes how your ad typically ranks against other ads. This rank determines in which order ads appear on the page. Position one is the first ad on the page.

Best Practices: Campaign, Bid, and Budget Management

Managing your paid search campaign involves the fine tuning of your keyword strategy, ad messaging, bids, and available budget. By manipulating these elements, the budget can be managed to allow you exposure all day or during the key hours you want to be displaying. Keep in mind that when the daily budget is depleted you will no longer be rotating and have no presence until the new budget period begins. The optimization of the campaign will come through changing ad copy and the keywords being utilized – in and of itself this process is a series of tests to find the correct balance of exposure and return.

Quality score affects your cost per click and ad position and therefore is a key component of the management of the optimal campaign. As a way of rating paid search keyword relevance, quality score ranks relevance on a scale from 1 to 10, with 1 being the worst and 10 being the best. The components of quality score are your CTR (click-through-rate), ad relevance, landing page quality and relevance, and expected impact from the use of extensions and ad formats. It is important because it is used to:

- Determine the actual cost per click (CPC) that you pay
- Estimate first page bids
- Determine if a keyword is eligible for the ad auction
- Rank your ad against other advertisers in the auction

Quality score will directly impact what you pay for a click, where you appear on the list of ads, and therefore how effectively your budget will be consumed.

Best Practices: Testing

Testing is an indispensable component of any marketing strategy. A challenge for certain channels, like email or direct mail, is that they take more time to test in setup and to receive test results. PPC tests can take less time depending on the volume we are able to drive. While nearly every element of Paid Search can be tested, following are some of the most common tests.

Keywords

Which keywords draw more quality traffic to your page? But also important is to measure if those visitors are staying and converting.

Headlines and Description Line

Changing one word in a headline can alter performance dramatically. Not unlike headlines in direct mail, certain words seem to compel action, like "new," "limited," or "free." The usage of rates, discounts, or other numerical ad components can also significantly improve your ad's performance. Again, it's important not only to measure traffic but the results of the traffic. Once you find the headline that works the best, that becomes your control and then test other headlines to see if they can beat it. The same is true for ad copy. A/B testing or split testing is a method of testing marketing strategy by which a baseline control sample is compared to a variety of single-variable test samples to improve response or conversion rates. You can change the settings to rotate ads indefinitely to ensure clean results.

Landing Pages

You can easily create multiple landing pages and see which has a higher conversion rate. More images? Fewer images? Placement of your call to action?

Testing can be an arduous process, but it is worthwhile as paid results can be expensive. In order to maximize your investment, always be testing and changing your purchases or copy based on results.

The data gathered from a test can be applied to all elements of the digital marketing strategy, but specifically it is most useful when developing organic optimization of keywords and even website content.

CHAPTER 18
Programmatic Display Media

KEY POINTS
- Display advertising and paid search advertising work best in a multi-channel campaign that also includes social media and affiliate marketing.
- Programmatic media is accomplished through an ad server and uses several data sources to target a user.
- Measure performance based on programmatic media metrics specific to hotels.

What is Programmatic Advertising?
Programmatic advertising helps automate the decision-making process of media buying by targeting specific audiences and demographics.

Programmatic display advertising platforms track consumer behavior through cookies placed on users' browsers. These cookies collect insights on users' behavior, and the data allows display platforms to deliver the right messaging to the consumer at the right time to convince them to buy your product.

For example, a travel-specific display network may have information about a consumer with a tendency to book luxury rooms who may be traveling to Chicago in 2 weeks. This creates an opportunity for luxury hotels in Chicago to advertise to this consumer. Alternatively, if your hotel's prime target audience is "college educated women aged 30-40 in the Southeast US," display networks will enable you to deploy ads to that audience with precision.

Why Programmatic Display?
There are millions of different combinations of target audiences – by age, geography, education, reading habits, personal hobbies, etc. Targeting specific audiences with this much detail is not feasible through manual optimization and would likely lead to a significant waste of advertising dollars. That's why programmatic advertising platforms use sophisticated algorithms, machine learning, and artificial intelligence to precisely target niche audiences at the most opportune time to drive high conversion rates[1]

Additionally, programmatic advertising platforms utilize machine learning to improve over time based on your current advertising performance and changing market dynamics.

Campaign Delivery
Programmatic based media can appear in a variety of digital environments, such as news sites, blogs, social networks, video sites, and mobile/tablet-based apps. Programmatic media is delivered to these environments via an ad server which allows an advertiser or agency to centrally manage the setup, trafficking, and reporting of their campaigns. An ad server is simply a web server backed by a database, which stores advertisements and delivers them to visitors of websites where advertising is enabled. Ad servers also perform important tasks like counting the number of impressions, clicks, and interactions for an ad campaign, as well as providing detailed reports that can help the advertiser determine the Return On Advertising Spend (ROAS) for ads on a particular website, platform, or network.

Programmatic Display Networks
The most common programmatic display networks for the hospitality industry include:

1. Google Display Network
2. Google Marketing Platform – Display and Video 360 (previously Doubleclick)
3. ADARA
4. Sojern

Google Display Network
The Google Display Network can help you reach people while they're browsing their favorite websites, watching a YouTube video, checking their Gmail account, or using mobile devices and apps. Google Display Network will put your ads in front of a user before they start searching for what you offer, which can be key for your overall advertising strategy. You can also remind people of what they're interested in, as in the case of remarketing to people who previously visited your site or app.

It is designed to help you find the right audience for your ads. Following are examples of how you can approach targeting:

- Find new customers or engage your existing customers using audiences – Similar audiences and in-market audiences allow you to target people who are most likely to be interested in your products, helping you find new prospective customers. You can also use data, like remarketing lists, to help you re-engage people who previously visited your site.

- Drive more conversions using automation – Automated targeting helps you get more conversions by finding high-performing audiences based on your existing audiences and landing page. By automatically optimizing over time, Google Ads can learn which audiences work for you. Automated bidding automatically adjusts your bid to help you meet your return on investment. Smart display campaigns combine the best of automated targeting, bidding, and creatives to maximize your conversions on Google Ads.

Display allows marketers to engage users with different ad formats, including:

- Responsive Display ads – Creating ads on the Google Display Network is partially automated with responsive ads. To create them, enter ad text, then add images and logo, and Google will optimize the ad to improve performance. Both new and advanced users benefit from responsive ads because they show as "native" ads, and blend into the font and feel of the publisher's site.

- Uploaded image ads – For more control, you can create and upload ads as images in different sizes or HTML5.

- Engagement ads – Run engaging image and video ads on YouTube and across the Display Network.

- Gmail ads – Show expandable ads on the top tabs of people's inboxes.

Google Marketing Platform – Display and Video 360 (previously Doubleclick)

Display and Video360 is Google's Enterprise level advertising platform which offers advertisers access to audience insights and targeting. According to Google, "Specialized options for keywords, demographics, and remarketing help you engage the right audiences. Manage your audiences in the same product where you execute media buys. Apply existing audience lists to your media plan, discover and create new audience segments, and reach the right people across screens by tapping into Google's unique understanding of intent. Apply machine learning to automate steps like bidding and optimization, helping you respond to customers' needs faster. Fueled by powerful machine learning algorithms, Display and Video360's automated bidding strategy drives performance at scale to help you reach your goals."

ADARA

According to ADARA, "ADARA offers people-based insights to increase marketing efficiency, foster growth, and maximize the value of your customer portfolio. The value-based understanding of your customers is fueled by travel patterns, trends, and behaviors representative of 750+ million monthly unique traveler profiles across more than 200 of the world's top travel brands. ADARA offers a full suite of media solutions, and uses predictive targeting to deliver on brand and performance goals. You can activate ADARA's traveler intelligence across your media plan to deliver on campaign objectives at scale."

Sojern

According to Sojern, "Sojern's platform is focused on travel, taking a true omni-channel approach that starts with building awareness. Your property is put in front of people who are in-market to travel to your destination, but may still be doing research. When these travelers are ready to book, Sojern drives them directly to your website where they complete the booking transaction. Sojern leverages the power of programmatic ad-buying technology across a wide-range of media channels including mobile, social, native, video, and the open web."

Key Elements of Implementing Programmatic Display Advertising

There are four important steps to take when implementing programmatic display advertising:

1. Setting your goals
2. Understanding your audience
3. Segmentation and targeting
4. Measuring performance

Setting Your Goals

A successful paid media campaign starts with your business goals. Depending on your business needs, map your digital media strategy by leveraging customer data to grow loyalty and business, using audience targeting and applying personalization strategies, continuous testing, and fine-tuning based on results and performance of your campaigns.

stages. If ROI is the primary focus, retargeting campaigns work well to drive higher ROI.

All major programmatic display advertising platforms provide opportunities for allocating marketing funds towards prospecting and retargeting. The actual split of funds between the 2 types of campaigns will depend on your goals.

Source: Milestone Inc.

As you are setting goals, it is important to consider that display campaigns can primarily be divided into two major categories: prospecting and retargeting.

Prospecting campaigns are focused on finding new customers for your hotel or business. Display campaigns are an ideal method of prospecting for new customers as the display networks enable you to enter detailed information about your audience profiles. Integrating your audience list (your email database, website data, etc.) enables the display networks to create audiences similar to your current audience, which means there is a greater likelihood of conversion. Typically, prospecting campaigns are focused on the top of the funnel or the "Awareness stage," hence they result in lower ROI. While this may be the case, it is still critical to allocate advertising funds to prospecting campaigns, otherwise you may not be attracting new customers to your property.

Retargeting campaigns focus on consumers who have already visited your website. These consumers have already expressed an interest in your company or product, and have proven intent; therefore, targeting them will result in higher ROI. These consumers are typically at the lower end of the funnel in the conversion

Understanding Your Audience

The core underlying strength of programmatic display strategies comes from precise targeting of your audience at scale. Prior to setting up display campaigns, it is critical for you to understand your audiences. In addition to the guest profile data in your hotel systems, there is a lot of data about your audiences available from social media channels such as Facebook or from Google Analytics.

Segmentation & Targeting

The next key element to implementing programmatic display advertising is segmenting your audience based on data and customer behavior. You must leverage the wealth of data and intelligence that are available – both from your own CRM data as well as from available advertising platforms – to create campaigns that are highly targeted based on customer behaviors and target demographics. Typical segmentations include:

- Geo-targeting
- Social interactions
- Psychographic attributes
- Incomes
- Likes and dislikes
- Hobbies

HOSPITALITY DIGITAL MARKETING ESSENTIALS:

Use your knowledge of your customer base to create targeted campaigns that focus on "like" consumers and provide offers to drive bookings to your website.

If your primary goal is to gain and retain a significant share of customers who are loyal to your brand, then your marketing strategies and tactics will be slightly different than if you are focused solely on acquiring new customers.

Before focusing on acquiring new customers, it is critical to create an action plan to retain brand-loyal customers. Own 100% of the share of impressions for your branded terms by allocating and maximizing budget for branded campaigns and consistent omnichannel personalized campaigns across devices. Deploy your marketing channel strategy based on CRM data, retargeting customers specific customers such as those who have visited your site but did not book.

Once you have gained a significant share of current and loyal customers, you can deploy strategies like in-market campaigns, business-focused and destination-specific "things to do," and FAQ campaigns across multiple online channels to attract new visitors with unbranded, yet targeted campaigns.

Measuring Performance
Display campaigns can be measured on their effectiveness using several KPIs. Several examples include:

- Advertising Metrics
  - Impressions (also called Views): How many people viewed the ad
  - Cost Per Thousand (CPM) Impressions: Cost/Impressions x 1000
  - Clicks: Number of people who click on the ad
  - Click Thru Rate (CTR): Number of clicks/ number of impressions served
  - Cost Per Action (CPA) or Cost Per Booking: Cost/Actions
  - Return on Ad Spend (ROAS): Revenue/ Spend
- Revenue Metrics
  - Total Room Nights Booked
  - Total Revenue
  - Assisted Revenue: Revenue booked via other channels after an interaction with the display ad

- Conversion Rate: Percentage of people who convert (book) compared to all users exposed to the ad
- Average Daily Rate (ADR): Revenue/ Number of nights
- Check Availability Rate: Percentage of people who enter the booking engine to check availability

Important Terminology to Know

The following definitions are taken from the IAB Wiki – Glossary of Interactive Advertising Terms.[2]

- AUDIENCE TARGETING: A method that enables advertisers to show an ad specifically to visitors based on their shared behavioral, demographic, geographic, and/ or technographic attributes.

- BEHAVIORAL TARGETING: Using previous online user activity (e.g., pages visited, content viewed, searches, clicks, and purchases) to generate a segment that is used to match advertising creative to users (sometimes also called Behavioral Profiling, Interest-based Advertising, or online behavioral advertising).

- CONTEXTUAL TARGETING: Targeting content that deals with topics, as determined by a contextual scanning technology.

- RETARGETING: A method that enables advertisers to show an ad specifically to visitors who previously were exposed to or interacted with the advertisers' creative.

- DEMOGRAPHIC TARGETING: A method that enables advertisers to show an ad specifically to visitors based on demographic information such as age, gender, and income which may come from site registration data or an inference-based mechanism.

- GEOGRAPHIC TARGETING: A method that enables advertisers to show an ad specifically to visitors based on zip code, area code, city, DMA, and state and/or country derived from user-declared registration information or inference-based mechanism.

- KEYWORD TARGETING: Targeting content that contains keywords.

- SEARCH RETARGETING: A method that enables advertisers to show an ad specifically to visitors based on one or more searches or search click events.

- SEMANTIC TARGETING: A type of contextual targeting that also incorporates semantic techniques to understand page meaning and/or sentiment.

- SITE RETARGETING: A method that enables advertisers to show an ad specifically to previous site visitors when they are on third-party websites.

- TIME-BASED TARGETING: A method that enables advertisers to show an ad specifically to visitors only on certain days of the week or times of the day (also known as Day Parting).

Chapter 18 Endnotes

1Programmatic Advertising & Media Buying. Marketing Land. https://marketingland.com/library/display-advertising-news/display-advertising-programmatic-media-buying. January 18, 2018.

2 IAB contributors. "IAB Wiki - Glossary of Interactive Advertising Terms." Interactive Advertising Bureau. Web. November 15, 2013.

Affiliate marketing is a performance-based advertising channel in which the advertiser rewards the publisher (affiliate) with a pre-determined commission for each lead or conversion that the publisher drives. Affiliates typically use online advertising methods (SEM, email, content, retargeting, display, etc.), which allows hotels and brands to extend their digital reach to attract potential guests. Typical affiliates include cash-back sites (Ebates.com), coupon/deals sites (Retailmenot.com), and blogs. Some affiliates offer a merchant's own website-enhancing technologies.

Many hotel brands offer affiliate programs geared towards driving direct traffic to their websites under a revenue share model. In the hospitality sector, affiliates predominantly operate on a commission model where the hotel/brand pays a percentage of revenue for every consumed booking delivered by an affiliate (typically a base of 3-5%). Other compensation methods include CPC (cost per click), CPA (cost per action), or CPM (cost per thousand views), although these models are not widely used in the affiliate channel.

Affiliate networks are often used for advertisers and affiliates to have a platform where they can more easily work together. Typically, the affiliate network allows merchants to quickly scale their programs by providing reporting, tracking, payment and refund processing, program management, and the access to a large database of publishers. For the affiliates, networks also offer easy registration for a merchant program and a central database of affiliate programs organized by category and popularity. Some of the biggest affiliate networks include ClickBank, Rakuten Linkshare, CJ Affiliate, ShareASale, Performance Horizon, and Impact.

Hotel advertisers can upload display banners and text links in which publishers can extract from the affiliate platform and place on their websites. All tracking elements are included into the creative to record the click or transaction. Advertisers can also purchase flat-rate media with the publishers for additional exposure. This includes Homepage placements, travel category placements, email blasts, and more.

Many advertisers are now working with Influencers and Influencer Networks through affiliate platforms to allow for a centralized set-up. The influencer agrees to the terms and conditions set within the platform, and reporting and payment happens within the network.

Hoteliers should consider this tactic as a part of their broader digital strategy offered through Performance Marketing. Across the globe, affiliate marketing has been proven successful to drive increased website traffic and revenues in a cost-efficient manner.

CHAPTER 20
Metasearch

Metasearch sites are shopping comparison sites that allow consumers to compare hotels' prices between suppliers and OTAs. TripAdvisor, Kayak, and Trivago are the largest traditional metasearch sites, and Google's Hotel Ads product follows the metasearch model as well. The cost model varies slightly per partner, but the most prevalent is CPC (cost per click) auction based (either 1st price auction or 2nd price auction).

Historically metasearch has been a channel shift product, where suppliers are competing against the OTAs to drive direct bookings. One of the recent trends has been the addition of share shift products that allow hotels to purchase paid placements that move their property to the top of the search results. Examples of share shift products include TripAdvisor Sponsored Listings, Google Promoted Hotels, and Kayak Inline Ads.

In addition to the traditional metasearch listings, TripAdvisor also offers a subscription plan called Business Advantage. Business Advantage is an annual subscription with which a hotel pays to have a link to their website, phone number, and hotel deal along with access to TripAdvisor's back end tools that allow a hotel to optimize their page.

Social media is distinctly different from all other forms of digital advertising. Social media-based ad placements are designed to integrate with the actual content and therefore the consumer experience within the site. This form of ad placement is referred to as an "in-stream" placement and, unlike traditional digital media placements, offers the ability for a consumer to both share, like, dislike, and comment on the ad unit. For this reason, it is often considered a best practice to create ad units which are not just content based but also informational and entertaining in nature to drive consumer interactions.

Examples of social media websites include Facebook, Instagram, Pinterest, Twitter, and Four Square. See Chapter 15 for more information on social platforms.

Native advertising placement shares many of the same characteristics of social media and is most effective when it is promoting the promise of rich content which offers both informational and entertainment value to the consumer. However, there are two distinct differences between social media and native ad placements. First, native ad placements historically live within the same websites where you would traditionally find programmatic-based display and video media. Second, native ad placements do not offer the same sharing or commenting functionality which social media-based ads have.

Both social media and native ad units are inherently mobile friendly in nature and therefore often the preferred methods when the desire is to target a consumer while they are on a mobile device.

Within social media advertising, each channel has its own unique opportunities and challenges. By far the most popular social channels for hotels are Facebook, LinkedIn, and Instagram, because hotels see high level of engagement as well as some revenue and leads being driven through these channels.

The approach to social media advertising is similar to any other ad campaign reviewed in Chapters 17 and 18. You will want to focus on the same key areas covered:

- Setting goals
- Determining the right audience
- Ad creation
- Budgeting for the initiative
- Measuring performance/testing

Setting Expectations & Goals

What is your desired outcome for your social media advertising campaigns? You first need to be able to answer questions such as: Do you want to focus on new guest acquisition? Creating brand awareness? Do you want to drive ancillary revenue on property (spa bookings, dining reservations, etc.)? Are you trying to increase your loyal customer base?

Once you have determined your objectives, then you can determine the best way to reach your goals. The strategy around setting goals for most social channels has multiple options such as:

- Drive clicks/traffic to website
- Drive clicks/traffic to social company page
- Boost the visibility of a specific post promoting an event or promotion
- Convert to a booking
- Increase social channel followers

For example, your desired outcome may be to promote a holiday weekend package on your website. You can drive people from your social ad directly to the landing page of your website promoting that package, or you can drive them to a products page on your social channel which encourages them to follow or like your page in order to qualify for future promotions. One outcome increases bookings, and one outcome increases your targeted list and helps build a bigger audience for future marketing efforts.

Understanding Your Audience

Social channels provide a multitude of targeting options. Most channels offer you the ability to target new customers, or communicate to your existing followers – or target an audience that has similarities with the audience that is already a follower of your brand. This is typically referred to as targeting "like" audiences. A few audience targeting examples you should consider follow.

Location

Is your hotel primarily visited by people from a certain location? For example, do you run a small hotel in the Adirondacks that draws primarily from the NYC area? Or perhaps the vast majority of the guests at your hotel in wine country come from LA?

Demographics

Does your hotel target a particular age group? Gender? College graduates? Married couples? Depending on your location, Facebook offers a range of demographic attributes to choose from.

Interests

What are the demand generators near you? Great sights, attractions, or even restaurants? Why are your current guests coming to visit your area? Make sure to target for those interests. What are your guests' hobbies? Are you looking for soccer players, knitting enthusiasts, or backcountry skiers?

Connections

Who is already connected with your brand? Do you want to reach these people who have an established affinity for your hotel? Or, do you want to specifically exclude them in order to focus on finding new people to (for example) like your page?

Ad Creation

Each platform offers different ad types and ad requirements. We cover some best practices in the specific areas of Facebook, Instagram, and LinkedIn later in this chapter but the same rules apply for all ad creation – be sure the visual component is compelling, use your keywords in your ad copy, and ensure you are communicating messaging that will most likely appeal to your target audiences. Every ad should have some call to action (CTA).

Budget

Most platforms allow you to determine a daily budget and a duration for your ad to run. You can also choose a total budget and duration and the daily budget will be automatically calculated. Most platforms offer suggestions on the probable response rate so you are able to determine if the amount of spend is going to reach the return you want.

Measuring/Tracking/Analytics

Most platforms provide robust tracking for your ad performance. If you have set up your goals correctly, most of the platforms will analyze exactly how close you are to meeting or exceeding your expectations, and you can adjust your budget or extend your promotion based on your success.

While every social media platform has unique offerings based on their user behaviors, we will go into a bit more detail for three of the more popular platforms in order to show the similarities and differences.

Facebook

Setting Goals

The first step in the Facebook advertising process is to determine what goal(s) you are aiming to achieve.

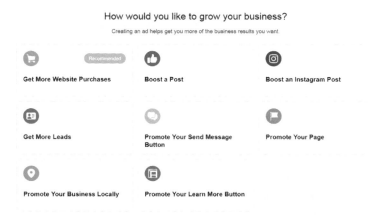

Source: www.marketing360.com

Before you reach this point, you should have determined your desired outcome for this promotion. Do you want to create awareness, increase leads, promote a specific event? The bigger answer should drive which route you want to take here. If you want to create awareness for your property, perhaps you should promote your page. If you want to increase leads for events, weddings, meetings and/or groups, select get more leads.

Following is a sample ad with the simple goal of increasing page likes – or page promotion:

This ad for Crown Reef Resort puts their 4-story oceanfront waterpark front, a unique and popular amenity that they offer, front and center.

TIP: Use high quality images that showcase unique property amenities or upgraded rooms and features.

Source: Fuel[3]

A strong caveat around promoting your FB page – yes, increasing likes on your page may seem fantastic on its own – but you must be sure to think strategically about your target audience because they will only continue to engage with you organically if you are reaching the right consumer for your property. If you simply buy "likes" or entice likes from people who have no real interest in your property, you will have low engagement rates which will harm your organic reach.

Facebook Lead Generation Ads For Hotels

Here are a few examples of lead generation ads that we have successfully run in the past:

The ads above ran for two Myrtle Beach resorts, Crown Reef and Captain's Quarters. Each ad features an enticing, high quality image that highlights one of the resort amenities and clearly communicates what the visitor can expect by joining the email list.

TIP: Test different form fields to find the sweet spot of information and length. The more info you can collect, the better, but be wary of asking for too much too soon.

Source: Fuel[4]

As you can see, based on your objectives, your approach to FB ads will vary greatly. So first, define your desired outcome or goal.

Your Audience

FB offers you a wide range of audience options. You first must choose between all of Facebook or only those members of Facebook who have previously interacted with your page. Within each, you can then narrow your focus by selecting age and gender, interests, education level, etc.

FB provides specific best practices for targeting audiences for hotels[1]. One best practice is to target your ads to people based on their travel dates and location:

- People with specific travel dates or booking windows
- People looking to travel on the weekends
- People with travel dates or with no travel dates
- People searching for specific destinations

To reach people who are interested in traveling, consider targeting:

- People with high travel intent signals (e.g., time spent on a site or the number of searches on a site)
- People traveling alone, in groups or with kids
- People who searched for or booked flights recently but haven't booked hotels
- High value audiences (e.g., loyalty members)

Also, consider excluding people who don't meet certain qualifications:

- People whose travel dates have passed
- People who have flights with the same departure & return date and won't need a hotel

One of the most interesting features in FB advertising is the ability to target lookalike audiences. You can import a mailing list of your best customers for example and ask FB to create a lookalike audience based on who is a current customer. You can then further adjust the demographics of that lookalike audience, but it is a fantastic tool if your end goal is to grow your customer base.

Creating Ads

FB offers multiple ad options – a single image, a video, a carousel (or several images), or a slideshow (which becomes a video with up to 10 images).

You will need to write a compelling headline. Make sure it appeals to your target audience. If you are searching for new customers, you want to make sure your headline matches what your research tells you might be appealing about your property to that audience. If you are retargeting existing customers, you want a reminder of why they like you. Typically you only have up to 25 characters for your headline. Headlines are a great way to test your ads – create two ads that are the same in every way but change the headline and see which draws better engagement.

Next you will write the body or text of the ad. Typically you have up to 90 characters for the text of your ad. That is not a lot of space so choose your text wisely. Keywords are important here too – and can make the ads compelling.

Finally you should have some call to action (CTA), based on your goals. Book now, Contact us, Learn more, download; these are just a few of the call to action options you have available. This CTA should be a logical next step based on your ad and your audience. If your audience knows you, Book Now might be a reasonable call to action, especially if you are promoting a specific event. If you are trying to create awareness, a simple "Learn More" might be your best option.

As you are creating your ad, you should always test to see how it will appear on a desktop or on a mobile device. You may also choose to target only mobile or desktop with ads.

Budget

FB allows you to allocate a daily budget and set a time limit for how long an ad will run. Based on the criteria that you set, FB will also let you know the projected results you can expect so you can make adjustments to your daily bid, duration, or placement based on their predictive analysis.

Measurement

Check your progress frequently on your results page in FB. You can see if your ad is resonating, if you need to make adjustments to the creative, or perhaps change your audience. You can make modifications to an ad in process if you feel it is required. You should always tie your end results back to your original intent. If you were testing your ad, which elements performed better? Make note to use that format again in the future.

Here is the typical data you will see:

- Number of people reached
- Number of engagements
- A breakdown of engagement metrics by action taken (comments, share, views)
- Demographic breakdowns by age, gender, location, and interest.
- How much you spent

You are able to sort this data in a pretty wide variety of views – by the hour or by the day for instance. You can also compare performances of ads over different time periods. In general FB makes it easy for you to evaluate when your ads are most effective.

Facebook Pixels

FB offers you the ability to retarget easily by creating a FB pixel. You can place this pixel on your website and FB can then track which visitors went from your ad to your website, but perhaps did not convert. This information allows you to see who has some interest but for a variety of reasons didn't convert. You can then create additional content and advertising to appeal to that specific audience – which has historically shown the best ROI for hotel marketers.

Instagram

As FB is the parent company of Instagram, most of the advertising information is the same. However, Instagram behaviors are different from FB so you have to take an Instagram-specific approach. Instagram is a much more visual platform and placing traditional ads will not be as effective. You will need to use visuals to tell your story much more so than text.

You can run ads in three ways on Instagram currently:

1. Run ads directly from Instagram
2. Create ads from your FB page
3. Create ad campaigns in Ads Manager (in FB)

You will need to set up a business profile in Instagram and ensure that it is linked to your FB account.

You can currently only add the following call-to-action buttons to your business profile on Instagram:

- Buy/Get Tickets
- Start Order
- Book (Book an appointment)
- Reserve (Make a reservation)

The following are currently the only Insights you can view from the Insights tab on your profile:

- Activity: This section lets you view important Insights on your profile, including Interactions (such as profile visits and website clicks) and Discovery (how many people see your content and where they find it).
- Content: This section lets you view Insights on your Posts, Stories, and Promotions.
- Audience: This section tells you more about your followers and audience.

Similar to FB, you can also boost your individual Instagram posts in addition to creating ads.

What about video? Instagram has recently launched IGTV. It is a quickly evolving platform and currently you can promote your IGTV channel (which hosts your pre-recorded vertical videos) via sharing on stories or on your FB channel – not through promoted ads. However, this area is new and changing quickly so be sure to check back as this could be a valuable resource for hoteliers in the near future.

LinkedIn

Not surprising, LinkedIn advertising follows along the same lines as the others. You want to set your goals, identify your audience, create your ad, and track results. However, while Instagram favors visuals, LinkedIn favors text – or really in the case of LinkedIn, content. In general, LinkedIn is a great way to reach more of a B2B audience: meeting and event planners and wedding planners for instance.

In terms of setting goals – you should be aware that there are currently several ways to advertise on LinkedIn.

Sponsored Content

While Instagram wants you to tell a story visually, LinkedIn sponsored content lets you use your words. You are able to write articles, share white papers, or use any content that your audience might find interesting.

HOSPITALITY DIGITAL MARKETING ESSENTIALS:

Here are a few LinkedIn best practice recommendations for sponsored content:

- Analyze industry news instead of just sharing it. Offering insights and key takeaways will keep your content from feeling generic, and help establish thought leadership in your field.
- Add content curation to your plan. Share information that is useful and relevant to your audience, without creating it all yourself. Always credit your source.
- Repurpose your own content. Remember to check your blog, website, and social media channels instead of creating new content every time.
- Use rich media (like video, audio, or other element) by incorporating YouTube, Vimeo, and SlideShare videos. They play right in the LinkedIn feed, so your audience can engage organically.
- Include human interest stories that connect to your brand, and you will help your audience establish an emotional connection.

Sponsored inMail

You can contact your potential audience via LinkedIn InMail. You can take a more personal approach by appearing to have sent an individual email, speaking directly to that prospect with this approach.

Best practices for sponsored InMail follow traditional prospecting email guidelines. Make it personal, make it relevant, make it interesting. Write for your audience. If you are targeting influencers, create value for them to share your content. If you are writing to decision makers, ask for next steps in your call to action.

LinkedIn suggests that the best performing subject lines use some of the following key words: thanks; exclusive invitation; connect; job opportunities; or join us.

Text Ads, Carousel Ads, Video Ads, Dynamic Ads

These ads will show up in newsfeeds and will be noted as sponsored.

Dynamic Ads are personalized ads tailored to each member based on each member's own LinkedIn profile data including profile photo, company name, and job title.

Advertisers only need to build their creative and write their ad copy once, and LinkedIn will automatically personalize their campaign for each person in their audience.

With that in mind, you can determine what your goal is and what avenue you should pursue based on those goals.

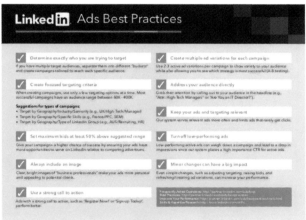

Your Audience

You are able to select your target audience in the following categories in the LinkedIn environment.

- Experience: Function, Title, Seniority, Years of Experience
- Company: Name, Industry, Size, Followers, Connections
- Education: Schools, Degrees, Fields of Study
- Interests: Skills, Groups
- Identity: Location, Age, Gender

Similar to lookalike audiences in FB, LinkedIn also offers advanced targeting via their Audience Expansion option. You can also use Matched Audiences to customize LinkedIn audiences with your own business data so that you can re-engage website visitors with website retargeting, nurture prospects with Contact targeting, and run account-based marketing campaigns with Account Targeting.

Enable Lead Gen Forms to capture more qualified leads. This feature pulls LinkedIn profile data (like job title, company name, and contact details) into a form that members can submit with one click.

Measure and Optimize

LinkedIn provides analytics similar to other networks. You are able to track your traffic, your engagement, and your conversions. You can see how your targeted audience is behaving and compare your results over different time periods.

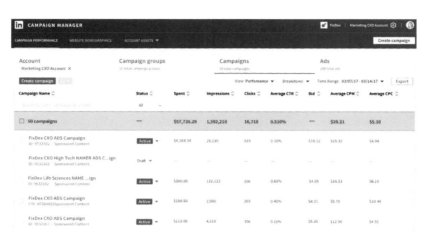

Source: Marketing Land

Install the LinkedIn Insight Tag on your website, so you can track conversions and enable demographic reporting on your website visitors.

You should also optimize for mobile. Make your landing pages an easy place to view, navigate, and submit information from a smartphone.

Always Be Testing[2]

- Run A/B tests to compare multiple messages or versions of your ad creative. You'll see which one resonates most with your target audience.

- Use A/B testing to optimize targeting, too. Create a campaign, duplicate it, and alter the targeting criteria slightly. Run both campaigns to learn which audiences are more receptive to your content.

   ▪ Include 2-4 ads in each campaign. Campaigns with more ads usually reach more people in your target audience.

   ▪ Every 1-2 weeks, pause the ad with the lowest engagement and replace it with new ad creative. Over time, this will improve your ad relevance score (based on indicators that LinkedIn members find the ads interesting, such as clicks, comments, and shares), which will help you win more bids.

- Use Direct Sponsored Content to test different ad creatives and targeting combinations. This ad type is only shown to the campaign target audience, never on your LinkedIn Page.

Chapter 21 Endnotes

1 *"Best Practices for Promoting Hotel Inventory Using Travel Ads." Facebook Business. Web. April 30, 2019. https://www.facebook.com/business/help/872000339596842*

2 *"Sponsored Content tips." LinkedIn Marketing Solutions. Web. April 30, 2019. https://business.linkedin.com/marketing-solutions/success/best-practices/sponsored-content-tips*

3 *"The Best Facebook Ad Formats For Hotels." Fuel. Web. March 20, 2017. https://www.fueltravel.com/blog/the-best-facebook-ad-formats-for-hotels/*

4 *"The Best Facebook Ad Formats For Hotels." Fuel. Web. March 20, 2017. https://www.fueltravel.com/blog/the-best-facebook-ad-formats-for-hotels/*

Additional Resources:

- *Hotel Facebook Marketing: Your Guide To Getting Results – https://otiumboutique.com/hotel-facebook-marketing-guide/*

- *Facebook Ads for Hotels: Everything You Need to Know – https://www.abacus.agency/facebook-ads-for-hotels-everything-you-need-to-know/*

- *Facebook Ads: Hotel Marketing Advanced Targeting – https://www.hotel-internet-marketing.com/blog/facebook-ads-advanced-targeting-hotel-marketing/*

Many of the OTA's have paid media models where you can purchase "media assets" that will try to drive bookings (in some cases within the "walled garden" of the OTA). These are helpful in need periods but one must be careful as the cost for acquisition needs to be calculated as your margin plus the media cost divided by your revenue. Not all options are available for all OTA's. Expedia Media Solutions has the largest collection of paid media options but all have some opportunity to pay for added visibility within their website. It should be noted some brands restrict the type of OTA paid media a hotel can participate in – for example, mobile and/or last-minute deals. It is important to note that some OTA campaigns allow you to drive traffic to 1) your OTA listing, or 2) your brand.com site to "book direct." The destination URL should be discussed when choosing a campaign and selecting the goal/ROI.

Following are some of the paid media options available by OTA.

Expedia Media Solutions

Expedia Media Solutions includes Expedia, Hotels.com, Travelocity, Orbitz, Hotwire, Cheaptickets, ebookers.com, wotif, lastminute.com.au, and Mr.Jet.se.

- TravelAds / Sponsored Listing is one of the most common forms of paid placements on Expedia and allows a hotel to pay for premium placement in addition to the organic listing. These are typically pay per click (PPC) models with a minimum bid. Ads can be targeted by country of origin, booking window, length of stay, etc.

- TravelAds Direct is a pay-per-click advertising program that drives shoppers to book directly with the hotel. The sponsored listings appear in premium placements alongside hotel search results and feature the hotel's brand logo and URL.

- Accelerator Program is a bid for placement commodity that hotels may opt into as a measure to move their ranking up from later pages into the first page of results in Expedia. A hotel pays an extra % in margin to get preferred placement, on top of what they already pay for commissions, to

ensure visibility for select, targeted dates.

- Display Advertising (other OTA's have versions of this) includes custom banner ads within the website. Ads can be customized within the booking funnel, responsive, or via sponsorships that allow the hotel to be the official brand sponsor for site-wide and holiday sales.

- Passport Audience Extension Ads allow a hotel to follow the consumer through the buying journey with targeted ads anywhere on the internet.

- Co-Op Campaigns combine display advertising with custom landing pages. While most often used with CVBs and visitors bureaus, hotels or a collection of hotels or brands could utilize.

- Email marketing is available through dedicated email to an Expedia Group targeted audience or via featured ad placement on specific Expedia Group brand newsletters.

- Egencia Travel Ads allows for advertising within Expedia Groups corporate travel program (similar to a GDS). Ads are pay per click and can be placed throughout the booking process.

Booking.com

- Genius Program (some version of this is available on other OTAs) allows hotels to pay an extra % in margin to get preferred placement, special tags, and ranking boosts.

- Preferred Program is status-based program that hotels qualify for, and they must maintain the criteria. There is an increase in commission to participate. Preferred properties get extra visibility in search results next to a thumbs up sign that indicates they have met the criteria.

- Visibility Booster is a short-term option to increase a hotel's ranking and visibility during short, specific dates.

Priceline

- Display Advertising using a pay-per-click (PPC) model that includes preferred placement and ads. Text or video options.

- Email Sponsorships allow you to pay for advertising within the brand newsletter.
- Custom Landing pages can be built at additional costs to drive ads directly to your hotel page.
- Click Off Campaigns – Available through some business listings but not common;

sometimes OTA's will allow you to buy display advertising that enables you to send clicks to your own website.

CTrip
- Pay for preferred placement to attract Chinese consumers.

CHINESE OUTBOUND TRAVELLERS

HSMAI has focused this publication on the best practices for hoteliers looking to apply digital marketing strategies to improve results. In most countries, there are several large players that dominate the search and travel landscape, so we have focused on processes and tactics which will work across local search engines and social channels regardless of which ones you use. The one large market that stands out is China; this is a market that needs to be addressed separately for two reasons: the sheer size of the market (China is already the world's largest outbound travel market) and because China has its own social and search engines.

FAST FACTS
- China is a country of 1.4 billion people and over 5,000 years of history. There are 33 provinces, municipalities, autonomous regions, and special administrative regions (SAR).
- The Chinese outbound market is set to grow further. By 2020 it is expected that more domestic travellers will graduate to overseas trips, pushing annual outbound traffic to 160 million1.
- Chinese Tourists are not homogenous; there are 8 archetypes with drastically different preferences and behaviours2.
- Chinese outbound travellers are getting younger, their spending behaviour is becoming more rational, and more are seeking quality instead of being price sensitive.
- Fifty-six percent of travellers across all segments look for mid-range hotels. In pursuit of quality, 21 percent of aspirants seek luxury hotels, and base their choice on key opinion leaders and social media. The same proportion of individuals opt for a luxury hotel in search of a unique travel experience. Budget hotel operators should be thinking about the 31 percent of unplugged travellers who don't care as much about accommodation.
- Websites should be hosted on servers in China so they can get the .cn domain. Though as noted below, most companies just create WeChat pages due

to expense and complications of creating websites in China.

WHAT CHANNELS DO CHINESE CONSUMERS USE?
- Mobile is the predominant channel consumers use to access the internet in China. WeChat, Weibo, Baidu, and Ctrip are among some of the more predominant online tools Chinese consumers use.
- WeChat
  - Owned by Chinese tech giant Tencent, WeChat has more than a billion monthly users, just behind WhatsApp and Facebook Messenger. But it offers so much more than messaging, allowing its users to do everything from payments to booking flights and hotels. One of its key features is "mini-programs," which are apps within WeChat. More and more, hotels are using mini-programs instead of developing a Chinese language website.
  - If you're buying something online in China, there will be an option to purchase with WeChat Pay. You will need to put in a passcode or use a biometric authentication tool to authorize the transaction. Instant money transfers to your WeChat contacts can also be made via the messaging function, which makes it easy to split bills or just move money around China. It is possible to be nearly cashless in China and actually go out for the day without a wallet.
- Weibo
  - Akin to Twitter in China, it is one of the largest platforms.

- Baidu
    - The predominant search engine in China, Baidu should be approached similarly to Google when it comes to advertising and SEO.
- Online Travel Agents for Chinese Consumers
    - CTrip – the second largest OTA in the world with almost 80% of all online travel transactions in China leading back to it3 – http://www.ctrip.com/
    - eLong – allows travellers to book hotels and air tickets –http://www.elong.com/
    - Zanadu – targeted to high-end travellers – https://zanadu.cn/site/partnership.html

HSMAI will continue to provide information and resources around this fast-growing source market. Follow developing information at https://hsmaiacademy.org/hotel-marketing-to-chinese-guests/

Chapter 22 Endnotes

1 *"Hu nyíng to the new Chinese traveller." McKinsey & Company. Web. November 2018. https://www.mckinsey.com/industries/travel-transport-and-logistics/our-insights/huanying-to-the-new-chinese-traveler*

2 *"Hu nyíng to the new Chinese traveller." McKinsey & Company. Web. November 2018. https://www.mckinsey.com/industries/travel-transport-and-logistics/our-insights/huanying-to-the-new-chinese-traveler*

3 *"Ask the hotel experts: 'Attracting Chinese tourists is no longer one-size-fits-all'." SiteMinder. Web. May 10, 2019. https://www.siteminder.com/r/marketing/hotel-digital-marketing/attract-chinese-tourists-hotel/*

PART 5: DIGITAL INTERMEDIARIES

CHAPTER 23
Online Travel Agencies (OTAs)

KEY POINTS

- History of the OTA segment and characteristics of the primary OTA models.
- Understand what makes OTAs a compelling choice in the journey of the consumer.
- Best practices in working with OTAs to deliver a long-term, sustainable ROI.
- How to think about content marketing and user experience on an OTA in addition to your direct strategy.

SUMMARY

There are four primary business models for Online Travel Agencies (OTAs) — retail, merchant, opaque/auction, and metasearch sites. It is critical to understand the differences of each in order to take full advantage of these channels for your hotel. As a part of an overall digital marketing strategy, determining how to reach consumers usually means working with OTAs as their websites are often a preferred research and booking point for consumers. Typically, consumers using OTAs are brand agnostic and often price-conscious, searching for a cheaper way to book their travel. Determining which OTAs will provide hotels with incremental revenues at long term sustainable cost requires a thorough understanding of the models and specific OTA marketing efforts. Recent consolidation in the OTA segment has resulted in a duopoly in the U.S. and Europe, while Asia still has several regional sites looking to expand beyond their primary countries.

OTAs contribute about 12% of hotel bookings, according to the report Demystifying the Digital Marketplace.[1] Overall, growth rates in OTA have outpaced Brand.com, however Brand.com is still a larger component of the revenue pie thanks in part to aggressive Book Direct campaigns launched by many hotel chains in 2016. According to the Demystifying the Digital Marketplace report, Brand.com across the industry is still almost twice the source of business for hotels compared to OTA (20% vs. 12%) although those percentages can vary widely depending on location, brand and size of hotel.

A Brief History

As the overall internet has evolved over the years, OTAs have proliferated as relevant research and booking channels. For a more complete history of the channel, Skift produced the Definitive Oral History of Online Travel[2] in 2016. Here are some highlights of how this segment of the digital marketing landscape has grown.

- In the 1980s, American Airlines subsidiary Sabre developed eAAsySabre to allow consumers to make flight, hotel, or car reservations through early internet service providers like Compuserve and AOL.
- In 1991, Hotel Reservations Network and Travelscape pioneered the wholesale model of buying blocks of rooms and reselling them through other channels, which became the "merchant model."
- In 1996, Sabre launched Travelocity.com, the first website to allow consumers to book directly and purchase airline tickets online without using a travel agent.
- Later that year, Microsoft launched the online travel booking site MSFT Expedia Travel Services, which later was shortened to Expedia.com.
- In 1997, Booking.com was founded in Amsterdam as booking.nl and Priceline.com was launched.
- Ctrip and eLong in China were both founded in 1999.
- Hotwire launched in 2000 and Orbitz in 2001.
- In 2001, Hotel Reservations Network was acquired by USA Networks (which then became InterActiveCorp or IAC). Hotel Reservations soon thereafter changed its name to the brand Hotels.com and later in 2001, IAC acquired a controlling stake in Expedia.com.
- In 2003, IAC acquired the opaque travel site Hotwire and in 2005, IAC spun-off its travel businesses — Expedia, Hotels.com, Hotwire, corporate travel site Egencia, and TripAdvisor — into what is today known as Expedia, Inc.

- In 2004, early stage team members from Orbitz, Travelocity, and Expedia co-founded Kayak.com as the first travel metasearch site.
- In 2005, The Priceline Group acquired the European hotel booking website Booking.com, and metsearch site Trivago was launched
- In 2007, Kayak bought metasearch competitor SideStep.com, which it shut down in 2011.
- In 2008, Expedia acquired the Italian OTA site Venere.com, giving them the backend system to launch the retail model in Europe in addition to their legacy merchant model.
- In 2010 and 2011, the growth of specialty metasearch engines continued with the launch of Hipmunk and Room 77. In 2011, Expedia Inc. spun off TripAdvisor.
- In 2012, Expedia bought Trivago, which it then took public in 2016. Also in 2012, Kayak went public and four months later was acquired by the Priceline group.
- In 2014, TripAdvisor launched its Instant Booking feature, enabling consumers to book directly with hotels, which was paired with a metasearch component which TripAdvisor had launched years before. Over the years, TripAdvisor acquired dozens of niche online travel companies, including Oyster.com, FlipKey, GateGuru, Viator, and Jetsetter, as well as restaurant review/reservation sites.
- In 2015 and 2016, the OTA market entered a phase of consolidation, with Expedia acquiring Travelocity and Orbitz. With these transactions, Priceline and Expedia control 90+% of the OTA marketplace, creating a duopoly for booking channel OTAs in the U.S. and Europe. In late 2016, CTrip acquired the metasearch site Skyscanner.

OTA Models

There are four primary OTA business models: retail (or agency), merchant, opaque/auction, and metasearch.

Retail Model

Much like a traditional travel agent, the consumer books through an intermediary and pays the hotel directly on checkout. The hotel then pays the intermediary a commission (or margin), typically 10-20%. This model is also sometimes referred to as the "published" or "agency" model. Room revenue for retail OTA bookings is captured on the hotel income statement as a gross rate, or what the consumer paid. In an example with a room revenue of $200 and a commission rate of 20%, the income statement would look like this:

Room revenue = $200
Commission paid (@ 20%) = $40
Net room revenue = $160

Booking.com is the leading site worldwide using the Retail model. Expedia's Hotel Collect or Expedia Traveler Preference (ETP) model also employs this method of reservation and payment. Typically, this model also operates more like a traditional reservation where the guest can cancel until the day of the reservation (or with a longer lead time if the hotel utilizes a stronger cancellation policy), which often results in high cancellation rates. Marketers and revenue teams need to monitor these cancellation rates as they plan their sellout strategies as markets with long lead times or days to arrival (DTA) can be impacted by retail model cancellations.

Merchant Model

The merchant model was created by former wholesale tour operators and later adopted by OTAs, most notably Expedia. Initially, OTAs would negotiate room blocks just like wholesalers and guarantee payment for those rooms, but today that practice has largely gone away. Here, the traveler pays the OTA by credit card directly upon booking, so the OTA becomes the "merchant of record" hence the model name. The OTA charges the traveler a room rate, which is a combination of the hotel's net rate and the OTA's commission (or margin). The net rate is the actual revenue the hotel receives for the room while the margin is the negotiated fee that the OTA charges for its service. Typically, in this model, the guest will pay the OTA up front on their credit card and, after the traveler's stay, the OTA pays the hotel the net rate via their own credit card or other payment processing system.

Under the merchant model, a hotel provides OTAs net rates that are typically 12 to 25 percent below published levels. This discount is usually consistent with the Retail model commission rate. The OTA will then offer the hotel on its site to make the room rate equal to the published rate. To maintain rate integrity, many hotels require that the room rate charged by OTAs equal the hotels' officially published rate, also known as rate parity. In the EU rate parity has come under fire, and now OTAs are not required to publish the same rate, which can lead to consumer confusion about what the lowest rate really is.

A variation of the merchant model is the package model. In the package model, the consumer is offered a bundled price where the hotel rate is combined with a rate for another travel product such as an airline ticket or car rental. OTAs often require a deeper discount (an additional 10% or more) for package rates versus hotel room only rates. Packages are typically booked farther in advance, for longer lengths of stay, and are often chosen by guests that will have higher incremental spend.

Room revenue for merchant OTA booking is captured on the hotel income statement as a net rate. The amount the OTA pays the hotel does not include the OTA margin, which some call a hidden marketing expense as it does not show up on the income statement directly. In our example with a room rate of $200, the net room revenue is still $160 but the commission paid at 20% ($40) is kept by the OTA up front. No marketing expense shows up on the hotel's P&L.

Since merchant model reservations are prepaid, typically their cancellation rates are much lower than the retail model.

Opaque/Auction Model

This model involves the consumer not knowing the name or brand of hotel chosen until after booking, hence the term "opaque" as there is no transparency about which hotel the consumer is booking. Priceline invented the "Name Your Own Price" opaque model in 1997 which employed an auction model where consumers would bid on discounted airline tickets. Priceline quickly expanded the model to include hotel rooms and other verticals. Hotwire launched its version of opaque travel products in 2001 using a posted price rather than a bidding model. Opaque/auction sites are popular with price-sensitive travelers who are not concerned about the brand they use.

In exchange for the 'opaque' nature of the transaction, typically hotels will offer discounts to these sites of 20% all the way up to 60% off of the best available rate. Most hotels using these channels only do so to yield last minute revenue when they are not going to fill, or over future slow period dates. Hotels must be mindful of using these channels however to ensure that they are truly opaque and that consumers are not 100% certain of which hotel they will get when making a booking. Analysis of reports provided by the opaque site will give the hotel insights about the opacity of their property.

In the opaque model, the consumer makes a non-refundable commitment to purchase based on the rate offered within a given competitive set which is defined as a specific star rating and a general location (e.g., 3-star hotels in Midtown Manhattan). Once the consumer has clicked "buy," the opaque site will select which of the hotels in the comp set with which to secure the booking. While this model is radically different relative to the traditional OTA model, from a transactional perspective it can be considered a variation of the merchant model, as the customer pays the OTA directly and the hotel bills the OTA for payment on a net rate basis.

Priceline continues to be the market leader in opaque hotel sales, and morphed its model to also include a posted price (yet still opaque) offering in 2012. Through its parent company Expedia, Hotwire has sometimes offered its inventory on Expedia, Hotels.com, and Travelocity. Recently the opaque model appears to be waning somewhat in consumer usage due to more sophisticated hotel revenue management systems and policies, and the availability of other last-minute booking channels like the mobile-only app HotelTonight.

Metasearch Model

As discussed in Chapter 21, metasearch sites now have many paid media options and several of the metasearch (and search companies like Google) are starting to test CPA models, thus blurring the line between media partner and travel agency/OTA partner. In reality, the OTAs have been doing this for a long time with both their travel agency model and their media model. The most important thing for marketers to consider is the **total cost of acquisition**. This calculation should be made regardless of whether it is a commission, net rate, or marketing expense.

Consumer Perceptions and Behavior

OTAs are popular because they simplify the search and selection process for travel consumers. Instead of researching multiple individual hotel or brand websites, a shopper can go to one OTA site and search many hotels in a specific location for a particular date, all at one time. The name, location, availability, and price of each hotel appears in an easy-to-read format to aid decision-making. Robust content including hotel details, high resolution photos, and traveler reviews are also key components to aid comparison shopping on OTAs.

Also, some OTAs offer the ability to search multiple travel products including flights, car rentals, vacation packages, and cruises, which make them a very viable "one stop shop" for many brand agnostic shoppers. This ease of shopping is enhanced as the OTAs are able to segment their traffic and conduct A|B (or multivariate) tests, as well as ethnographic consumer research. Given their broader reach beyond just one vertical (hotels) or brand, they are typically able to innovate much faster than brands can. In 2015, a Bloomberg article reported that Expedia processed over 7.5 billion air searches and ran over 1,750 tests on their sites.[3]

Fueling this strategy to test and learn is the OTA's relentless passion for consumer marketing. Even a small uptick in conversion on an OTA site can mean millions in bookings and revenue for large OTAs. Funded by the commissions and fees they collect on travel bookings made on their sites, OTAs are able to take that revenue and put it back into their marketing strategies and technology. Often, OTAs have deep expertise in offline and online marketing and spend billions each year to market their sites. These significant resources and powerful marketing abilities allow them to optimize spend and cost of customer acquisition, typically far more effectively than hotels can.

Many OTAs also include loyalty marketing as part of their acquisition and retention strategy. Offering perks for VIP customers, additional discounts, or buy X rooms get one free are all ways that OTAs try to lock in the consumer and build loyalty to their sites. Often these benefits are being funded by the OTAs marketing budget (which again is funded by the travel suppliers) or in some cases offered by the hotel or supplier directly. Hotels participating in VIP programs should do so with a clear ROI in mind and a strategy to create loyalty with that guest to their property on future visits.

For hotel only rates, most OTAs offer a best rate guarantee. This means if a customer finds a lower rate for the same booking, the OTA will match the lower rate found and often provide additional compensation. Similarly, most major hotel chains also offer a best rate guarantee. These practices have moved the industry toward rate parity across multiple channels, although in Europe this practice was outlawed in 2015. Often, an opaque model offers the best rate available, but since a consumer selects the hotel based solely on price before they ever know the brand in this model, the hotel's best rate guarantee does not apply to these bookings. In addition, in cases where hotel rates are bundled with other travel components in the package model, the best rate guarantee does not apply.

Sometimes OTAs will use deceptive practices to lure guests to their site rather than a hotel's site. Examples of these deceptive practices include:

- promoting a toll-free "800" number, which some guests mistakenly believe is a direct line to the hotel.
- bidding on brand terms on Google.
- creating URLs with the brand name in them, further confusing customers and leading them to believe that they are booking directly with the hotel, not with an intermediary.

As part of their overall search strategy, hotel marketers must stay on top of these practices and raise red flags to their OTA partners, brand, and/or Google [and, if in the U.S., the American Hotel & Lodging Association (AH&LA)] if they see that their traffic is being misappropriated. Some hotels resort to making test bookings with suspicious sites to find out how they are accessing inventory, and then have serious, direct conversations with the partner responsible for that inventory about not allowing rates and availability to the offending OTA.

The Importance of Strategy

The primary job for a hotel marketer is to find and convert travel shoppers. When travelers are shopping for hotel information, whether it is for business or personal travel, they go through a process from the point that a trip is under consideration to the post-travel dialogue they may have with their family, friends, or colleagues.

Given the current dynamic with many players vying to be the guide of choice for the consumer through the travel shopping journey, a hotel must not only ensure its content is well represented across all channels, but that its rates and availability are also accurate. Attracting travelers to any single hotel in a place where tens of thousands are visible is one of the most challenging jobs for the hospitality marketer. And it is not just about making the available information accurate and timely, but it has to be equally compelling and relevant. The travel search process involves multiple steps of inspiration, planning, searching, validating, and sharing before the shopper even gets to booking and experiencing, making it even more crucial for marketers to ensure they are represented well on OTAs.

In addition to having a solid strategy for positioning a hotel on an OTA, it must be determined which and at what margin OTAs make financial sense for your property. Each model can bring value as long as you approach it strategically. OTAs can bring benefits to a hotel.

- INCREMENTAL/NEW CUSTOMERS: The OTAs can help hoteliers extend their reach and visibility to millions of consumers domestically and all around the world. These customers can help build RevPAR, GOPAR, and market share. OTAs can be an effective channel for hotels to acquire new customers and turn them into brand loyal customers by signing them up for loyalty programs, and some brands have taken aggressive strategies to grow their loyalty bases via deep partnerships with OTAs.

- MARKETING: Historically OTAs have outspent brand and independent hotels in marketing. OTAs deploy a wide variety of online and offline marketing efforts to inspire travelers around the world and to connect these travelers directly to hotels. These marketing efforts are even more beneficial for hotels with smaller budgets to reach audiences that they would otherwise not be able to reach.

- PAY FOR PERFORMANCE: While some online referral or affiliate partners charge an upfront listing fee, OTAs are a pay for performance marketing vehicle as hotels only pay the OTA once a booking has been made. Hotels that are listed on OTAs may also gain a reservation benefit in addition to direct sales. That benefit, often called the billboard effect (and often hotly debated), involves a boost in reservations through the hotel's own distribution channels (including its website), due to the hotel being listed on the OTA website.

- CUSTOMER DIFFERENTIATION: Online travel agents can bring unique types of customers with regards to booking window, days to arrival (DTA), length of stay (LOS), and price point. OTAs can help hotels across the entire booking curve (short-term, mid-term, and long range) as well as provide promotional opportunities to fill need dates and complement the hotel's own revenue strategy.

- DATA AND INSIGHT: The global OTAs and many regional OTA's offer valuable market data and insight either by way of self-service tools or local account managers commonly referred to as market managers. Increasingly the OTAs offer rate, conversion rate, market dynamics, and other insights on their hotel-facing portals.

Generally speaking, sort order on an OTA is based on a variety of factors including offer strength (a benchmark of your hotel price relative to value), quality score (a measure of how attractive your property is to travelers), and commission (similar to other marketplaces or auction models, the commission you are paying the OTA will influence your rank). Some OTAs also offer avenues to improve your ranking or placement via paying an additional override commission. Hotels should weigh these options carefully as they evaluate the overall ROI of the channel. Staying on top of your scores, commission rate, and conversion rate compared to the competitors in your market are key aspects to having a winning strategy with an OTA.

Best Practices for Digital Marketing Through OTAs[4]

While the daily room allocation and rate offering for the OTAs typically falls under the responsibility of the revenue manager, the digital marketer has a key role to play in this booking channel.

Know the models inside and out, and understand your pricing.
Work in tandem with your revenue management counterparts to understand the points of differentiation, their costs, how (and when) revenue will be recognized, and the payment terms. Understand that for your market or competitive set some sites or models have strengths, which you should look to capitalize on when you need to drive occupancy, rate, or both. If a consumer pays $200 for your room, exactly how much of the $200 will the hotel see? Will you incur any connectivity or channel management costs to get your rates and inventory to the OTA?

Read and adhere to contracts.
If you do not have a clear understanding of the terms, then ask for additional clarification or do not participate. Each OTA model is different, with some requiring daily minimum room availability and some not. Some require last room availability for a promoted rate. Rate parity is a typical requirement in the U.S. OTAs generally have language around how they will market the hotel; if you have a trademark you want protected then ensure the rules of engagement and marketing are clear in the contract.

Understand the nature of any opaque offering.
If it is not truly opaque, the consequences of offering a significantly lower rate are far reaching as regular guests might book the hotel at a deep discount rather than at the best available rate. Ensure your hotel is opaque and not getting too much of its share in the opaque site's comp set as it can impact not just your nightly RevPAR but your overall brand value proposition.

Get to know your market manager.
An OTA market manager is analyzing trends across markets, and working with him or her to identify opportunities or just understand key market trends is an essential part of any marketing strategy.

- You'll stay on top of their promotions and the market segments they specialize in. You'll understand if and how they align with your customer mix targets. For instance, Booking.com has a significant presence in the European market, Expedia can deliver package guests with long lead times, and Hotel Tonight is focused on guests arriving tonight.

- If reviews are attached to listings and if for example your property received many negative reviews prior to your renovation, the market manager may be able to remove them once your property is upgraded. They are more likely to help your hotel if they know you and you have established some credibility with them.

- Ask for more opportunities, placement, and advertising. With your revenue management team, develop your need date strategy and determine ways that online sites can help you fill them. Often there are win-win initiatives that can be implemented. Placement on a results page is important and will have a direct impact to the volume of business you receive from an OTA.

Be willing to test strategies.
Once you've identified need dates and talked it over with your revenue management counterpart, be willing to try things out of the box. Online sites can often provide immediate feedback on specific rate, advertising, promotion, or channel strategies. So test, learn, and test again.

Analyze your results.
Conversion numbers are the primary tool to use to analyze results, but they are certainly not the only tool. While some travelers are searching dozens of websites prior to booking, conversions will only track the last site visited. Even if you have a lower direct conversion rate than an OTA, did presence on the OTA contribute to a conversion rate bump on your site? Was there a "billboard effect"5? The OTAs are constantly improving the tools for hotels to use so they can be smarter marketers on the site.

Be strategic in your use of OTAs as a part of your marketing strategy.
Every OTA wants to inspire customers to book more travel. Converting more business through these sites is usually not just in the site's best interest but the hotel's as well. Understanding how to use these partners effectively can help grow RevPAR and market share. That said, understand the overall costs of the OTA and weigh that versus your other marketing costs to ensure you are delivering the right mix of business for your property. Expedia and Booking.com also offer ways to improve your position via an additional commission on top of the base commission.

Align your OTA participation with your current customer base or need segments.

If you are a predominantly weekend leisure hotel, you may not want to affiliate your property with an OTA primarily targeting weekend business. Or if you are a corporate Monday through Thursday hotel, a weekend leisure stay may be exactly what you need to win at your hotel. Also, attracting international travelers can be a boon for your RevPAR but make sure your operations teams are set up to succeed with guests who may not be fluent in your local language.

Offer compelling and consistent content.

Just like anything on the web, content matters. If you are participating with an OTA, be sure your content is accurate. Have high quality photos, and as many as are allowed. Note that other third-party databases may be feeding content to an OTA. Ensure that your content and photos are updated in the primary data aggregators like GDS/HOD/Leonardo. Content can be pulled from a number of sources, some of it beyond your control, so take precautions to ensure that the data you can control is accurate and compelling.

Connect with guests.

Also make sure you monitor your OTA traveler post-stay reviews as many OTAs allow you to write a management response. More and more OTAs are also providing channels for guests to connect with hotels before and during their stay, so ensure your teams are equipped to answer those queries as well.

Best Practices: Content and User Experience

Content and user experience are key variables that can drive online consumers to one site over another. However, it is important to keep in mind that because travel shoppers visit so many sites and are touched by so many promotional contacts in the research process up to a booking, a presence on multiple sites and at multiple consumer touch points is likely to be a good strategy for your hotel. Additional points to keep in mind include:

- Know Your Customers: Research the path the different customer groups take on their way to a booking with you. Examine each step along that path for opportunities to have a meaningful presence that engages

and builds the relationship, whether that is online or offline.

- Build an Online Strategy: Review your online strategy alongside the travel process customers use to research and book your hotel to ensure you have considered actions at each step to create a bias among your customers and prospects to consider you.

- Offer Compelling Content: Make your content compelling and relevant, whether it is on your own website or on OTA sites where you have a presence. Investing in great visual and written content is a highly effective differentiator given the number of hotel websites from which a traveler can choose. Content is a form of merchandising and should be developed with that in mind.

- Create Bias for Your Preferred Channels: You can't make travel shoppers choose one channel over another, but you can put out bread crumbs along their path that are so compelling that they will choose your route because it is appealing and helps them accomplish their goals better than the alternatives. This doesn't mean only using your own website. By collaborating with others, you can get travelers to choose sites on which you can deepen your relationship with them as you lead them to your booking engine, whether that is on your own website or embedded in an external one.

- Get Social: Many consumers these days are all about social media. Master the social sites your consumers use. Think of social sites as places to build relationships, and if you sell or incorporate your booking engine into a social site (e.g., Facebook), put it in a place that makes sense for the way the social site is naturally used.

- Test and Monitor: Whatever you do online, you should track results in all places possible. If you partner with a website (social, transactional, or informational) to promote your hotel, be sure you can track the results from it, whether it is a booking or other form of interaction. If you decide to test a new option, try to remove other factors that would muddy the results.

- Consider Attribution Models and the "Billboard Effect": Be sure to calculate promotional lift from all your marketing channels, not just the ones that are claiming credit for it. It is likely that every one of them, including promotional messages like email, banner, or display ads, and some off-line campaigns, are contributing to making the cash register ring. Before assigning credit, look hard at the data to be sure you can quantify what each channel brings in terms of benefit from an added presence, and ideally test various hypotheses until you figure out which ones get you the bookings at the lowest overall cost.[5]

- Distinguish Yourself: It is helpful to think about how your brand (independent or chain) differs from the others. Hotel brands have a tendency to look very similar in their content and messaging. It is hard to cut a unique swath from that cloth; this has been most successfully done with boutique brands in major metro areas or in resorts. On a national or international basis, there is a tendency to dilute a brand's uniqueness with messages that resonate with so many consumer profiles that they fail to distinguish the brand for any particular customer cohort. Ensure that your content sets you apart with the audience(s) that matter most to you.

- Seek Sustainable Profit: As much as every hotel would love the simplicity of one-step promotions that deliver immediate revenue, few consumers buy without having some kind of relationship first, so while a booking usually requires multiple interactions, it's important to understand which channels deliver a sustainable ROI.

- Focus on Engagement: A customer that does not refer others or return is worth far less than those who do. Spend your time and money on those who will refer or repeat. If you allocate resources in terms of acquisition, persuasion, and retention, remind your team that if you are spending too much time on the first two steps, you may find yourself cycling through too many customers and chasing your tail. Focus your resources on the channels that contribute the most profit and have long-term potential.

Conclusion

OTAs currently generate on average about 12% of all bookings and roughly 40% of all online bookings. Third party sites use a range of models to generate bookings for their partners and use that revenue to develop exceptional technology systems and marketing strategies. Many brand-agnostic customers turn to OTAs for their research and booking, so it's incumbent upon the hotel marketer to develop strategies and use best practices when working with OTAs. When considering a relationship with any OTA, it is important to understand your brand's position or if you are an independent hotel, you may want to seek a partner who can help you navigate OTA deals and requirements. Ensuring you have content that supports your hotel's positioning is key, and merchandising your property is as important on OTA sites as it is your own. Lastly, OTAs are typically the fastest growing segment for a hotel, so it is paramount to constantly monitor and manage the percentage of bookings that come from third party partners.

Chapter 23 Endnotes

[1]   *All information quoted from Demystifying the Digital Marketplace is reprinted with permission. Demystifying the Digital Marketplace: Spotlight on the Hospitality Industry PART II, March 2017.*

[2]   *Schaal, Dennis. "The Definitive History of Online Travel." Skift.com. June 2016.*

[3]   *Bennett, Drake. "Expedia Relentlessly Tests the Science of User Experience and Vacation Planning." Bloomberg. February 2016.*

[4]   *Portions of the Best Practices section are adapted from the HSMAI white paper "Best Practices for Your Online Distribution & Marketing Strategy" published December 2010.*

[5]   *For more information on the "billboard effect," see page 131 of Distribution Channel Analysis: a Guide for Hotels and "The Billboard Effect: Online Travel Agent Impact on Non-OTA Reservation Volume."*

KEY POINTS

- What is a group intermediary and why are group intermediaries important?
- How should a hotel optimize its presence on group intermediaries?
- How can digital marketers craft campaigns to attract business through group intermediaries?

SUMMARY

Before the introduction of online sourcing technology, meeting planners often struggled with finding the right venue to meet their event needs, and hotels found it difficult to target their marketing dollars to book incremental group business. Over the past several years, meeting planners have shifted from the traditional means of venue sourcing and adopted online methods to save time and money. As a result of this shift, hotels are receiving more group business than ever before via online group channels. However, this also means that hotels must work to build a stronger online presence on these platforms through distinguished and eye-catching profiles, and increased digital marketing efforts.

A group intermediary is a company or Software-as-a-Service (SaaS) platform that connects event and meeting planners with venues, and vice versa. Similar to other online marketplaces like Amazon or Expedia, group intermediaries provide a way for meeting and event planners to easily compare venues, and send and receive RFPs. They benefit hotels and venues by increasing qualified demand for group business, and allowing hotels and venues to manage that demand more efficiently.

The Importance of Group Intermediaries

Cvent, a leading group intermediary, recently surveyed over 800 planners in a wide-ranging study on sourcing behaviors. It found that the top sourcing channel for planners was through online sourcing tools or group intermediaries.

To help quantify that trend, Cvent reported that their online sourcing platform has seen a 999% increase in the number of planner organizations that sent an eRFP for the first time between 2009 and 2014, and in 2017 they said that over 300,000 people actively use their platform.

Group intermediaries have changed the meetings and events business by unifying venue sourcing into a few sourcing platforms that planners now rely on to search. They've been able to do so because it used to be particularly time-consuming for a planner to research venues at scale. While one-to-one relationships remain an important part in the decision-making process, the increased volume and velocity of meeting requests paired with gains in technology have made it easier to use online tools to make faster decisions. Also, hotel websites are typically focused on transient leisure and business travelers, treating group business as an afterthought, and in some cases, ignoring it entirely. That also makes it difficult for search engines like Google to return relevant pages to a meeting planner.

Group intermediaries allow planners to search through databases of venues whose profiles only display information relevant to a planner. In a few clicks, they can find pertinent details about a hotel including the square footage of meeting space, what those spaces look like, and the number of sleeping rooms it provides.

Meeting planners now have access to tools that allow them to research and act (send an RFP) immediately. This would not have been possible in the not-too-distant past. If you went to a hotel to find out more about it, you still had to go back to the office, prepare the RFP, print it out, put it in a binder, and mail it. That is not the case in today's connected and mobile world.

For hoteliers, it means creating and maintaining a presence where planners are researching because the competition is not just across the street anymore. Hotels are each competing with a universe of choices. And who is the planner going to choose: the hotel that is marketing itself everywhere and telling a great story, or the one whose profile is empty and whose ads do not catch the planner's eye? The rapid migration to online sourcing supports this concept.

Additionally, group intermediaries have created more competition. Considering it's so easy for planners to find new properties that match their needs, a hotel is no longer just competing with their competitor across the street. In the meeting planner's consideration set may also be a property across town, in another the state, or another country, or a unique new the independent boutique the planner hadn't heard of before.

This means hotels cannot rely on having a basic presence (profile) on group intermediaries. They must aggressively pursue opportunities that ensure their property's advertising is displayed where the planners are. Furthermore, the property must identify themselves as unique, showcasing what differentiates them from the competition. The only platform that allows for that kind of specific targeting is a group intermediary.

Planners are also turning to group intermediaries because they pioneered the rise of eRFPs. Instead of a planner creating separate paper RFPs for each property from which they want a proposal, they create a single electronic version that they send to multiple properties with a single click. Rather than manually creating excel sheets to compare venue pricing, group intermediaries also automate the response process and allow planners to collect and analyze their responses in a single, easy to access location. It also centralizes all the communications between them and venues, ensuring that miscommunications are limited and responsibilities adhered to.

For the hotel, the tools also assist with responding quickly, managing their lead flow, and using analytics to optimize their own response behaviors.

Should you incorporate group intermediaries into your marketing strategy?

If the group market is an existing segment, or targeted segment, there may be some marketing opportunities in this area. As established above, planners are no longer reaching out directly to venues to source their meetings and events, but are instead turning to group intermediaries. Hoteliers must demonstrate to meeting planners that they are willing to participate in the client's preferred channel. By not participating in the channel, the venue's chance of consideration is significantly diminished.

Similar to paid advertising on search sites, advertising on a group intermediary channel allows venues to gain a leg up on competition by placing their venue front and center in the planner's search process. Venues have the opportunity to target planners by showcasing their unique qualities and differentiators.

Best Practices: Building a Group Intermediary Presence

With more and more planners turning to online sourcing platforms, it's crucial that a hotel's online presence on group intermediaries is as strong as on their own website or their on-site tour. Unfortunately, many hoteliers don't treat or invest in their group intermediary's profile like they do their own website. This is problematic because to many planners, a hotel's profile on a sourcing platform is the only web presence about that venue that they'll see before moving to the next step in the consideration process.

Your presence on online sourcing channels begins with your hotel's profile content. To ensure your listing on these sites can be found easily and is interesting, take the time to incorporate some of these best practices to your profile.

Make it complete.

This profile should be an event planner's one-stop-shop for all things group related. By limiting the amount of information on your profile, you are encouraging the planner to move on and look elsewhere. Keep their attention by offering as much information as possible and being accurate in your listing.

This task can be simpler than you think if you focus on relevant information and keep your target audience in mind. First and foremost, ensure the content about your hotel is accurate and up to date. Focus on including the relevant information that a meeting planner would care most about (meeting space, airport transportation, F&B minimums, etc.) and ensure your content reads easily. If relevant, adding information about local attractions can be helpful, but go beyond just listing the names of as many points of interest as you can think of. Instead, include a short description, the address, and website of some of the top attractions that drive demand to your location. Always remember that meeting planners are likely scanning dozens of listings, or using filters to hone in on their key needs, so make sure your listing is complete.

Make it visual.

Your online profile must be visually enticing. The image gallery is one of the most visited portions of your profile, and the main image is the first and last thing a planner notices. Make sure the images are of good quality, sized correctly, and accentuate your property's best features.

Additionally, pay special attention to every image you include on your profile. Think about your audience and what they would want to see on an onsite tour. Would you spend time showing them the hotel room bathroom or would you spend more time in each meeting room? Would you show them only one room setup or several? Do you have inspirational images merchandising your hotel effectively for meeting planners that want a memorable event? Answering questions like these will help you organize your ideal image gallery.

Make it valuable.

Now that planners are paying more attention to your profile, add the little something extra that will encourage them to take the next step. Although your property may provide everything their event needs, they may not believe right away that yours will offer the best deal — unless you tell them so.

Including planner specific deals directly on your profile is an important part of spreading the word about new promotions or incentives available at your property. Even if you are not running specific promotions consider highlighting your property's key differentiators. Also, simply stating that your property is willing to negotiate any contract over 200 attendees or F&B minimums are negotiable with a large enough sleeping block can be enough to convert a planner's initial consideration into a genuine lead for your sales team.

Make it unique.

The last step of managing a successful profile is getting noticed. To stand out from the several hundred other properties in your area, your listing should offer something unique and different. Among the photos of hotel rooms and static square footage stats, your profile can more easily catch a planner's eye by doing something different. If your hotel's greatest selling feature is the picturesque landscape, incorporate that as a visual element. No picturesque landscape? Turn it into an opportunity to use creativity to inspire meeting planners to give your hotel a second look.

Like your property website, the URL to your profile should be leveraged as a sales tool. Whether that's including the link in social media posts, saving it to your email signature, or pulling it up during a face-to-face meeting, the most important thing is not to neglect it.

Best Practices: Digital Group Marketing Campaigns

Today's digital group marketing campaigns often involve a multitude of moving parts. From brand awareness to lead generation, campaigns should be multi-faceted, trackable, and have clear expectations of results. As a result, consider these actions when implementing a digital group marketing campaign.

Understand your opportunities.

Fully understanding the promotional vehicles at your disposal and matching that with your goals is key to evaluating what campaigns you may wish to undertake. Intermediaries often have levels of promotion, offering additional exposure or content depending on your investment level, and traditional display advertisements or other CPM or CPC models are often offered to lure advertising dollars. Fully evaluate your options before moving ahead with your plan.

Have a plan.

As with all campaigns, know what your Key Performance Indicators (KPIs) are at the beginning of your campaign, and what your expected outcomes are. Are you improving your branding and want impressions, or need specific leads? Do you have a specific ROI in mind? Remember that group sales funnels and booking lead times will impact your ability to measure ROI. Chart a course and refer to it regularly in order to measure your performance from beginning to end as a need to adjust your strategy may often arise.

Lead with the big idea.

Advertising campaigns are often run in order to push awareness of a new group promotion or offering. It is important to ensure that all advertisements running speak to these offerings. Even if the promotion contains a lot of caveats and details, some small piece of it can be woven into all advertising elements. For image based advertisements, include a short amount of relevant teaser text. In a more content based placement, use the extra words to provide more of the key highlights of your offering.

Of course, this isn't to say that the ads should only represent the big idea. Don't forget about your own company's branding as well. Often, these ads only capture a quick glance. With each eye-catching opportunity, you want to make sure the planner knows who you are and what you are offering. These two details are essential to helping a planner determine if the advertisement is relevant to them. And if that isn't enough to convince them, a good tag line doesn't hurt.

Create clear calls to action.

When the planner is ready to learn more about your offer, be sure your campaign allows them to do so easily and without confusion. For example, including phrases such as "Learn more" or "Book now" will encourage viewers to actually click on your ad versus simply seeing the placement as branding.

In some cases, a planner may need to take additional steps to claim an offer, which makes it important to be clear about what is expected. Whether that be mentioning a code within their RFP details or submitting an RFP within a certain date range, the clearer your messaging is, the more effective your campaign will be.

Eliminating confusing variables within the advertisements will also lead to additional success. For example, if one of the images in your ad campaign says "click here" but does not link anywhere, the planner is more likely to stop the process and move on to another hotel.

Lastly, request a mock-up or proof of your advertisement before it goes live. This will help you stay one step ahead of your campaign instead of being forced to change elements at the last minute. The best way to make sure your ads follow this rule is to view and test them yourself.

Keep it visual.

One of the biggest trends in hotel marketing right now is the visual experience. Almost every new website update or social media platform incorporates more visual elements, and for good reason. Humans process images 60,000 times faster than words. When your advertisements may only have a moment to make an impression, it's important to keep this fact in mind.

Keep a look out for image-based advertising opportunities. Most advertising campaigns require a visual component, but if it's optional take time to analyze whether it makes sense to add imagery to it. These opportunities can be the best way to feature your hotel and impress your potential clients. If your hotel needs to update its visual gallery, make sure you allocate time and financial resources to take some new, updated pictures of your property or destination.

Provide a seamless experience.

A common mistake in digital marketing campaigns is a broken buying path. For example, the advertisement says there is a "pick your incentive" program with your hotel, but the landing page outlines no details about the incentive. Promotions change, and with that, so should the advertisements. The planner experience must be fluid, with an advertisement leading to additional relevant details directing them to submit an RFP.

Once your campaign launches, click through the advertisements as if you were the meeting planner to get a feel for their process. This practice will help ensure you are utilizing all placements correctly and effectively. And if your campaign will be running over a long period of time, make a note to check on it every month or so to ensure everything is still accurate, up to date, and functioning correctly.

Track your success.

Implementation should not be the terminus of your group marketing campaign. While it's easy to click the completed check box and move on, tracking the overall success of the campaign by comparing its performance to your group business goals is a key criterion for success. Know what your Key Performance Indicators (KPIs) are at the beginning of your campaign, and refer to them regularly in order to measure your performance from beginning to end. No matter how well-executed your campaign, there will always be room for improvement. The trick is to stay ahead of the game and never rest on your laurels.

Monitoring success of using intermediaries.
While it is easy to fall into a 'set it and forget' path with your group strategy, it is important to always monitor your results. Regularly check lead volume and conversion rates in addition to your offers and content. Solicit feedback from meeting planners who book your hotel. Make test bookings — how easy is it for attendees to use the tools provided to actually book your rooms? Just like the strategies and tactics digital marketers put into place for websites and transient channels, it is incumbent upon them to manage and measure these channels as well to drive value for the hotel.

Conclusion
Meeting and event planners are notoriously short on time, which is why most planners have made the switch to group intermediaries to handle the RFP process. By investing time and resources into group intermediaries, hotels can build a stronger online presence, run more effective digital marketing campaigns, and ultimately receive more group business leads because hotels can place themselves in front of meeting planners more easily and more frequently.

PART 6: TRENDING TOPICS

A Note About the Bright and Shiny

Before we jump off into the "trending" section, it is important to note that that not all that glitters is gold. The term 'Bright and Shiny' is both a positive and a negative. Something that is bright and shiny new and cool captures our attention, but it can also be distracting and lead us down a path of spending time and money on something that might not be worthwhile. It is extremely important to look at new and innovative ways of doing things but one must be careful of how much time, money, and effort is put into something without knowing the potential return or long-term viability.

So many in our industry do not perform the fundamentals of good integrated marketing, the "low hanging fruit" if you will. At first marketers should ensure their blocking and tackling is in place before they look to the latest and the greatest. It takes a very unique set of circumstances for emerging technologies to be tested and implemented for positive results. It can range from the need to be a major brand with the resources and the scalability to bring a project to market, or it may be a leading edge product or property that has in place all the pieces of a solid foundation of strategy and can afford to expand into these new realms of opportunity. Whatever the conditions that may exist, one thing is absolutely certain: without a solid marketing foundation in which to venture into the "bright and shiny" your efforts may cost you more than just the expense of trying. On the bright side, seeing what the future could hold allows for preparation and anticipation of progress. Just imagine if you had the ability to venture back in time by even 11 years knowing what you know now, and try to explain even what your current phone does to anyone back then. They might just look for your spaceship.

With this in mind, please enjoy the next few chapters about some interesting trends and innovations we are seeing in the hotel digital marketing space.

CHAPTER 25
Location-Based Marketing

KEY POINTS

- The difference between location-based and proximity marketing.
- Key steps to ensure your location is optimized in search.
- Three critical components of proximity marketing.
- Gamification as a part of proximity marketing.

SUMMARY

Location has always been key to marketing, and the mobile age makes it even more valuable. Not only does it play a crucial role in search marketing, it also opens the door for location-based and proximity marketing. The tools and tactics for both vary widely and should be considered separately in your overall digital strategy.

Not long ago, billboards controlled the marketplace for location-based marketing. If you were a roadside hotel you would put a billboard up a reasonable distance from your exit to capture the drive-by market. You may have participated in advertising in exit guides to take advantage of the proximity of travelers to your property. You would also have advertised in directories so that area visitors could find your property.

Today, drive-by traffic is more likely to locate a property based on a smartphone app, which can provide information on amenities, check-in details, local attractions and restaurants, rates, and user reviews. Billboards may help point the way for some drivers, but the planning and booking have likely already taken place.

Search and Property Location

In the last few years, local search has begun to dominate the search engine results and this trend appears to be intensifying. You can now take a photo of the Paris Casino in Las Vegas and visual search tools within Google will return search information on the property. There's no need to even type in the name — the photo is enough. Google's local search results appear directly below the pay per click ads, the local map appears in the top right, and most of the paid search terms are location driven. Most significantly, Google's Hotel Finder has changed the face of local search marketing dramatically.

Location plays a role in how prospective guests search for your property online. Unless the property itself is the destination, guests want to stay close to area attractions, facilities, or meeting locations in the case of business travel. As a result, they might use terms such as "hotels near" or "accommodations within walking range of," or some other long-tail keyword phrase that helps them find convenient locations near their actual point of interest.

The addition of Google Hotel Price Ads has made the landscape even more competitive. Once available only to OTAs or brands, any property can now create a listing that will show up on relevant searches, and allow guests to book directly on your property website. You bid for ad placement just as you would with other search ads, and if your property shows up in a search, the guest can click on your hotel listing to see any relevant location information as well as user reviews, pricing, and a click-through to book their selection. You will need to set up live inventory and a daily budget to appear in the results.

In addition to incorporating Zagat reviews and Local Guides — over 50 million individual contributors who provide updated photos, reviews, and other relevant information about a given destination — Google has incorporated hotel rates and availability into its search results. This integration, called Google Hotel

Price Ads (HPA), has turned Google Search results into a metasearch channel for customers to research and book hotel rates. As with all metasearch, these ads require connectivity with Google through your central reservations or channel manager to make rates and inventory available within the listing. However, hoteliers now must view Google as a potential booking channel and not just a website traffic referrer.

Whether through paid search or organic search, your property details must be correct, consistent, and linked to physical address, nearby attractions, arrival directions, and any other details which could link your digital content to your location. Ideally you could input your information in one spot and populate every site on the internet, but the world doesn't work that way. Instead, sites pull property information from data warehouses such as InfoUSA, Acxiom, Switchboard, Superpages, Localize, and Datacom. Search engines, online directories, and hundreds of other sites draw their data from these different sources, which may not always contain identical listings for your property.

As a result, it's vital to identify all relevant directories online where your information might appear, and do periodic audits to ensure your property's Name, Address, Phone Number, and Website information (known as your NAP listings or NAP+W listings) are up to date and, most importantly, consistent not only in terms of content, but also in terms of spelling, punctuation, abbreviation, and so forth. Consistency of NAP listings represents one key factor in your property's rankings within local search, which in the age of mobile plays an increasingly important role in your guests' overall experience.

Your website should consistently and thoroughly communicate your location to search engines through things like Schema markup, meta descriptions, image tags, and on-page content. Consumers should have a clear sense of your property's location from reading your website. Include directions from multiple points of travel (e.g., airports, public transportation terminals, major roadways) and maps that are integrated with mobile navigation apps. Even images of your hotel should be tagged with location information.

Location-Based Marketing

According to Marketing Land, 80 percent of all social media activity now occurs on mobile phones — which means that people are posting, socializing, and broadcasting their location more than ever before. From a marketing standpoint, that means properties now have opportunities to connect with guests and prospects on a much more individual and customized level not only when they're searching for a location, but also when they're in the immediate area, and even in specific locations on property. Because of location services available on smartphones, we can now not only collect data, but also utilize location to create specific contact messages, notifications, and offers through a range of wireless technology.

Location-based marketing is essentially the act of locating a prospect's mobile device through GPS or cell phone signal, and activating services on a mobile app or website through a "geo-fence." A geofence is a virtual perimeter created around a real-world location such as a hotel or attraction location. When a location-based service user enters or exits a geofence, their location-aware device receives a generated notification through text or email, which can include any type of information relative to the real-world location. Imagine your guests receiving a push notification from you when they're a mile away from your property, welcoming them and letting them know that you are preparing their registration information.

Most proximity-based apps allow a hotel, or any business, to claim their venue. This allows the property to perform any number of tasks such as make offers, or provide and receive information. The apps often include rating services which produce user-generated reviews about the business. In most, users can create a network of friends to share travel information and updates — including notification, photos, or videos. Each common component provides multiple opportunities for a hotel's digital marketing strategy.

A growing number of companies are taking advantage of this capability, often employing "gamification" strategy. Foursquare's Swarm app allows members to "check in" at a location and earn collectibles for visiting different location types, or "mayorships" for checking in frequently at the same location. It shares information with the City Guide app, where Foursquare users can view and create reviews (called "tips"), post photos, and locate specific details about the business or location.

A growing number of museums, landmarks, and parks are employing augmented reality experiences that can offer guided tours, interactive maps, and additional details based on user location — all through the user's smartphone. For example, visitors to the National Mall in Washington, D.C. can download an app that shows their location in relation to the various attractions, take them on specifically arranged self-guided tours, and even utilize their smartphone camera to identify the building or tagged location in front of them.

Location-based marketing works well over a larger area of space, and requires the mobile device to have an installed app, with location services turned on, or triggered by a social post which requires geo-tagging (such as "checking in" at an event or location).[1]

It's worth noting that you can create geofences anywhere you want — even in your competition's location! That means you can activate special offers in areas where you might be able to divert customers to your door. The Pokémon Go app is a wonderful example of one company layering augmented reality across a variety of real-world locations, sparking exploration into different neighborhoods and even places of business.

Proximity Marketing

Proximity marketing allows much more customer-specific targeting and offers, because it employs much more precise location techniques. Whereas GPS and cellular are limited to outdoor use, you can utilize beacon technology to create essentially a localized indoor GPS system to track movement and location throughout a property. And the good news is, 80 percent of customers currently using location based services want to get alerts on their mobile devices.

So when a guest is onsite and gets a message telling him that the restaurant has a special appetizer offer for him, or the concierge offers to pick up tickets for an event in the area, you're providing a welcome service that increases the value of your relationship to your customer, enhances their stay, and provides an incentive to come back again.

Bluetooth low energy beacons or WiFi sensors don't require an accompanying app in order to function, so they don't depend on having your own location app — or the guest installing it. With sensors or beacons, you can set up a network with more precise location, triggering offers or notices when someone is in a gift shop, restaurant, pool, or any other specific area while on your network. Marketing Land reports that nearly 90 percent of all airports are now utilizing sensors and beacons on property, so the process is quickly becoming mainstream for travelers.[2]

Although nascent, technologies like Google Lens or Apple's Siri should be closely monitored for opportunities to market your hotel. In addition, a growing selection of beacon sensors are available from providers such as Apple (iBeacons), Facebook (Bluetooth Beacons), and Google (Eddystone Beacons). In addition to "active engagement" — pushing offers when a customer is within their proximity — beacons can also assist in passive engagement by collecting user data which can help refine other marketing efforts.

There are three critical criteria for proximity marketing: 1) the location of the guest, 2) the timing of the offer, and 3) the relevance of the offer to the guest. All three must be considered within the creation of any digital strategy that will incorporate proximity marketing. By utilizing collected data and building customized customer profiles, you can create timely offers for your guests at the right place and right time.

"SoLoMo" Has Become the Norm

Location-based marketing, both local and proximity, is the natural outgrowth of social, local, and mobile platforms coming together on unified platforms to provide relevant information to consumers based on their locations at a specific point in time. Today, those platforms are expanding the reach of mobile devices into augmented reality and other interactive location-based technology.

For marketers, this convergence is key because it allows much more robust tracking and attribution for campaign activities, which in turn allows more opportunities to assign measurable ROI based on more sophisticated attribution models.

The hospitality industry should pay special attention to this trend, and look for ways to optimize and personalize the multitude of digital and face-to-face touch points with their guests and prospects. Regardless of the property tier, inbound guests are going to be booking, sharing, and documenting their visits, and that provides multiple opportunities to create brand advocates and cultivate additional sales opportunities.

Traditional marketing tactics of understanding your unique location, your specific market mix, and your existing and targeted customer demographics will all direct how much of your marketing budget and human resources should be applied.

As consumers adopt mobile as their de facto internet access point and constant companion, the hotelier should focus on mobility and engagement with consumers as they move about through their daily lives. By installing basic building blocks that enable these mobile strategies, you can ensure that your property is prepared to leverage new location-based engagement opportunities as they emerge.

Location-based marketing takes a village. Not only should you engage your fellow employees to monitor comments on Google Places or your location on maps, but you might want to engage your most loyal guests as well. Not everyone enjoys checking in on Foursquare Swarm, but those who do are often zealots. Find your zealots and solicit their help.

Chapter 25 Endnotes

[1] *"Location-based marketing: Where is it today, and where is it headed." Marketing Land, Nov. 21, 2016. Web.* https://marketingland.com/location-based-marketing-going-195732

[2] *Sterling, Greg. "Report: Nearly 90 percent of airports deploying proximity sensors, beacons." Marketing Land. November 7, 2016.* https://marketingland.com/report-nearly-90-percent-airports-deploying-proximity-sensors-beacons-197511. *January 20, 2018.*

CHAPTER 26
Virtual Reality, Augmented Reality, & 360 Views

SUMMARY
The technology that drives virtual reality, augmented reality, and the ability to view multiple directions on any screen is developing quickly. How hospitality enterprises can leverage this technology is limited only by the imagination, and the budgets, of its developers.

As for right now, using this technology is not as elusive or cost prohibitive as it might first appear. But as of yet it has not been adopted by the majority of the traveling population past the stage of novelty. All that aside, unless a particular set of circumstances exists, so much more should be done in digital marketing before you explore the world of VR and AR marketing.

Virtual Reality

Offered by almost every manufacturer of smartphones to date, VR (Virtual Reality) viewers are rapidly becoming a legitimate engagement platform for many brands. But are they really as valuable to the hospitality industry as VR advocates suggest?

By definition (from www.merriam-webster.com), virtual reality is "an artificial environment which is experienced through sensory stimuli (such as sights and sounds) provided by a computer and in which one's actions partially determine what happens in the environment; also the technology used to create or access a virtual reality."

Clinical definition aside, VR is at its core an artificially created environment. This artificial environment can be a location previously recorded with 360 cameras that allows the user to view in a virtual way the experiences recorded by the camera, but the user cannot 'interact' in that environment in real time unless the experience is truly generated to be interactive. This can be produced in two ways: computer generated graphics, such as immersive technology like Oculus currently owned by Facebook; or 'live' 360 broadcasts like Periscope by Twitter. The term 'interaction' is quite dissimilar in these two examples. One refers in part to the amount of technology needed to create both, and the second to the options available to interact with what is being shared. Oculus requires not only the unique equipment it has developed, but a minimum level of computing power to render the complexities of the engagement. With Periscope TV 360 a variety of cameras can be used to display both the image and sound associated with the location of the camera, but your interaction is limited to simply changing the POV (Point Of View) shared by the camera. Ironically the latter holds the greatest potential for VR in hospitality.

Virtual Reality in Use Today

Google Street Maps
Who hasn't used Google street maps? The ability to provide a spherical view of a particular location is one of the most adopted forms of VR use, both with flat-screen navigation as well as using Google Cardboard for a more immersive experience.

Google Street View
This is content generated by users and shared with the same technology as Google's Street Maps. But unlike Street Maps, the user recorded the 360 still image and placed it on Google's Map app. Also available is Google's Cardboard Camera app that allows you to capture sounds while recording the 360 image.

Some notable features of all of these apps is the ability to create your own content and then share it based on the location where it was taken, allowing anyone looking for a view of that location to access it from Google's search function. You can also create connecting 360 images that allow the viewer to 'progress' from one location to a connected second location. For example, you can create a picture of your hotel's entrance with a connection to your lobby then move onwards to a meeting room, etc., all for free, and findable on Google for your location.

Google's Museum View
This is a notable 360 development by Google that allows the user to experience in 360 view the great museums of the world.

Google Expedition

This application of VR takes children on field trips around the world in 360 view.

With the entry cost already low and usable by owning a smartphone, the cost to do more robust engagements such as live meetings, with platforms like Liveit Now which allow live streaming in 360, is falling quickly. You can see why virtual reality is expected to be a $70 billion industry by 2020.

VR Implications for Hospitality

For all of its potential uses, VR has mostly languished in the realm of novelty. Brands have been dabbling in VR, like Marriott's testing of innovative ideas like VRoom Service and Hilton's offering "Our Stage Your Story" 360 video introductions to some of its select properties around the world. However, none of these initiatives have been sustained on a large scale.

Some variations have been expanded such as VR tours of hotels, for instance the GCH Group with 120 of its European based hotels on display, which does not include 360 views but 360 viewed navigation. Is this due to early attempts done too soon or an indication of VR's inability to transcend to mainstream use? Time will tell.

Currently its strongest potential uses are for:

- property visual exposure
- destination exposure
- research and discovery

Augmented Reality

Holding the brightest promise for hospitality, AR (augmented reality) has become the rising star of visual interaction.

According to Wikipedia, augmented reality is "a live direct or indirect view of a physical, real-world environment whose elements are augmented by computer-generated sensory input such as sound, video, graphics, or GPS data."

To see where AR is heading, look at Google's launch of its Tango project. Although not directly related to hospitality, projects like this offer insight into what AR has to offer when it comes to interaction in physical spaces. An AR project that has been around for a while is a not-well-known feature on the Yelp mobile app called Monocle. This radar-like app uses your phone's camera to indicate locations around you with their Yelp listings.

There is an array of useable AR apps that can do things like help you find the stars in the sky or where you parked your car, provide language translations of anything written, or give you movie times and let you buy tickets through a poster for that movie. Another notable AR tool is Amazon's visual product finder which, when opened within the Amazon app, will identify what you are pointing at with your camera and show you if you can buy it with a one-click purchase.

AR Implications for Hospitality

With apps already running like Time Traveler, an AR application that allows you to discover Berlin with historic images overlaid with present day locations similar to the Grand Central Station tour, augmented reality is already in use in hospitality. Some applications like WallaMe allow you to leave AR messages at locations to be discovered by others using the app. An artist or docent can virtually stand beside a piece of artwork and explain its creation. Let's not forget how the whole world went a little crazy for a few weeks when it was introduced to the biggest launch of an AR platform with Pokemon Go.

As developers continue to work on wearable technology like Google Glasses, AR will remain in the world viewed through our handheld devices. Menus could be in your native language, visual directions can be provided, reviews and displays can be on the outside of businesses — creating a kind of hyper-reality.

Currently its strongest potential uses are for

- guest engagement
- guest education
- guest travel enhancement
- guest communication
- destination exposure

We see in things present today glimpses of what AR and VR may become. Imagine advanced rides at theme parks that immerse its riders in a sensory controlled environment if even for a brief few minutes. Will that become an adapted way of exploring travel? Will we attend concerts or sporting events via a VR viewer? All possibilities are not too far from current technologies.

CHAPTER 27
Artificial Intelligence (AI)

SUMMARY

AI is everything we fear and desire all in one. As we crave personalization, AI is able to better deliver everything unique and of interest to each one of us. But as we allow more AI into our lives, we continue to surrender human control over how that gets accomplished.

For hospitality, our interest has always been in improving the guest experience. AI has the means to do that, where it would take a significant increase in staff-to-guest ratio to offer such personalized service. AI offers the hope of allowing for that heightened level of attention with a fraction of the staff needed to deliver it. There is a caution however. As more and more data is being collected and used to provide personalization, and consumers allow their specific identities to be used for these purposes, we surrender our privacy to a larger, uncontrolled audience of developers who may not have our individual interests in mind.

From *Star Trek* to the *Terminator* and HAL to the *Matrix*, we have been envisioning what artificial intelligence will 'look' like.

If you haven't been introduced to AI yet, allow me to introduce you to SIRI, Google Assistant, Cortana, Alexa, Bixby, and Watson. Yes, AI (artificial intelligence) is here, and most of these AI's are already tucked in your pocket or purse; all of them (plus a host more) reside in your computers; many of them are in your home. But not all AI is equal. Some AI products are single function, and some just a series of specific tasks. This chapter will review the variances, and their impact and use in hospitality.

AI in the Macro

Artificial Intelligence, AI, or 'machine learning' refers to computers created to learn and make connections between information. In machine learning, AI computers are able to teach themselves how to perform an action instead of following programmed or human instruction.

AI has already had a huge influence on our daily lives. For instance, with Google's Deep-Mind, at its core is the Google Assistant, but it is also an ever-growing part of how search results are rendered. With its use of the Rank-Brain machine learning tool, this AI uses 200 'ranking signals' and 10,000 variations for each positioned result, learning each time better ways of doing it. How does that affect hospitality? As with any SERP result, if we do not rank in relevancy, we don't show on the results at a level seen by or of interest to its user. And when it comes to Google's Assistant, the answer to the question posed to it may not render our product in the results offered.

Extend that concept into SIRI, Cortana, Alexa, and Bixby and you can see how much Macro AI can help or harm your business.

AI in Bots

As mentioned earlier, all AI is not equal. Most of the specialized use of AI is in bots which are applications that perform automated tasks, such as setting an alarm, telling you the weather, or searching online.

Bots are everywhere: there are malicious bots that we see in the news as malware; we have bots that automate conversation like chatbots (see Chapter 9 for more information); and we have bots that can order food, shop, and compare prices.

Most bots are currently being used in human interaction, whether it's in the use of an app or in platforms like Facebook Messenger. Some large hotel brands are exploring the use of bots in booking rooms and checking in guests. Already in place is the ability to make dining reservations and ticket purchases.

The year 2016 will go down as the 'year of the bots,' given that every major platform such as Google, Apple, Amazon, and Microsoft released the ability to developers to construct programs using their AI platforms. As the technology for bots improves, so does its range of potential applications.

AI Implications for Hospitality

As we become more comfortable talking to inanimate objects like our smart phones and <u>Amazon Echo</u>, using these devices will increasingly become a part of our daily life — including when we travel.

These devices are being tested and added into hotel rooms to better the guest experience, giving rise to a host of legalities and functionalities related to privacy. Inasmuch as these devices can be used to control everything from the temperature in the room to the TV and even order room service, they must always be 'listening' to know when you need them. Already in courts is the legal use of this type of data in civil and criminal cases, meaning the legalities are currently undefined. Many questions about AI data and its ownership and use need to be addressed.

Other aspects of AI are already enhancing the guest journey, including the use of travel apps and the specific services they offer. Brands and platforms like Google are using AI to help facilitate some of the more standard services like check in, or making a reservation. These represent the tip of the iceberg in eventual uses.

Also impacting hoteliers is the use of AI in marketing. No greater example of this can be found than in Watson's marketing sister LUCY, a cognitive computer (AI) that learns from the data provided to make advanced marketing decisions in a human interactive way.

One of the major influences in our current business and personal worlds is data. Gathering it, understanding it, and acting on that understanding is one of the greatest focuses in technology development today. As an industry, we have so many functions that rely upon data and its use. Whether revenue management, accounting, guest services, marketing, or operations, no department is untouched by the use of data. AI is a means of understanding that data so that it can be acted upon in meaningful ways to benefit our hospitality businesses.

KEY POINTS

- It is important to examine, measure, and manage online channel performance to maximize marketing effectiveness and ROI.

- Understand best practices for owned-media analytics, especially as they relate to websites and email.

SUMMARY

Digital marketing analytics involves examining, measuring, and managing online channel performance to maximize marketing effectiveness and ROI. As digital marketers are faced with mountains of real-time customer data, it is increasingly vital to focus on the most significant and relevant information available. In this way, hotels can best determine which consumers to target, the most attractive offerings to convey, the most appropriate channels to use, and the most effective ways to communicate to the target audience.

The most common website analytics metrics typically seek to measure:

- Visitor statistics indicating the quantity and quality of traffic received by your website.

- The sources of website traffic, particularly organic (SEO), direct, PPC, and referral.

- The top keywords driving traffic to your website.

- Conversion and revenue-related website statistics.
  - Effectiveness of content/website:
  - Performance of offers, merchandising,
  - Usability of the website, and/or
  - A/B testing.

The following table illustrates metrics many analysts recommend, as well as their suitability to answer key marketing questions. While this list is by no means comprehensive, it identifies metrics available in most tools and immediately applicable to marketing challenges.

Metric	Goal Served	Rationale
Visits, Unique Visitors	Marketing effectiveness, brand awareness	Visits, sessions, unique visitors, and similar metrics count the volume of traffic a site receives. They help marketers identify when customers come to the site and whether various marketing activities increase awareness of the hotel's brand.
Bounce Rate	Guest interest, engagement	Bounce rate – defined as the percentage of visitors who leave the site after viewing only one page – provides insight into guest interest in marketing offers. Pages with high bounce rates fail to engage customers and point marketers to ineffective messaging, poor customer experience, or both.
Referrers, Traffic Sources	Identify valuable traffic sources	Referred traffic – that is, visitors who followed a link from another site – highlight guest interests and potential marketing opportunities to your hotel's team.
Search, Search Terms	Guest interest, traffic sources, marketing effectiveness, brand awareness	Most analytics tools provide easy access to the search terms guests used prior to coming to your site. Reviewing these terms helps marketers understand what their guests care about and how to speak to guests in their own words. For instance, few guests ever search for "accommodations," no matter how often hotels may use the term internally. Similarly, changes in how often guests search for a hotel's name, brand, or location may point to the effectiveness and reach of marketing activities.
Top Content, Top Pages, Most Viewed Pages	Guest interest, engagement	Whether called top content, top pages, or most viewed pages, the concept is the same: where are your guests spending their time on your site? Marketers can then use these pages to promote the hotel's benefit to the greatest number of site visitors.
Conversions Delivered to Booking Engine (CDBE)	Purchase intent	Guests who enter the booking engine typically signal purchase intent or an interest in comparative rate shopping. High abandonment rates from the booking engine may result from poor user experience, limited content, ineffective value proposition, high rates or, often, the combination of these factors.
Conversion Rate, Reservations, Revenue	Business results	Conversion rate – as is typically defined in the hotel industry – measures the percentage of visits or unique visitors resulting in a reservation. Reservations represent the ultimate measure of marketing success for many hotels.
Reservations, Revenue, Cost per Conversion	Business results	The number of bookings, room nights, and revenue produced by your website should be tracked on a monthly basis and analyzed on a year-over-year basis due to seasonality. If at all possible, cost per conversion should be tracked from referral sources to determine the best marketing strategies.
Entry, Consumption, Analysis	Website optimization	Website clickstream analysis helps to better understand visitor behavior and improve the user experience. The website should be organized to efficiently and effectively guide the customer journey. Web analytics tools track the visitor flow including: 1. Entry: top entrance pages for visitors, where visitors come from, the best sources for visitors 2. Consumption: count of pages with the greatest number of visitors, how long they stay, how deep they go, what they do, what they 'consume' 3. Exit: last page view, most common last page views, where visitors left, why they left

Today, the most popular analytics tools are Google Analytics, Adobe Analytics, and Webtrends. Regardless of which tool you use, there are many similarities.

As with most analytics reporting systems, there are four main components to the Google Analytics system:

1. DATA COLLECTION: Collecting your users interactions from your website, from your mobile app, and any digitally connected environment like your PMS system.

2. CONFIGURATION: In this step, Google Analytics applies your configuration settings, such as any filters you might want to introduce to the raw data it has collected. Once this data is processed, it is housed in a database and cannot be changed historically.

3. PROCESSING: Once the interactions from a user have been collected according to your configuration in the database, the next step is data processing. This is the "transformation" step that turns your raw data to something useful that you will be able to look at and share in order to make future decisions.

4. REPORTING: Typically, you will use the web interface at www.google.com/analytics to access your data. However, most brands will use proprietary reporting systems that have simply pulled the data from Google but put it in a format that is brand-specific.

Below are the reporting categories and their subcategories that Google currently has in place (as of January 2018):

 HOME

 CUSTOMIZATION

Dashboards

Custom Reports

Saved Reports

Custom Alerts

In this section you have access to a number of different reports:

- *Real-Time Report:* Gives you popular metrics including top referrals, top social traffic, top keywords, top active pages, and top locations.

- *Audience Report:* Delivers a variety of visitor statistics including the number of visits, pages/ visit, % new visits, unique visitors, average visit duration, page views, and bounce rate. This report also categorizes visits by demographics (e.g., language, country), system (e.g., browser, operating system), mobile (e.g., operating system, screen resolution), and language.

- *Acquisition Report:* Allows you to examine data which reveals the sources of traffic, keywords, and campaigns that drove traffic to your site. This Google Analytics report breaks out traffic by Direct, Referring, or Search, each with its own report. The keywords report reveals the keywords used to drive traffic. These can be broken out into organic and paid search. There are also reports for each campaign (for example, paid search, email, display, social media) and results for each ad being run for paid search campaigns. The traffic results can be linked with booking information to determine the efficacy and success of each channel.

- *Behavior Report:* Shares insights on your website usability from the visitor perspective by tracking behavior flow, site content, navigation, speed, and search. Content reports reveal the pages being viewed along with their exit rates, entry rates, and bounce rates. The navigation summary sub-report analyzes the path taken by visitors in the site and highlights trouble spots. There is also an in-page analytics section that overlays a specific page from the website with key metrics for each link on that page, indicating which links drive sales, traffic, and conversions.

- *Conversions Report:* This report enables you to track ROI by attaching goals which you assign with specific conversions. With the proliferation of referral sources, and the fact that website visitors use numerous sources before eventually booking, multi-channel funnels and attribution models allow for values to be assigned to sources even if they are not first-click or last-click on the path to purchase. Multi-channel funnels give insight into how customers reach your site and convert – from all your channels. They allow you to conduct attribution analysis on your online marketing activities, looking at them as combinations of channels and steps of varying success, rather than last-clicked channels in isolation. Historically most common analytics have only allowed the last site visited to be tracked, which was obviously limited in evaluating the ROI on digital marketing efforts. If the average consumer visits 18 sites before making a booking decision, how valuable is getting information only on the last site? Now analytics allow you to trace the steps of your visitors to evaluate the value of Facebook in the research phase, or display ads, etc. Attribution modeling is only in its infancy stage currently and will certainly continue to shape the way we market digitally.

Attribution Models

In recent years, marketers have begun exploring how to quantify what was historically known as the billboard effect – what factors, other than the very last click, contribute to visitors arriving at your website. Based on this need, more data can be reported based on attribution. Google Analytics provides the following default attribution models in the Model Comparison Tool. You can also create your own custom models in the tool.

Last Interaction

The Last Interaction model attributes 100% of the conversion value to the last channel with which the customer interacted before buying or converting.

When it's useful: if your ads and campaigns are designed to attract people at the moment of purchase, or your business is primarily transactional with a sales cycle that does not involve a consideration phase, the Last Interaction model may be appropriate.

Last Non-Direct Click

The Last Non-Direct Click model ignores direct traffic and attributes 100% of the conversion value to the last channel from which the customer clicked through before buying or converting. Google Analytics uses this model by default when attributing conversion value in non-Multi-Channel Funnels reports.

If you consider direct traffic to be from customers who have already been won through a different channel, then you may wish to filter out direct traffic and focus on the last marketing activity before conversion.

When it's useful: because the Last Non-Direct Click model is the default model used for non-Multi-Channel Funnels reports, it provides a useful benchmark to compare with results from other models.

Last AdWords Click

The Last AdWords Click model attributes 100% of the conversion value to the most recent AdWords ad that the customer clicked before buying or converting.

When it's useful: if you want to identify and credit the AdWords ads that closed the most conversions, use the Last AdWords Click model.

First Interaction Model

The First Interaction model attributes 100% of the conversion value to the first channel with which the customer interacted.

When it's useful: this model is appropriate if you run ads or campaigns to create initial awareness. For example, if your brand is not well known, you may place a premium on the keywords or channels that first exposed customers to the brand.

Best Practices: Analytics Implementation

As you begin implementing an analytics focused approach across your organization, use the following checklist to ensure you're on the right path.

Identify 3 or 4 strategic goals for your marketing efforts. Tracking just for the sake of tracking makes no sense. Ensure you understand the goals important to your organization before you start measuring. Limiting this set to 3 or 4 enables you to focus on only those measurements most important to the organization as you develop your analytics capabilities.

Determine conversion actions that support those strategic goals. While reservations likely remain your most important conversions, email sign-ups, loyalty enrollment, RFP requests, and other key visitor actions represent useful business outcomes. Determine which actions matter most and include them in your analysis.

Work with your analytics vendor to configure your defined conversion actions within your reporting tool. Include segmentation to evaluate where your most valuable traffic comes from. Additionally, review the Metrics table in this publication for additional measures and the goals with which they best align.

Identify the segments producing greatest conversion for each conversion action. Start with your most important conversion action, measuring activity during peak and shoulder periods to determine your core segments. Note any variation in your conversion patterns on a monthly basis with year-over-year comparisons and look for possible causes. Repeat this step for each conversion action as you move forward.

Set improvement targets. Once you understand both your conversion rate and the segments driving those conversions, set a clear, measurable target for improvement. Ultimately, the point of any analytics efforts is to produce improved business results.

Develop an action plan for achieving performance improvements. Using the identified segments, determine specific actions focused on each segment to drive desired improvements.

Evaluate changes in metrics based on outcomes from your action plan. Share these results across your organization to build support for ongoing efforts.

Best Practices: Email Campaigns

Email marketing is one of the most established forms of online customer engagement. Chapter 11 covers email marketing best practices, including the benefits it can deliver, including:

- direct communication with prospects and customers
- interactivity/call to action
- increased loyalty
- low cost

To evaluate the effectiveness of email campaigns, there are key metrics, which are normally provided by the mailing platform, that need to be tracked and compared across campaigns.

- TOTAL SENDS: the number of emails to whom the message was originally sent, before any bounces or failed notifications.
- SUCCESSFUL SENDS: the number of emails that have not been returned (for whatever reason).
- HARD BOUNCES: the number of emails returned because the recipient address was invalid.
- SOFT BOUNCES: the number of emails returned because the recipient's mailbox is

full, the server is temporarily unavailable, or the recipient no longer has an email account at that address.

- TOTAL OPENS: number of times the email was opened (not the best indicator of success because the total opens reflect multiple opens by a single recipient).
- UNIQUE OPENS: number of individual recipients who open the message (a better measure of success because you know exactly how many subscribers are interested enough to open your email).
- OPEN RATE: the percent of unique opens divided by emails sent or emails received.
- REPEAT OPENS: how many times the email was opened by one recipient. This is an interesting metric since if an email is opened many times it means that either the recipient is returning to the email again and again, or that the recipient forwarded the email intact to others who are opening it. Either way, it suggests an "engaged" reader.
- CLICK RATE: number of emails in which content was clicked on within the message divided by emails delivered.
- EMAIL UNSUBSCRIBE RATE: number of unsubscribes divided by the total number of email subscribers conversion rate – the percentage of people who clicked through and took the desired action (e.g., booked, subscribed, forwarded, etc.).

The first four metrics above test the quality of the email list used and guide the "cleaning" of the list to ensure the maximum number of emails are delivered to valid addresses.

You can track email campaigns, using Google Analytics for example, by adding parameters to URLs in each email marketing message. These will denote which visitors arrive as a result of each email marketing campaign. The values contained in each link will report back:

- CAMPAIGN SOURCE: who is sending the message (an e-mail provider, for example)
- CAMPAIGN MEDIUM: which instrument is being used to send the message
- CAMPAIGN NAME: each campaign should be named, so one can differentiate the results and effectiveness of each one. Usually for an email campaign, it is the subject line.

CHAPTER 29
Analytics & Attribution Modeling

KEY POINTS

- Identifying and assigning credit to sources of business has become more challenging as the buyer's journey to purchase evolves into a multichannel process.

- Four of the more popular attribution models are last interaction, last non-direct click, first interaction, linear.

- Choose one model and use it consistently, but find methods to account for different contributions.

- Segment channels by the type of impact they have on each phase of the purchase process. We can no long only focus on the final purchase point.

SUMMARY

Measuring the effectiveness of marketing campaigns is critical to any successful digital strategy. The multi-channel and multi-device customer journey makes it harder to determine ROI and the effectiveness of any one channel. There are different attribution modeling schemes that can be used to report results, but regardless of the approach used, be sure to report and track the impact of all channels that influenced the reservation. Segmenting the effectiveness of channels by each stage of the customer journey provides a good alternative methodology to fully understand the impact of your digital marketing strategies.

Analytics

"You cannot manage what you cannot measure," is an adage most marketers live by. It's critical to measure the effectiveness of each marketing initiative and constantly monitor the ROI you are achieving from those channels. As we discussed in the earlier sections, there are different KPIs that can be used to measure the effectiveness of the campaigns and their ROI. Despite the ability to clearly track and measure your performance, the customer journey of a typical hotel consumer poses some challenges for measuring the true ROI of different channels.

The Evolving Customer Journey

The typical hotel customer journey involves multiple touch points across multiple channels and devices. For example, let's go through the customer journey for Amy, who is visiting San Francisco and is looking for hotels with a spa in the financial district.

Amy starts on Google by searching for "San Francisco financial district hotels with spa." She might click on the top search result – a paid listing for your hotel. It's highly unlikely that Amy will book a hotel the first time she is browsing since at this stage she is still "discovering" her options. She gets tired of browsing and moves on to other things including her yoga class and dinner.

If you are doing retargeting across search engines and social media, you will have an opportunity to show her your hotel's display ads on her Facebook feed as well as other sites she visits later. Perhaps at this stage you might be presenting an enticing stay and spa offer that might convince her to book.

She next types your hotel name in the search browser and finds your hotel's organic listing and clicks on it and books a room. This scenario is very typical of the complex customer journey and is every marketer's biggest challenge in measuring return on investment reports across marketing initiatives.

The Marketer's Dilemma

The challenge in this scenario is that even though it was your Paid Marketing advertisement that got Amy familiarized with your hotel, and your Facebook offer convinced her to book, the booking step happened directly on your website through an organic search. Which channel should get the credit for booking? Was it your paid ad? Your social ad/post? Or was it your organic search channel that got the booking credit? You could probably choose any of the 3 answers above and your answer would be right. Marketing gurus have come up with different attribution models on how to address this challenge.

HOSPITALITY DIGITAL MARKETING ESSENTIALS:

Attribution Models

For reference in this publication, we will use the attribution models defined by Google at https://support.google.com/analytics/answer/1662518?hl=en. For the sake of simplicity, only a few of the models are covered in the following material. For a complete list of models, review the article in the link above.

- **LAST INTERACTION** attribution model: the last touchpoint – in the case of Amy's scenario, the *Organic Search* channel – receives 100% of the credit for the sale.

- **LAST NON-DIRECT CLICK** attribution model: all direct traffic is ignored, and 100% of the credit for the sale goes to the last channel that the customer clicked through from before converting – in Amy's story, the *Social Media Channel (Facebook)*.

- **FIRST INTERACTION** attribution model: the first touchpoint – in the case of Amy, the *Paid Search* channel – receives 100% of the credit for the sale.

- **LINEAR** attribution model: each touchpoint in the conversion path – in the case of Amy's scenario, the *Paid Search*, *Social Network*, and *Organic* channels – would share equal credit (33% each) for the sale.

- **MULTI-TOUCH** attribution model: In this model each touch point in the conversion gets credit. In the case of Amy's scenario, the Paid Search, Social Network, and Organic channels would all get credit for the sale. There are various forms of multi-touch attribution, with the main difference being how much credit is given to each touch point. Some examples are:
  - Linear: Each touchpoint in the conversion path gets equal credit.
  - Time Decay: Each touchpoint in the conversion path gets different credit based on when the event took place.

- Custom: Each touch point in the conversion path gets varying degrees of weighting based on some logic, often using previous data (big data). Machine learning and AI is starting to be used to develop very complex, accurate, and custom multi-touch attribution models.

Best Practices: Use an Attribution Model Consistently

As a marketer, you can choose to use any of the models if you are consistent in your approach. In the hotel industry, the most commonly used model is the last interaction model. You now understand that in the last interaction model, organic search would receive 100% of the credit in our example. It is critical, however, to remember and report that even though the booking was realized through organic search, the paid search campaigns had the most critical role to play in bringing awareness of your property to Amy. Likewise, some of the programmatic display channels track the consumer through cookies and take credit for the intermediate interactions with the consumer. Though there is nothing wrong with that approach, you must be aware as a marketer that there is a likelihood of double counting that revenue as you may be counting it a second time through the last interaction channel.

Best Practices: Calculating ROIs and Effectiveness by Stages of Customer Journey

As a marketer, it is important for you to understand and communicate the impact of each digital channel clearly. For example, social media channels such as Facebook and Instagram are less likely to be the channels from which the consumer initiates the purchase transaction vs. paid search queries — like directly looking for hotels in San Francisco. However, the social channels play an important role in increasing the awareness of your property and should be an important component of your digital marketing mix. Some analytics software breaks down the impact of each digital initiative by stages of customer journey which helps the marketer understand the effectiveness of each channel and not just strictly focus on the overall ROI metric.

Source: Milestone Analytics

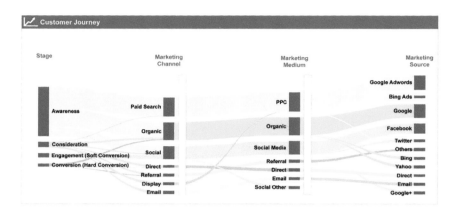

KEY POINTS
- Vendor management allows hotels to choose the right way to scale resources quickly and easily.
- Most hotels use a combination of in-house and outsourced service providers to achieve their digital marketing and distribution objectives.
- Vendor management allows hotel marketers to achieve the greatest value for their property by ensuring the right mix of vendor and in-house resources.

SUMMARY

Even if you work for a large brand with a capable team you will often be utilizing vendors to assist you with various tasks and objectives. If you work with a smaller brand or independent hotel, in all likelihood you will be utilizing vendors as an extension of your team. Since vendors and vendor relationships are so vital to the success of the digital marketer is important that these relationships be optimized. This section can be applied throughout the study guide.

What is Vendor Management?
Due to the wide variety of skills and resources needed to market a hotel today, most hoteliers rely on one or more vendors to help them achieve their digital marketing objectives. For instance, for digital marketing alone, a given hotel might ask vendors to supply at least some of the following:

- strategy consulting
- web development
- an internet booking engine (IBE)
- content development
- graphic design
- photography and videography
- organic search engine optimization
- paid search engine marketing
- display media and remarketing campaigns
- OTA distribution and channel management
- metasearch connectivity and marketing support
- social media marketing
- email and database marketing
- mobile marketing
- analytics support

Some hotels choose a single vendor for all these services to streamline their management overhead while others choose multiple vendors in hopes of finding "best of breed" for each required discipline. No single approach – no single vendor, for that matter – guarantees success or failure. But failing to plan for how to work with your vendors often makes it difficult to achieve your objectives effectively, efficiently, or both.

Vendor management is the process of finding and managing the right vendor, or set of vendors, to help achieve a property's objectives, deliver excellent results, make the best use of the internal team's time and efforts, and do all of this for a reasonable cost.

In-House or Outsource?
The first question facing many hotel digital marketers revolves around whether to use a vendor at all. Are you more likely to succeed by finding a vendor to help you meet your hotel's digital marketing needs? Or are you better off in the long run to build your digital marketing capabilities in-house?

As noted previously, no one answer works for every property or hotel company. You must assess your own situation and determine the best solution for your unique needs. However, first acknowledge that the decision to use in-house or outsourced resources is not an "either/or" decision. Most successful hotel marketers rely on a blended approach, choosing to develop talent in-house in some areas, and using vendors to supplement and enhance their internal capabilities.

Additionally, you can shift your approach as your needs change over time. Businesses frequently choose to use outsourced vendors while they build their internal capabilities, then gradually move those functions in-house. Alternatively, specific functions may be outsourced over time to free internal resources due to shifting strategic priorities.

When deciding whether to use vendors or in-house resources, consider the benefits and limitations of each approach[1].

Outsourcing Benefits

- **Access to a larger talent pool.** Marketing agencies, consultancies, and technology vendors often attract talent focused on each organization's core area of expertise. For example, few hotels require enough graphic design work to make hiring a dedicated designer practical. A design agency, by contrast, may have many graphic designers on their staff to meet client demand.

- **Experience with a variety of projects.** Because most outsourced vendors work on projects for more than one client, they often have insights and experience beyond those a single hotel or hotel company would gather.

- **Rapid time to market.** Building in-house capabilities usually takes time due to the need to attract, hire, and train staff. Outsourcing often allows hotel marketers to quickly supplement their teams with needed experience and expertise — and to reduce commitments as priorities shift.

Outsourcing Downsides

- **Lack of independence.** By definition, when choosing a vendor to augment your team's abilities, you rely on the expertise and knowledge that vendor provides to accomplish your objectives. This creates a dependency that may cause issues for your business in the longer term if you shift directions or find that they cannot effectively meet your needs.

- **Limited control.** While you of course have the ability to reject work from vendors that fails to meet your brand or business standards — at least within the constraints of your contract — vendors have significant control of the processes and products they provide. Any disconnect between their processes and vision and your own may reduce your ability to achieve your goals.

In-House Benefits

- **Better understanding of your business.** No matter how closely a vendor works with you, it's likely that internal resources will have a deeper understanding of the details of your business. Many vendors focus exclusively on the hospitality industry to mitigate this limitation, but the very nature of most vendor relationships definitely provides in-house personnel an advantage here.

- **Total control of process and priorities.** When working with your own team, you have full control of your working processes — the ability to decide what, when, and how your resources will accomplish your goals. Vendors must split their priorities across multiple clients and may not provide you the level of control you may require for some aspects of your digital marketing and distribution activities.

- **Maintain knowledge and skills.** Vendors can help you get access to resources and skills quickly and easily. Unfortunately, those resources and skills remain with your vendor and introduce the risk of losing access if your vendor relationship changes.

In-House Downsides

- **Fewer available resources and tools.** Typically, an in-house solution gives you access to fewer resources — human, process, and technological — than you can acquire from a vendor.

- **Staff retention issues.** While bringing components of your digital marketing in-house gives you the ability to grow your institutional knowledge, frequently the loss of a single key individual from an internal team can hurt overall productivity.

- **May be more expensive.** When working with a vendor, your costs are typically borne across their clients, lowering your overall expenses. Any functions you bring entirely in-house come with salaries, benefits, and training for your human resources, plus technology, additional implementations, and the need to keep up tools in line with industry standards on your own. These factors often — though not always — result in higher costs overall.

The key question when evaluating whether to manage a function in-house or outsource it is, "Is this tool, technology, and/or role strategic to our organization?" Hotel marketers often use vendors so they can focus on the big picture, the strategy, and the operation of the hotel itself. Vendors play a complementary role, providing hotel staff the bandwidth to focus on those areas most important to the business overall.

No matter which direction you choose, your success depends on your ability to manage your vendor relationships and your overall strategy. As noted in Harvard Business Review,[2] "Outsource the work, not the leadership…when outsourcing, you can't manage through the contract, you have to manage through the people. Delegating to a vendor is no different, on a day-by-day basis, than delegating internally."

The Vendor Management Lifecycle

Once you have decided to engage a vendor, you can use a straightforward process for selecting the best possible one. This process (illustrated in Figure 1) allows you to determine the right vendor for your needs and ensure you get the greatest return on your spend.

1. Assess needs.
2. Identify qualified vendors.
3. Evaluate fit.
4. Negotiate contract.
5. Onboard and manage the vendor relationship.
6. Divest (if needed).

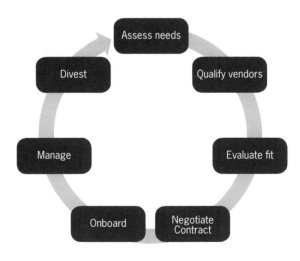

Figure 1: The Vendor Management Lifecycle

STEP 1: Assess Needs

As you begin your search for a new vendor, the first step is to discuss and document in detail the services and products you need for your hotel. While it is perfectly acceptable to have exploratory calls with vendors to "see what's out there" – sometimes you may not know what products and services exist to support your needs, let alone what your needs are – you should draft some basic requirements at your earliest opportunity in the process. As RFP 365 notes,[3] "What does their optimal size, location, and service portfolio include? Clarify which traits and features are necessities and which are on the 'wish list.' Be as specific as possible. The clearer the picture of your 'ideal' solution, the easier it will be to recognize…" the vendor who best meets your needs.

Meet with all affected members of your team to ensure you've thought through all requirements you have of your vendor. Determine who within your organization will help you assess potential vendors. Make sure that you define your decision-making process with your team. Will only one person make the final decision based on input from other stakeholders? Will you choose based on consensus? Clarify roles for the evaluation process to streamline your final decision. Additionally, develop a project plan and set expectations with your internal stakeholders around their time commitment to the process.

Finally, establish a target budget for your outsourced services. While you may not know what individual vendors or services cost, you will save yourself time later if you can at a minimum estimate what you can afford to spend to meet your needs.

Once you've defined your needs, begin formally contacting vendors to assess their capabilities and fit with your organization.

STEP 2: Identify Qualified Vendors

After defining your needs, create a target list of potential vendors. Scout them out in the exhibitor showcase at HSMAI conferences, review trade publications, conduct online searches, and talk with others in your market and industry colleagues about which vendors they use. What do they like about their existing vendor? What would they like to see work better? This will help you determine the appropriate vendors to meet with for your situation.

For simpler requirements, you may choose to simply contact the vendor directly and begin discussing your needs. For more complex engagements, you may want to draft a request for information (RFI) or request for proposal (RFP) instead. An RFI is a preliminary document that asks vendors to detail their products, services, and capabilities. Hotel companies use this information to evaluate potential vendor candidates, who may then be invited to present their qualifications in-person or to participate in an RFP response. RFI's and RFP's help you manage the expectations of the candidates, but require a fair bit of work on your end. Ensure you are using a process that aligns with the size of the desired engagement.

STEP 3: Evaluate Fit

Once you have reached out to potential vendors, whether directly or via an RFI/RFP, begin to evaluate their ability to support your needs. As ContractWorks states, "focus on fit, not flare."[4] You can easily be dazzled by robust presentations or sophisticated sales techniques. Focus always on your relationship with the vendor's team. As you're likely going to work closely with these individuals for a period of years, your ability to get along with them is as important to the success of the partnership as their technical or business skills.

Ensure each affected member of your team you identified during the requirements phase has the opportunity to meet with the potential vendors and have their questions answered. Gather feedback from internal stakeholders and work with potential vendors to identify and address any problem areas early to minimize or eliminate conflict later. No one likes surprises. While contract negotiation typically follows the evaluation phase, it is often worthwhile to discuss potential terms during the evaluation itself to ensure alignment and fit.

For larger vendor searches, many hotel marketers choose to use an evaluation scorecard (see Figure 2). This allows stakeholders an easy way to consistently assess each candidate vendor, while also providing a simple way to reduce conflicting opinions. Additionally, you may wish to speak with references. If others in your market or network use the vendor, speak with them too about their experience as it's rare that a potential vendor will connect you with a client who is dissatisfied with their service.

EQUIREMENT (Score 1-10)	WEIGHT	VENDOR A	VENDOR B	VENDOR C
Quality	3.0	8	8	7
Chemistry/Fit	3.0	7	8	9
Trust	3.0	6	7	7
Scalability of Resources	3.0	9	7	8
Relevant Experience	3.0	9	9	9
Development Methodologies	3.0	5	5	6
Technology Focus	3.0	8	8	8
Proximity	2.5	7	7	7
Size	2.0	8	5	6
Cost	2.0	8	6	7
Compliance	2.0	8	8	8
References	2.0	4	7	7
Warranties/Guarantees	1.5	8	8	9
Financial Position	1.0	8	7	7
Certifications	.5	8	8	8
TOTAL SCORE		253.5	248.5	260
RANKING		2	3	1

Figure 2: Vendor evaluation scorecard example[5]

HOSPITALITY DIGITAL MARKETING ESSENTIALS:

Take the time to find the vendor who best suits your needs. When possible, establish a pilot program, working with one or more vendor candidates on a low-risk, small-scale implementation of their service to determine how well your teams work together in practice, and how well their solution meets your needs.

Once you've determined the best candidate, move on to negotiating a contract.

STEP 4: Negotiate Contract

Contract negotiations can range in complexity from a few simple discussions and rounds of review to weeks or months of back-and-forth to find mutually agreeable terms. As the legal implications of contracting fall outside the scope of this program, we will offer just a few tips for effective negotiation.

- SERVICE LEVELS: What is an acceptable service level from your vendor? How regularly will you interact? How rapidly do you expect them to respond to you? Do you expect faster response during particular periods? What remedies do you expect if they fail to meet agreed-upon service levels? What remedies are you prepared to offer if you fail to meet some portion of the agreement?

- PRICING: What pricing model does your vendor use? Are costs fixed or do they scale based on room count, property count, use, marketing spend, or other factors? How will their charges to you change as your company grows (or shrinks)? Can pricing change while the agreement is in effect or only during renewal periods? Remember that you're not always looking to achieve the lowest cost; you're looking to receive the greatest value.

- TERM AND RENEWALS: How long is the agreement in effect? Does the contract auto-renew at the end of its period or are you (or the vendor) required to explicitly agree to renew? Which party, you or the vendor, can terminate the agreement and for what reasons? What resources do you own at termination? If your relationship doesn't work out, are you able to move to an alternative provider – or move services in-house – without violating the agreement?

Obviously, there are many other elements to include in a contract that will help you meet your goals and protect you from risk. Consult with your attorney or qualified legal counsel before signing any agreement with a vendor. But remember, your lawyer can only do so much. It will often be your responsibility to represent the business and ensure the contract specifies what you expect of the vendor. Make sure you have negotiated and reviewed the contract carefully to get what you need.

STEP 5: Onboard and Manage the Vendor Relationship

Congratulations! You've signed a contract with your vendor. At this stage, your primary concern is building a healthy relationship with the outsourced team. In fairness, you have likely been working on that relationship throughout the selection and contracting process. But now they're not "some vendor;" they're your partner, an extension of your team. Ensure effective onboarding and ongoing management.

- CLEAR ROLES AND RESPONSIBILITIES: Are you and your vendors clear on your respective roles and responsibilities? Ensure you've outlined expectations and have a clear understanding of who on the vendor's team will deliver on those. Similarly, make your team easy to work with too. Keep the lines of communication open so your vendors know who to contact when they need something.

- SHARED ACCOUNTABILITY: Have you consistently outlined what success looks like for your vendors? Do you hold each other accountable for reaching those objectives? Use regular checkpoints to review progress and hold one another accountable for delivery against your goals.

- REPORTING AND FEEDBACK: Do the measures exist that show you and your vendor the progress towards your goals? Who is responsible for validating those measures? If you're relying on your vendor to produce reports of their progress, do you fully understand those reports? While it is absolutely the vendor's responsibility to track its progress, you are ultimately accountable for the business results. Make sure you can effectively evaluate their activity and results – and that you are providing your vendor with actionable feedback of how their actions are working for your property.

The keys to a successful relationship are communication, trust, and integrity. Do you trust what your vendor tells you? Do they trust you? Can you rely on one another to do what you say you'll do? Can you have difficult conversations, focused on solving problems? In the words of Harvard Fellow William Ury, "Be soft on the person, hard on the problem."[6] The stronger your professional relationship, the better your results will be.

STEP 6: Divest (If Needed)

Unfortunately, vendor relationships don't always work out. Whether your needs change or the vendor's services evolve, sometimes your vendor can no longer meet your needs. This will require transitioning to a new vendor, taking the service in-house, or dropping the service altogether. The following questions can help you prepare for that situation.

- What does it take to terminate the contract? Many contracts have some form of termination clause or the ability to buy out the rest of the contract period. If you're unhappy with your existing vendor be aware of any auto-renewals and prepare to terminate prior to those going into effect.

- When is it appropriate to alert your existing vendor? While you typically would rather not blindside an existing vendor, and would prefer to leave on good terms, you also must protect your business. Existing service level agreements in your contract should require your current vendor to continue support during any transition. At the same time, ensure you have everything in place as soon as possible to make the transition as smooth as you can.

- Do you have an alternative provider? Assuming you still will require the service your existing vendor provided, are you prepared to move to a new vendor or are you ready to move the services in-house? Have you identified who will do the work and when they are available to take over? Do you have a project plan for the transition?

- What support do you require from the existing vendor during transition? Often during transition, you may require your existing vendor to continue providing

support. This may include day-to-day operational service and training for your team and/or new vendor. Talk through how this will work in practice with your existing vendor once you've informed them of your intent to cancel, then hold each party accountable to ensure a smooth transition.

- How long will transition take? Are you ready for the transition? Do you have a project plan to guide you through the transition? Are all stakeholders aware of the transition and what it requires of them?

- What costs will you have to account for during transition? Frequently during a transition you may have to pay both the new vendor and the existing one at the same time. Ensure you have the budget to support the transition fully and minimize any unnecessary risks.

- What lessons have you learned that you can apply to the new situation? Finally, what can you take from the existing relationship to help you get better results from the new vendor or your internal team?

- Handling your vendor relationships from needs assessment through to day-to-day management and, when necessary, divestiture takes effort. But done well, it also yields excellent results for your hotel(s). Work closely with your vendors throughout the lifecycle to ensure they have all the information they need. Then manage them effectively to ensure they will help you achieve all the goals you have.

Conclusion

Vendor management represents a critical component of your digital marketing skills. Due to resource constraints and other factors, few hotel marketers do everything by themselves. Instead, they use the right blend of in-house and outsourced team members to reach their goals.

Vendors ideally represent partners for your hotel, as dedicated to your success as any other member of your team. You should hold them accountable just as you would a member of your team. But ultimately, you're looking to work together to achieve results. Manage your vendors effectively and efficiently and you'll be able to do just that.

Chapter 30 Endnotes

1 Adapted from "CMO's Boost In-House Marketing Skills." The Wall Street Journal. May 2, 2017. http://deloitte.wsj.com/cmo/2017/05/02/cmos-boost-in-house-marketing-skills/; Robles, Patricio. "In-house agency versus on-site agency: Weighing the pros and cons." eConsultancy. June 9, 2017. https://econsultancy.com/blog/69148-in-house-agency-versus-on-site-agency-weighing-the-pros-and-cons; and, Smale Thomas. "In-House or Outsourced? How Do You Decide?" Entrepreneur. March 1, 2017. https://www.entrepreneur.com/article/289844.

2 Cramm, Susan. "Outsource the Work, Not the Leadership." Harvard Business Review. July 19, 2010. https://hbr.org/2010/07/outsource-the-work-not-the-lea.

3 Duin, Anna. "Strategic Sourcing & Other Vendor Management Best Practices." RFP 365. September 3, 2015. http://www.rfp365.com/blog/vendor-management-best-practices-strategic-purchasing.

4 Naughter, Tara. "4 Vendor Management Best Practices." ContractWorks. July 20, 2017. https://www.contractworks.com/blog/4-vendor-management-best-practices.

5 Used with Permission by Tim Peter & Associates.

6 Fisher, Roger and William Ury. Getting to Yes: Negotiating Agreement Without Giving In (New York: Penguin Books, 2011), 11.

PART 8: GLOSSARY OF DIGITAL MARKETING TERMS

GLOSSARY OF DIGITAL MARKETING TERMS[1]

301 Redirect	A method of redirecting a visitor from one web page to another web page. This type of redirect is to be used for permanent redirects. For example, you own websiteA.com and websiteB.com but you only want one website. You can 301 redirect all the traffic from websiteB.com to websiteA.com so that all visitors end up on websiteA.com.
302 Redirect	A method of redirecting a visitor from one web page to another web page, used for temporary situations only. For permanent redirects, instead use a 301.
404 Error	The error message that appears when a visitor tries to go to a web page that does not exist.
Ad Extensions	Additional pieces of information that can be added to Google Adword ads, including reviews, address, pricing, callouts, app downloads, sitelinks, and click-to-call. Ad extensions help advertisers create richer, more informative ads that take up more on-page real estate, which generally lead to higher Click Through Rates.
Ad Manager Account	An advertising account on Facebook that allows you to run ads on the Facebook Ad Network.
Ad Network	A grouping of websites or digital properties (like apps) where ads can appear. For example, Google has two ad networks: the search network (text ads that appear in search results) and the display network (image ads that appear on millions of websites that have partnered with Google).
AdWords	Google AdWords. A Google owned program that is used by advertisers to place ads on Google search results pages, on YouTube, and on Google ad network sites. AdWords is the primary platform for PPC advertising.
Algorithm	A process or set of rules that computers follow to perform a task. In digital marketing, algorithm usually refers the sets of processes Google uses to order and rank websites in search results. The SEO industry gives various Google algorithms their own nicknames like Penguin (which analyzes the quality of links pointing to a website) and Panda (which assesses the quality of the content on a website). The main ranking algorithm in SEO is referred to as "the core algorithm."
Algorithm Update	A change made to a Google algorithm. Updates typically affect the rankings of websites. Google makes hundreds of adjustments to their algorithms throughout the year, as well as several major updates each year.
Alt Tag	Describes what is in an image on a website, and its function on the page. Screen readers for the blind and visually impaired read out this text to make an image accessible. Alt tags and title tags strengthen the message toward search engine spiders to improve the visibility of the site within search engines. The alt and title attributes of an images are commonly referred to as alt tag or alt text and title tag.
Google Analytics	A Google platform that allows webmasters to collect statistics and data about website visitors. Sometimes abbreviated "GA," Google Analytics allows webmasters to see where web traffic comes from and how visitors behave once on the site.
Anchor Text	The visible, clickable text in a hyperlink.
Average Position	A metric in Google AdWords that helps advertisers understand where, on average, their ads are showing in Google search results pages. There are usually 4 available ad slots at the top of a search result page (where 1 is the first ad, 2 is the second ad, etc.), so for the best results advertisers typically want an average position between 1-4. Average position 5+ indicates that your ads are showing at the bottom of the search results page.
Backlink	Also known more plainly as a "link," this is when one website hyperlinks to another website using html href code. Backlinks are used by Google in their SEO ranking factors, with the basic idea being that if "website A" has incoming backlinks from other strong websites (websites B, C, and D), the links are votes of trust for website A, and website A gains some authority from B, C, and D through the links.
Banner Ad	A popular type of digital image ad that can be placed across various websites.
Bing	A search engine that provides search services for web, video, image, and map search products. Bing is owned and operated by Microsoft, and it powers Yahoo! Search.
Bing Ads	A platform that provides pay-per-click advertising on both the Bing and Yahoo! search engines. The service allows businesses to create ads, and subsequently serve the ads to consumers who search for keywords that the businesses bid on. This platform also offers targeting options such as location, demographic, and device targeting.
Black Hat	Slang for unethical tactics to influence website rankings, like article spinning, mass directory link building, or negative SEO.
Blog	Short for "web log." A web page or a website that is regularly updated with new written content. Blogs are an important section of a website in digital marketing, as they offer fresh new content on a regular basis which can help attract new visitors, engage existing visitors, and give authority signals to Google.

Bot	Sometimes referred to as a "crawler" or "spider." An automated program that visits websites for specific reasons. A spam bot visits websites for nefarious reasons, often showing in Google Analytics as junk traffic. However, Google uses a bot to crawl websites so that they can be ranked and added to Google search.
Bounce Rate	The percentage of visitors to a website that leave without clicking or interacting with any portion of the page. For example, if 100 people visit a website, and 50 of them immediately leave, the website has a bounce rate of 50%. Websites aim to have as low a bounce rate as possible, and averages tend to be between 40-60%.
Campaign	A series of advertising messages that share a theme, and market a product or service. In the context of digital marketing, campaigns can be run through search and display network advertising platforms (e.g., Google, Bing), social media, email, and/or other online platforms.
Code	The languages used to build a website. The most commonly used languages in web design are HTML, CSS, JS, and PHP.
Content	Any form of media online that can be read, watched, or interacted with. Content commonly refers specifically to written material, but can also include images and videos.
Conversion Rate	The rate at which visitors to a website complete the predefined goal. It is calculated by dividing the number of goal achievements by the total number of visitors. For example, if 100 people visit a website and 10 of them complete the conversion goal (like filling out a contact form) then the conversion rate is 10%.
CPA	Cost Per Acquisition. A metric in paid advertising platforms that measures how much money is spent to acquire a new lead or customer. It is calculated by dividing the total spend by the number of conversions, for a given period. For example, if in a month a PPC account spends $1000 dollars and gets 10 conversions (leads), then the cost per acquisition is $100.
CPC	Cost Per Click. The amount of money spent for a click on an ad in a Pay-Per-Click campaign. In the AdWords platform, each keyword will have an estimated click cost, but the prices change in real time as advertisers bid against each other for each keyword. Average CPCs can range from less than $1 for longtail or low-competition keywords, to upwards of $100 per click for competitive terms, primarily in legal, insurance, and water damage restoration industries.
CPM	Cost Per Thousand (M is the roman numeral for 1,000). The amount an advertiser pays for 1,000 impressions of their ad. For example, if a publisher charges $10 CPM, and your ad shows 2000 times, you will pay $20 for the campaign ($10 per 1000 impressions x 2). Measuring ad success with CPM is most common in awareness campaigns, where impressions are more important than conversions or clicks.
Crawler	An automated program that scans websites. The name reflects how the software "crawls" through the code, which is why they are sometimes also referred to as "spiders." See also "Bots."
CRO	Conversion Rate Optimization. A branch of digital marketing that aims to improve the conversion rate of web pages, thus making the pages more profitable. Conversion rate optimization combines psychology with marketing and web design to influence the behavior of the web page visitor. CRO uses a type of testing called "A/B split testing" to determine which version of a page (version A or version B) is more successful.
CTA	Call to Action. A type of online content that drives the user to click-through to engage with a brand. This can be an image, button, link, etc., that encourages someone to book, download, register, call, or act in any way.
CTR	Click Through Rate. The ratio of how many times an advertisement was clicked on, versus how many times it was shown. It is calculated by dividing the ad's clicks by the ad's impressions. For example, if an ad is shown to 100 people, and 10 of them click the ad, then it has a click through rate of 10% (10 clicks / 100 impressions = 10%).
CRM	Customer Relationship Management. The practices, strategies, and technologies that companies use to manage and analyze customer interactions and data throughout the customer lifecycle, with the goal of improving customer relations, retention, and sales growth.
Dashboard	A web page that contains and displays aggregate data about the performance of a website or digital marketing campaign. A dashboard pulls information from various data sources and displays the info in an easy-to-read format.
Description Tag	A piece of HTML code that provides a short description of a web page and is included in the code, but is not visible on the page itself. If a web page has a description tag, Google shows it if there is semantic similarity between the description tag and the content of the web page, and there is similarity between the user's search query and the content of the description tag. If a page does not have a description tag, Google typically shows sentence fragments on the page that contain the search query.
Digital Marketing	A catchall term for online work that includes specialized marketing practices like SEO, PPC, CRO, web design, blogging, content, and any other form of advertising on an internet-connected device with a screen. Traditionally, television was not considered digital marketing, however the shift from cable television to internet streaming means that digital advertising can now be served to online TV viewers.
Direct Traffic	Website visits with no referring website.

Directory	A website that categorically lists websites with similar themes. Some directories like chambers of commerce (a list of businesses in one geographic area) can be helpful for SEO; however widespread abuse of spam directories led Google to discount links from directories whose sole purpose was selling links.
Display Ads	Ads on a display network which include many different formats such as images, flash, video, and audio. Also, commonly known as banner ads, these are the advertisements that are seen around the web on news sites, blogs, and social media.
Display Network	A network of websites and apps that show display ads on their web pages. Google's display network spans over 2 million websites that reach over 90% of people on the internet. Businesses can target consumers on the display network based on keywords/topics, placement on specific webpages, and through remarketing.
Duplicate Content	Refers to instances where portions of text are found in 2 different places on the web. When the same content is found on multiple websites, it can cause ranking issues for one or all the websites, as Google does not want to show multiple websites in search results that have the exact same information. This type of duplicate content can occur because of plagiarism, automated content scrapers, or lazy web design. Duplicate content can also be a problem within one website — if multiple versions of a page exist, Google may not understand which version to show in search results, and the pages are competing against each other. This can occur when new versions of pages are added without deleting or forwarding the old version, or through poor URL structures.
Ecommerce (or E-Commerce)	Electronic Commerce. A classification for businesses that conduct business online. The most common form of ecommerce business is an online retailer that sells products direct to the consumer.
Email Automation	A marketing system that uses software to automatically send emails based on defined triggers. Multiple automated emails in a sequence are used create user funnels and segment users based on behavior. For example, an automation funnel could be set to send email 1 when a person provides their email address, then either email 2a or 2b would be sent based on whether or not the person clicked on the first email.
External Link	A link that points at an external domain.
Facebook Ads Manager	A tool for creating Facebook ads, managing when and where they'll run, and tracking how well campaigns are performing on Facebook, Instagram, or their Audience Network.
Facebook Business Page	A public webpage on Facebook created to represent a company. Using a business page gives users access to Facebook Ads Manager. It also allows businesses to engage with users (i.e., page likes, message responses, post content).
Featured Snippet	A summarized piece of information that Google pulls from a website and places directly into search results, to show quick answers to common and simple queries. Featured snippets appear in a block at the top of search results with a link to the source. Featured Snippets cannot be created by webmasters; Google programmatically pulls the most relevant information from an authoritative site. Most featured snippets are shown for queries like "what is _____" or "who invented _____."
Filter	Popular social media and personalized search sites can determine the particular content seen by users, often without their direct consent or cognizance, due to the algorithms used to curate that content.
Friendly URL	A web address that is easy to read and includes words that describe the content of the webpage. This type of URL can be "friendly" in two ways. 1) It can help visitors remember the Web address, and 2) it can help describe the page to search engines. This is one of the most basic search engine optimization techniques.
Google	Company behind the search engine giant Google.com. Founded in 1998, Google now controls approximately 80% of the search market. Google has also expanded to include many software services, both directly related to search, and targeted towards consumers outside of the search marketing industry like Google Chrome (a web browser), Google Fiber (internet service), Gmail (email client), and Google Drive (a file storing platform). Google is owned by parent company Alphabet.
Google AdWords	Google's online advertising service. This system allows advertisers to reach customers through their search and display networks. AdWords offers several cost models which vary by bidding strategy and company goals. Advertisers can bid on keywords which allows their ads to show in Google search results and on Google's network of partner websites.
Google Algorithm	A mathematical programmatic system that determines where websites will appear on Google search result pages for any given number of queries. Sometimes also called the "Core" algorithm, though this is a less specific term. Google's algorithm is constantly updated (approximately 500-600 times a year, or two times per day), which can have varying levels of impact on the rankings of websites across the world. Google's actual algorithm is kept deliberately secret to prevent webmasters from manipulating the system for rankings, though Google does publicly state their suggested "best practices" for appearing higher in search results.

Google Analytics	A free software platform created by Google, which is used to analyze nearly every aspect of users accessing a website. Website traffic, conversions, user metrics, historical data comparisons, and effectiveness of each channel of marketing can all be managed using this tool.
Google Maps	The location and navigation service provided by Google. Using maps.google.com, users can search for stores, restaurants, businesses, and landmarks anywhere in the world. Typically, users will find routes to nearby establishments including local businesses using Maps.
Google My Business	A free tool for businesses and organizations to manage their online presence across Google, including Search and Maps. By verifying and editing business information, the owner can help customers find their business or any relevant information about it. Most brands own this listing, but hotels can manage/submit updates.
Google Partner Agency	An agency that is certified by Google for meeting certain requirements.
Google Reviews	Reviews left using the Google My Business platform. Reviews are on a 1-5-star scale, and include a brief message written by the reviewer. Reviews can show up in the knowledge graph in Google searches, and have been shown to positively correlate with SEO rankings. (See also Google My Business)
Google Search Console	Previously Google Webmaster Tools. A no-charge web service by Google for webmasters. It allows webmasters to check indexing status and optimize visibility of their websites.
Hashtag	A phrase beginning with the symbol "#" used in social media as a way for tagging content for users to find. Adding hashtags to a post allows users to find that post when searching for that topic. This can be used for finding users looking for broad topics on social media, as well as niche, detailed topics.
Header	Can refer to either the top portion of a webpage that typically contains the logo and menu, or the section of HTML in a website's code that contains important information about the site.
Header Tags	Used in HTML for categorizing text headings on a web page. They are the titles and major topics of a web page and help indicate to readers and search engines what the page is about. Header tags use a cascading format where a page should have only one H1 (main title) but beneath can be multiple H2s (subtitles) and every H2 can have H3s beneath (sub-sub titles) and so on.
HTML	Hypertext Markup Language. A set of codes that are used to tell a web browser how to display a webpage. Each individual code is called an element, or a tag. HTML has a starting and ending element for most markups. Hyper means it is not linear, so it is possible to go to any place on the internet and there is no set order.
HTTP	Hypertext Transfer Protocol. The protocol used by the world wide web to define how data is formatted and transmitted, and what actions web browsers and web servers should take to respond to a command. When you enter a website into your web browser and press enter, this sends an HTTP command to a web server, which tells the server to fetch and send the data for that website to your browser.
HTTPS	Hypertext Transfer Protocol Secure. A secured version of HTTP, which is used to define how data is formatted and transmitted across the web. HTTPS has an advantage over HTTP in that the data sent when fetching a webpage is encrypted, adding a layer of security so that third parties can't gather data about the webpage when the data is sent from the server to the browser.
Hyperlink	An HTML code that creates a link from one webpage to another web page, characterized often by a highlighted word or image that takes you to the destined location when you click on that highlighted item.
Impression Share	Used in pay-per-click advertising, this metric refers to the percentage of times viewers have seen an advertiser's ad, in relation to the total possible amounts that ad could have been seen. If an ad campaign's impression share is 70%, then the ads showed 7 out of 10 possible times.
Inbound Marketing	The activities and strategies used for attracting potential users or customers to a website. "Inbound" is a more recent euphemism for what has traditionally been called "SEO." Inbound marketing is crucial to having a good web presence, as it's used as a way to attract prospective customers by educating and building trust about your services, product, and/or brand. See also "Organic."
Index	When used as a noun, index refers to all of the web pages that Google has crawled and stored to be shown to Google searchers (e.g., "The Google index has billions of websites"). When used as a verb, it refers to the act of Google copying a web page into their system (e.g., "Google indexed my website today, so it will start appearing in their search results").
Keyword	A word or phrase that describes the contents of a web page. Keywords help search engines match a page with an appropriate search query.
Keyword Density	The percentage of how often a keyword appears on a webpage in relation to the total words on that webpage.
Keyword Phrase	A group of two or more words that are used to find information in a search engine. Sometimes, when searching for something, one single keyword does not provide the information you seek, where a keyword phrase allows you to string multiple words together to find better information.

HOSPITALITY DIGITAL MARKETING ESSENTIALS:

Keyword Priority	An overall score that combines keyword metrics to create a single, sortable number you can use to effectively prioritize keywords.
Keyword Stuffing	When a web page uses a keyword too often or superfluously, with the intent of manipulating search engines. This type of behavior is frowned upon and can lead to either algorithmic devaluation in search, or a manual penalty from Google.
Knowledge Graph/Panel	A system that Google launched to understand facts about people, places, and things, and how these entities are all connected. A knowledge graph displays on the SERP and is intended to provide answers, not just links, to search queries so that users do not have to navigate to other sites to gather the information.
Landing Page	The destination webpage a user lands on after clicking on a link (either in an ad or anywhere else). Some landing pages are designed with the purpose of lead generation, and others with the purpose of directing the flow of traffic throughout a site.
Latent Semantic Indexing (LSI) Keywords	Keywords that are semantically related to your primary keyword. They are not limited to synonyms or words with similar meanings. Google rewards websites which include relevant LSI keywords with higher rankings and more traffic.
Link Profile	The cumulative grouping of all links pointing to a particular website. A link profile can be used to determine a website's power, trust, subject matter, and content. Link profiles are important for determining where a website ranks in Google search results. If a website has a high number of links from websites that are not trusted, adult in nature, spammy, or against guidelines, the link profile will have a negative effect on rankings. If a website has a high number of links from websites that are strong providers of content or reputable sources of information it will have a positive effect on rankings.
LinkedIn	A social networking website oriented around connecting professionals to jobs, businesses, and other professionals in their industry. LinkedIn is also a strong platform for marketing, job posting, and sharing professional content.
Local 3-Pack	The top three results Google determines most geographically relevant to a local search. These three results will show at the top of the SERP in a special list accompanied by a map. The map pack shows up for queries with local intent, a general business type, or a "near me" search.
Local Citation	Anywhere online that a business is mentioned by name. Business directories like Moz, Foursquare, or Yelp are made of local citations. Being listed correctly on these sites is an important ranking factor for local search. They provide search engines with credible information about your business so the search engine understands the business exists, is legitimate, and that what you say about your business is true and accurate.
Local Search	A search to find something within a specific geographic area, such as "downtown hotel DC." Local search results can appear in many different places on a SERP but are typically accompanied by map pins. These results show the address and phone number of the company with a link to directions, if appropriate. Sometimes these listings are grouped into a "local pack."
Long Tail Keyword	A keyword phrase that is longer in length and hyper-specifically matches a user search query. A long tail keyword gets fewer searches per month but has a higher search intent, and typically less competition by companies looking to serve up content to that search query. For example, a regular keyword might be "Austin web designer" but a long tail keyword would be "affordable Austin web designer that makes WordPress sites."
Lookalike Audience	A targeting option offered by Facebook's ad service. This audience is created from a source audience (e.g., fans of your Facebook page, an email list), and from this list Facebook will identify common characteristics between audience members. Facebook will then target users that exhibit similar interests or qualities.
Meta Description	One of the meta tags that gives a description of the page in 160 characters. The meta description is an important aspect of a webpage because it is what appears in Google searches and other search engine results.
Meta Keywords	A specific meta tag that displays the specific keywords addresses in a page. After meta keyword markup was abused on some websites, listed keywords no longer apply to how a page is categorized by Google and other search engines.
Meta Tags	HTML snippets added to a webpage's code that add contextual information for web crawlers and search engines. Search engines use meta data to help decide what information from a webpage to display in their results. Example meta tags include the date the page was published, the page title, author, and image descriptions.
Metasearch Engine (or Aggregator)	A search tool that uses another search engine's data to produce its own results from the internet. A typical meta search engine pulls off the results from a number of search engines, say Google and Bing, and then applies its own algorithms in most cases to re-order the results. A hotel metasearch compiles the room rates from numerous booking websites and OTAs onto a singular platform. This focuses the shoppers/users onto one site, reducing the need to browse multiple sites. Examples: Trivago and Kayak.
Moz Local	Software that creates and maintains business listings on the sites, mobile apps, and directories that factor into local search engine results. Moz Local makes it easy to push business listings to the major data aggregators, plus other important sites and apps. Similar to YEXT.

Organic	A source of traffic to a website that comes through clicking on a non-paid search engine result. Organic traffic is a main measurement of an SEO campaign and grows as a site ranks better for keywords, or ranks for more keywords in search engines.
OTA	Online Travel Agency. Allows users to book hotel rooms, flights, train tickets, etc. These sites may be focused on travel reviews, trip fares, or both. Examples include Expedia and Booking.com.
PDF	A digital document format that provides a digital image of text or graphics. PDF's are the preferred document type when uploading documents to the internet because of the ease of use and the ability to import or convert them easily. PDFs can be read and indexed by Google just as a normal web page can.
Personalized Search Results	Results a user sees in a search engine that aren't just based on the traditional ranking factors, but also on the information that the search engine has about the user at the given time, such as their location, search history, demographics, or interests.
Position	The placement in Google search results that a site is in for a specific query. • Featured Snippet: When content within a web page is pulled into Google search results to instantly give the information a user is looking for. • First Page: when a site ranks on the first page of Google search results. • Map Pack: the first through third result on a Google SERP result page that serves up local businesses for a query.
PPC	Pay-Per-Click. An online advertising model in which advertisers are charged for their ad once it is clicked. The PPC model is commonly associated with search engine and social media advertising like Google AdWords and Facebook Ads. Advertisers bid for ad placement in a search engine's sponsored links when a user searches a keyword related to the business offering.
Quality Score	Google AdWords' rating of the relevance and quality of keywords used in PPC campaigns. These scores are largely determined by relevance of ad copy, expected click-through rate, and the landing page quality and relevance. Quality score is a component in determining ad auctions, so having a high score can lead to higher ad rankings at lower costs.
Query	The term given for what a user types and searches using search engines like Google, Bing, and Yahoo. Examples of queries include "Austin electrician," "how do I know if I have a raccoon in my attic," "distance to nearest coffee shop," and many more.
Rankings	A general term for where a website appears in search engine results. A site's "ranking" may increase or decrease over time for different search terms, or queries. Ranking is specific to each keyword, so a website may have keywords that rank on the first page, and others that don't. Google ranking is made up of 200+ components or ranking factors to determine where a website ranks.
Readability	Readability is the ease with which a reader can understand the written text.
Reciprocal Link	Two websites linking to each other, typically for the express purpose of increasing both search engine rankings. These types of links are sometimes deemed manipulative by search engines, which can incur a penalty or devaluation against both sites.
Redirect	A way by which a web browser takes a user from one page to another without the user clicking or making any input. There are various types of redirects (the most common of which is the 301 redirect), which serve different purposes. Typically, this helps improve user experience across a website.
Referral	A medium denoted in Google Analytics that represents a website visit that came from another website (as opposed to coming from a Google search, for example). When users click on a link to another, external webpage, they are said to have been "referred" there.
Remarketing	Also known as retargeting, a type of paid ad that allows advertisers to show ads to customers who have already visited their site. Once a user visits a site, a small piece of data called a "cookie" will be stored in the user's browser. When the user then visits other sites, this cookie can allow remarketing ads to be shown. Remarketing allows advertisers to "follow" users around in attempts to get the user back to the original site.
Responsive Web Design	A philosophy of creating a website that allows all of the content to show correctly regardless of screen size or device. Your website will "respond" to the size of the screen each user has, shrinking and reorganizing on smaller screens, and expanding to fill appropriately on large ones.
Rich Snippets	Describes structured data markup that operators can add to existing HTML so that search engines can better understand the information that is contained on each web page. Major search engines use this markup to present richer search results, allowing users to more easily find the information they are looking for.
ROAS	Return On Ad Spend. A PPC marketing metric that demonstrates the profit made as compared to the amount of money spent on the ads. Similar to ROI.

ROI	Return On Investment. In order for a business to receive a positive ROI, they must earn more money using marketing channels than they are spending on the marketing itself.
RSS	Really Simple Syndication. A way for users to keep track of updates to multiple websites (news sites, blogs, and more) in one place, as opposed to having to manually check in on every single site individually. An RSS Feed is a place where all updates are tracked together, in an easily viewable format.
Schema Markup	Code that is added to the HTML of a website to give search engines more relevant information about a business, person, place, product, or thing. Also known as rich snippets or structured data.
Search Engine	A program that searches an index of information and returns results to the user based on corresponding keywords. The most well-known search engines are Google, YouTube, Bing, and Yahoo.
Search Network	A group of websites in which ads can appear. Google's Search Network, for example, is a group of Google & non-Google websites that partner with Google to show text ads.
SEM	Search Engine Marketing. A nebulous term that can apply to either 1) any digital marketing that involves the use of a search engine, or 2) only paid digital marketing that involves a search engine. There is not an industry standard as to which definition is correct, however the latter is most commonly used.
SEO	Search Engine Optimization. The process of getting traffic from the free, organic, or natural search results on search engines. Primary search results are listed on the search engine results page based on what the search engine considers most relevant to users.
SERP	Search Engine Results Page. The page that search engines show in response to a query by a searcher. This page will look different depending on the search engine (Google, Yahoo, Bing, etc.), but the main component is the list of websites or blue links that provide answers to the query.
Sessions	A metric in Google Analytics that measures one user interacting with a website during a given period of time, which Google defaults to 30 minutes. A session is not dependent on how many pages are viewed, so if a person goes to a website and looks around at different pages for 20 minutes, it would count as 1 session.
Sitelink	An ad extension in Google AdWords that appears below the main ad copy which links to a specific page on the website (e.g., Contact Us, About Us, etc.). Ads can have from 2-6 sitelinks.
Sitemap	An XML file or page on a website that lists all of the pages and posts for search engines to see. This document helps search engines quickly understand all of the content that they should be aware of on a particular website.
Slug	A portion of URL that comes after .com (or .org, .edu, etc.).
Source	A term in Google Analytics that helps webmasters classify where traffic is coming from (i.e., the "source" of the web traffic). Source can be a search engine (for example, Google) or a domain (website-example.com)
Spam	A broad term that includes many different nefarious activities in digital marketing that are done either to help a website rank better or to harm a competitor website. Spam is often seen in the form of hundreds or thousands of low-quality backlinks that were built by a black hat SEO to manipulate rankings.
Spider	See Bot and Crawler.
Structured Data	A system of pairing a name with a value that helps search engines categorize and index your content.
Title Tag	An HTML element that is used to describe the specific topic of a web page. Title tags are displayed in the tabbed top bar of a web browser. In SEO, it is best practice to have descriptive title tags featuring your main keywords, rather than something basic like "home." In addition to the SERP, they also appear in web browsers and social networks.
Tracking Code	A script, often placed in the header, footer, or thank you page of a website that passes information along to software tools for data gathering purposes. Tools like Google Analytics and Google AdWords utilize tracking codes so that they can track information about users who view a site.
Twitter	A social media platform where users interact, or "tweet," by posting a message or replying to a message in 140 characters or less. Each keystroke on a keyboard is considered a character. Twitter is used to share information and links, and utilizes hashtags to categorize information. Tweets are typically public and can be seen by anyone. If you are followed by another user, that user will see your tweets in their feed. Similarly, you will the see the tweets of anyone you follow in your feed.
Twitter Advertising	Allows marketers to promote a tweet on users feeds without that user having to follow your brand for it to appear on their feed. These advertisements can be used to grow brand awareness, gain more followers, extend social media reach, and/or reach out to prospective customers about a product or service.
UNAP	URL, Name, Address, Phone Number. An important ranking factor for search engine optimization. Consistency in website address, name, address, and phone number citations is an important piece of a local SEO Campaign.

Unique Visitors	A metric used in web analytics to show how many different, unique people view a website over a period of time. Unique visitors are tracked by their IP addresses. If a visitor visits the same website multiple times, they will only be counted once in the unique visitor's metric.
URL	Uniform Resource Locator. The address of a web page. The URL refers to what specific web page a web browser is viewing.
URL (Link) Shortener	A website that will create a short URL or web page address from a long one so that the short version, which is easier to remember and enter, can be used instead.
UX	User Experience. A customer's experience when interacting with a product (e.g., a website). User experience design is the process of enhancing user satisfaction and loyalty by improving the ease of use and pleasure provided in the interaction between the customer and the product. The concept most commonly applies to digital fields today.
Visitors	A metric in Google Analytics that quantifies a user of a website over a particular period of time. Visitors are often broken down between "new visitors" who are browsing for the first time in the allotted time period, or "returning visitors" who have already browsed at least once in the given time frame.
Visits	An old term in Google Analytics which was recently changed to "sessions."
Voice Search	Search queries that are performed by a user speaking into a mobile device, digital assistant, or computer.
Web 2.0	The second major phase of development of the World Wide Web, marked by a shift from static web pages to dynamic content, as well as social media and user generated content.
Website	A document or group of documents that are accessible on the World Wide Web.
Wireframe	A cursory layout drawing of a webpage that acts as the first step in the design process.
Yahoo! Advertising	Yahoo and Bing ads are both run through the Bing Ads platform. These search engines share advertising networks.
Yahoo! Search	The third largest search engine in the U.S., owned by Yahoo and powered by Bing.
Yelp	A social review platform and search engine that allows users to leave reviews for businesses. Yelp also offers an advertising program which gives advertisers the ability to show their marketing assets to qualified Yelp users based on keyword searches.
Yext	A software tool designed to manage a business's location-related information on multiple directory websites. It uses a process called Power Listings so multiple listings and sites can be managed in one spot. Similar to Moz.
YouTube	A video sharing website bought by Google in 2006. YouTube is part of Google's ad network. YouTube is currently the 2nd most used search engine in the world.
YouTube Advertising	YouTube offers advertising in 6 different formats. Display ads, overlay ads, skippable video, non-skippable video ads, bumper ads, and sponsored cards. These ads can all be created and run through the Google AdWords platform.

Glossary Endnotes

1The following sources were used and sometimes quoted to compile this glossary.

Weber, John Leo. (July 7, 2017). The Ultimate List of Digital Marketing Terms. https://www.geekpoweredstudios.com/digital-marketing-glossary/

Cline, Mary. (March 28, 2017). Digital Marketing Glossary. https://www.mdsdecoded.com/blog/digital-marketing-glossary/

Digital marketing in 2018: A glossary every marketer should have. (September 12, 2018). https://www.tworiversmarketing.com/blog/blog-entry/2018/09/12/digital-marketing-in-2018-a-glossary-every-marketer-should-have/

The Ultimate List of Digital Marketing Glossary of Terms to Know. (October 15th, 2018). https://www.punith.com/digital-marketing-glossary/

ACKNOWLEDGEMENTS

This publication on digital marketing for hotels would not have been possible without the help, insight, and contribution of many in the travel industry who were called upon for their insights, best practices, case studies, and feedback along the way.

HSMAI thanks the following individuals for their contributions, their insights, and their willingness to share their expertise in order to make this publication a more valuable learning tool.

Anil Aggarwal
CEO
Milestone Internet Marketing

Aimee Cheek, CHDM
Director of eCommerce
OTO Development

Robert Cole
Founder-CEO
RockCheetah

Chris Copp
VP, Global Digital Marketing
IHG

Jackie Douglas
President
HSMAI Asia Pacific

Loren Gray, CHDM
Founder
Hospitality Digital Marketing

Carolyn Hosna
Vice President, Marketing
White Lodging

Jay Hubbs, III, CHDM
Senior Vice President, eCommerce
Remington Hotels

Ryan Hudgins
Director, Performance Marketing
IHG

Diane Jackson
Marketing & PR Manager
OTO Development

John Jimenez, CHDM
Director of E-commerce
Interstate Hotels & Resorts

Juli Jones, CAE
Vice President
HSMAI

Delana Meyer, CHDM
Owner
DRM Consulting, LLC

Tim Peter
President
Tim Peter & Associates

Dr. Donna Quadri-Felitti, CHDM
Director and Associate Professor
Penn State University

Mariana Safer, CHDM
SVP, Global Marketing
HEBS Digital

Kathleen Tindell
Program Director & Publications Editor
HSMAI

Paolo Torchio, CDHM
VP Digital Operations
Hyatt Hotels & Resorts

Dan Wacksman, CHDM
Principal
Sassato

Holly Zoba, CHDM
Owner
Influencer Sales

All members of HSMAI's Marketing Advisory Board 2018-2019

Notes:

_____

_____

_____

_____

_____

_____

_____

_____

_____

_____

_____

_____

_____

_____

_____

_____

_____

_____

_____

_____

_____

_____

_____

_____

_____

_____

_____

_____

_____

_____

_____

_____

_____

_____

Notes: